Learning Outside the Box

Learning Outside the Box

A Handbook for Law Students Who Learn Differently

Leah M. Christensen

Carolina Academic Press
Durham, North Carolina

Library of Congress Cataloging-in-Publication Data
Christensen, Leah M.
 Learning outside the box : a handbook for law students who learn
differently / Leah M. Christensen.
     p. cm.
 ISBN 978-1-59460-692-2 (alk. paper)
 1. Law schools--United States. 2. Law--Study and teaching--United
States. 3. Law students with disabilities--United States. I. Title.

 KF283.C48 2010
 340.071'173--dc22   2009051500

Carolina Academic Press
700 Kent Street
Durham, NC 27701
Telephone (919) 489-7486
Fax (919) 493-5668
www.cap-press.com

Printed in the United States of America

Contents

Part II
Maximizing Your Academic Success While You're
Deep *IN* the Trenches

Introduction

There are a number of excellent books that give law students advice about how to navigate through the first year of law school. This book strives to be something slightly different. It is meant to help the law student who learns differently. What do I mean by the phrase "law student who learns differently?" I use this phrase broadly to mean any law student who may have a learning disability, a reading disability, ADD, ADHD, Asperger's syndrome or any other diagnosed or undiagnosed learning disability that affects the way in which they learn.[1] I *also* mean any student who might simply process information differently than the norm—or even someone who might just need a new approach to law school to maximize their success.[2] If you are a smart, creative student who tends to think "outside the box" more often than 'in the box,' law school may initially be challenging for you.

---

1. "Learning disability" is a general term that describes specific kinds of learning problems. A learning disability can cause a person to have trouble learning and using certain skills. The skills most often affected are: reading, writing, listening, speaking, reasoning, and doing math. Learning disabilities (LD) vary from person to person. Researchers think that learning disabilities are caused by differences in how a person's brain works and how it processes information. The formal definition of "learning disability" comes from the Individuals with Disabilities Education Act (IDEA). The IDEA defines a learning disability as:

> "… a disorder in one or more of the basic psychological processes involved in understanding or in using language, spoken or written, that may manifest itself in an imperfect ability to listen, think, speak, read, write, spell, or do mathematical calculations, including conditions such as perceptual disabilities, brain injury, minimal brain dysfunction, dyslexia, and developmental aphasia," 20 U.S.C.A. § 1400 (2005).

2. I use the phrases "law students who learn differently," "non-traditional learners," and "traditional learners" very broadly throughout this book. We all learn differently. However, some of us tend to process information in a way that lends itself more easily to success in law school. By "traditionally learning" law students, I mean those law students who tend to meet the traditional law school demographic, i.e., 22 to 25 years old, no learning disabilities, auditory learners (learns by listening), processes information easily and quickly, etc. I use this phrase broadly because the idea of a "traditionally learning" law student is rapidly changing in our society for the reasons I discuss in Chapter 2. I believe that everyone in law school can benefit from the learning strategies in this book, but I do tailor the learning strategies more specifically to those law students who tend to process information differently than their peers.

The purpose of this book is to provide research-based learning strategies for law students who learn differently. In my experience, it is precisely those students who learn differently that make the most successful lawyers. But sometimes students who learn differently need a more proactive way of approaching the study of law.

More law students than ever before are diagnosed with learning disabilities during their first year of law school. Why? Law school requires a large volume of complex reading and analysis, and you may have been able to compensate for any learning differences up until this point in your education. Perhaps in undergraduate courses you could keep up with your schoolwork by studying more than your peers, doing more drafts on papers or taking additional time to prepare for exams, etc. In law school, the volume of reading coupled with its inherent complexity makes "taking more time" almost impossible. Therefore, if you learn differently, you will need to develop different reading and study strategies to get you through your first year. You may need to outline differently, read cases differently, and approach law school in a more active, engaged and efficient manner. If you come to law school with a learning disability (or if you simply approach learning differently), you *can* learn the skills to help you succeed in law school. The key to success in law school, however, is to develop a proactive learning plan as soon as possible.

As a law professor, I have been very interested in how law students learn. I have had the opportunity to research what the most successful law students do differently than the less successful law students. I have also researched how law students with ADD approach law school. The good news is that law students with ADD, ADHD or any other learning disability can be very successful in law school. But in order to achieve your goals, you may need to work differently than you have in the past.

The purpose of this book is to focus on the reading, studying and testing strategies that are particularly helpful to law students who learn differently. This book is more than advice—it is a learning guide based upon empirical research and statistical correlations between learning strategies and law school GPAs. Although these cognitive techniques will help any law student, these suggestions are particularly relevant to law students who learn differently. Further, I attempt to *show* you what the most successful law students do by using interviews and examples from actual students. It is one thing to *read* about how to read a judicial opinion— it's another thing entirely to *see* how a first year law student accomplishes this task. This book is full of examples of how students read, write, outline, and take exams. In addition, it will guide you through the disability accommodations process if you find that you need classroom or testing accommodations during law school.

There are two main parts to this book. Part I helps you get acclimated to the new world of law school. Part I explains why law school is so different—particularly for students who learn differently. Part I also addresses learning styles, legal reading, case briefing, class preparation, and how to apply for disability accommodations.

Part II of the book focuses specifically on the details of maximizing your potential in law school. Part II addresses specific learning strategies to master legal writing, legal research, outlining, and essay and multiple-choice exams. Part II is full of examples of actual student exam answers and my critiques of those exam answers. Further, there are example research logs and legal memoranda written by real law students.

I believe that with drive and determination, *every* student can get through law school. I also believe that law students who learn differently are extremely important to legal education and to the practice of law. Our world needs lawyers who think "outside the box." In my experience, non-traditional lawyers tend to have more empathy for their clients and are able to think of creative solutions to problems in new and important ways. Law students who learn differently become exceptional lawyers! This book is meant to help you navigate through law school so that you can achieve your maximum potential as both a law student—and a lawyer.

Part I

Getting Used to Law School: The Basics

Chapter 1

The New World of Law School: What Makes Law School So Different?

Every year I begin the fall semester asking my students what they know about law school. Most of them have seen movies like "The Firm" or television shows like "The Practice" or "Law and Order." Even on the internet, there are numerous websites devoted to instructing students on how to manage their first year of law school, including advice on how to read an opinion or brief a case.

In addition, most of my beginning students have been very successful in their undergraduate careers. They have tested well in the past (on the LSAT or other exams) and they all believe they will be just as successful in law school. Even though law school is a new experience, almost all law students begin their experience believing that if they work just like they did in college, they will be equally successful in law school.

However, even for traditionally-learning law students, using the same reading and study strategies in law school that worked in college will not necessarily translate into success. Every fall semester, I watch first year students struggle with reading a legal opinion for the first time. Despite their hard work and effort, most law students are left confused and frustrated. Further, law students who learn differently may experience even more initial confusion. This confusion comes not because these students lack skills or intelligence, but because of the unique characteristics of law school—the high volume of complex reading coupled with a strange new teaching methodology called the Socratic Method.

The purpose of this first chapter is to provide you with a better understanding of how law school is unique. And if you tend to learn differently, you may experience these differences more acutely—and they may affect you to a greater degree. This chapter will describe five characteristics of law school that make it a very different experience for all law students: (1) an increased workload; (2) the Socratic Method; (3) the need to direct your own learning; (4) intense peer competition; and (5) feelings of isolation.

If you understand these unique characteristics of law school—particularly if you learn differently—you can be better prepared to make the transition into law school more easily.

3

A. The Increased Workload in Law School

You have no doubt heard tales about the amount of work expected from law students. These stories are true. You will have a great deal of reading and thinking to do in order to prepare for each of your classes. And the reading will be difficult and time-consuming—because law school reading is a whole new vocabulary and format. In your first year courses, you will likely be assigned at least 20 pages of reading per class period—per *course*. You will likely have five courses at a time. That doesn't sound like too much, right? *Wrong.* If law school reading were like the reading you've done before, it wouldn't be a problem. However, *legal* reading, i.e., reading judicial opinions, is *very* time-consuming—particularly during your first semester. And if you tend to read more slowly than average, you may feel particularly daunted by the volume of reading in law school.[1]

Consider the following scenario. Typically, each law school class is between 50–80 minutes per class period (depending on whether you meet two or three times per week). And you will typically have 2–3 class periods per week in each course. And you may have up to five courses each semester. Therefore, you will likely be in class an average of 15 hours per week.

A law student without a learning disability will spend at least three to five hours of study time for each hour you will spend in class. Therefore, if a student is in class 15 hours per week, the student will likely need to study 45 hours per week *in addition* to the 15 hours per week she is in class. This means that a full-time, traditionally-learning law student begins law school with a 60 hour-per-week time commitment *just* for getting the basics done.

For any new law student, this is a tremendous work load. And for those students who learn differently—this new time commitment can be overwhelming (and you may need to budget additional time). The good news is that you can learn to study efficiently. However, you need to begin law school with a plan. I've seen too many students simply study for endless hours—working desperately to keep up with their classes. They think that if they can study *more* than their peers, they will succeed. But studying *more* is not always studying *better*. The actual number of hours you study is far less important than the quality of your reading and thinking.

Consider the words of one of my prior students, Alexa. Alexa was a second year law student with ADD. She was very successful in law school despite her learning disability. Although she became an efficient and successful student during her second year, she felt like she studied too much during her first year of law school.

---

1. We will discuss legal reading (and the optimal/necessary reading speed) in Chapters 4 and 5.

I would say that looking back [over my first year in law school], I spent all my time studying. I thought I wasn't [just studying], but I did.

... I think I studied every Friday, Saturday and Sunday. And thank goodness for my "study buddies." My study buddies also studied that much. We would pick Fridays where we would go to dinner. So, we would work all Friday afternoon and then eat dinner. And that felt like we were "going out." I didn't really make a lot of friends....

First year, we had classes at 9 a.m.... Then at 3 p.m. [after classes], I would go straight to the library. Do reading. Later in the semester, I would do less reading and more just sitting and talking to the "study buddies" or something. So, I probably would just get dinner and then come back and stay ... until like 10:30 p.m. or 12 a.m., and then go home and start all over again ... I would do that all week. Seven days a week. I would pick one day a week where I would go out or something like that. Later in the semester, I would be able to go to dinner or something like that. But, I would make sure it would be one.[2]

Alexa also recognized that she learned differently than other law students. She felt that she had to work harder than law students without ADD.

... I definitely think it took me longer [than other students to complete assignments] the first year. I definitely think first year I put more effort into it. This year I'm—I haven't been putting as much effort. But then I pull all-nighters. So, it's kind of like I've kind of reverted back to college.

Despite Alexa's ADD diagnosis, she ended up in the top 5% of her law school class. There is no doubt that she worked incredibly hard in law school. But after some trial and error, she also figured out how she learned best in law school. And *that* was the key to her success—not her long study hours. We'll return to Alexa's experiences in law school later in the book and, in particular, how she used her learning style to her advantage.

My main point is that many law students—particularly those who struggle during their first year—attempt to compensate for the high work load of law school by simply working longer hours, reading more cases or buying more outlines, hornbooks or supplements. The strategy of

---

2. This transcript was part of a larger study I completed on law students with ADD and their experiences in law school. The students signed waivers and agreed that their comments could be published. *See* Leah M. Christensen, *Law Students Who Learn Differently: A Narrative Case Study of Three Law Students with Attention Deficit Disorder (ADD)*, 21 J.L. & HEALTH 45 (2008).

working *more* may backfire in the end.[3] The most successful law students—whether they learn differently or traditionally—need to balance law school with their lives outside of law school. This means that in order to allow yourself that all-too-important free time, you will need to read and study efficiently and effectively. This book will give you some strategies to accomplish this task.

B. The Socratic Method, or in Other Words: The Strange Way Classes Are Taught in Law School

Another unusual aspect of law school is the strange way that many professors teach first-year classes. It is called the "The Socratic Method." Socrates (470–399 B.C.) was a Greek philosopher who engaged in the questioning of his students in order to uncover "truth." He sought to get to the foundations of his students' and colleagues' views by asking continual questions until a contradiction was exposed, thus proving the fallacy of the initial assumption. This became known as the Socratic Method.[4]

In 1973, there was a movie called "The Paper Chase" in which a famous actor, John Houseman, struck fear in the hearts of all current and future law students with his portrayal of a fierce law school professor who used the Socratic Method to torment his students. Although many law professors still use the Socratic Method, they like to think of it more as a tool to engage a large group of students in a classroom discussion.

The Socratic Method is supposed to be a conversation between the law professor and the law student. During this conversation, the professor and the student assist one another in finding the answers to difficult questions. In law school, it will often play out in the following manner. The professor will stand in the front of the room and call on a student. All students are expected to have read and briefed the case or cases before class. If you are called on, you are typically "on" for a series of questions from the professor. Your professor will ask you questions about the case assigned for that day, including basic questions like which court wrote the opinion, the facts, the result or conclusion of the court, etc. In addition, your professor may ask you additional questions about the rea-

---

3. Students may spend hours in the library devoting a *substantial amount* of time reading their assignments. But the students may not be reading *efficiently*. Are they getting distracted? Talking to friends? Falling asleep? If you are not reading efficiently, you are not extracting the relevant information out of the cases. Further, you may be exhausting yourself and this inhibits effective learning. Studying more is not always better. We will discuss how to study *efficiently* throughout the next several chapters.

4. Ironically, Socrates was tried, convicted, and executed for corrupting the young.

soning of the case or perhaps about the policy that the court used to come to its conclusion. These are often more difficult questions. Law professors use the Socratic Method in order to develop your analytical thinking skills.

In college, your job as a student was to give information *back* to your professor. You read the material, the professor lectured about it—you memorized it and then gave it back to your professor in the form of a test. However, in law school, law professors hope to teach you to 'think like lawyer.' What does this mean? It means that we want to train your brain to read judicial opinions, extract the legally relevant rules from the case, and apply those rules to new situations or hypotheticals. 'Thinking like a lawyer' is really asking you to become adept at text-based reasoning and this new skill involves a very precise method of reading and analysis.

Most law students would be able to talk to their professor about a case they had just read *if* the discussion were one-on-one with their professor. But in the law school classroom, you are discussing the case in front of 75 to 100 of your law school peers. This *is* intimidating for almost any law student—and it may be particularly challenging if you learn or process information differently than a traditional student. Not many of us are adept initially at the skill of "thinking on our feet."

Some students dislike the Socratic Method because they feel that the professor is "hiding the ball." In other words, the professor knows what he or she wants the student to say—and will keep pressing the student until the student gives the 'right' answer. But the student has no idea what the professor wants her to say! So law students feel like they are being lead on a fishing expedition—except that they are the fish on the hook—and it's very uncomfortable.

Here's an example of the Socratic Method used in a typical first year Constitutional Law class:[5]

> Professor: Ms. Smith, suppose the California state legislature passes a statute banning "the making of any statements critical of the state government." You write an editorial for the student newspaper in which you state that the members of the legislature who voted for the statute thereby violated their oath to support the Constitution. You are prosecuted for violating the statute. Do you have a constitutional defense?
>
> Student: Yes.
>
> Professor: What is your defense?

---

5. This excellent example of the Socratic Method at work in a first year Constitutional Law class is based upon Professor Michael C. Dorf, *How To Think Like a Lawyer: Advice to New and Prospective Law Students,* at http://writ.news.findlaw.com/dorf/20010822.html (last visited October 1, 2009).

Student: It violates the First Amendment.

Professor: But the First Amendment says that "*Congress* shall make no law ... abridging the freedom of speech, or of the press." Is the California legislature the same body as Congress?

Student: No.

Professor: So is the prosecution permissible?

Student: Uh ... I'm not sure. I don't think so.

Professor: Why not?

Student: The First Amendment applies to the states.

Professor: Yes it does. We'll talk later about a series of cases in which the U.S. Supreme Court ruled that when the Fourteenth Amendment prohibits any state from denying a person "liberty" without "due process of law," it implicitly includes within "liberty" most of those rights that are spelled out in the Bill of Rights. But I'm troubled by something else today. Why should a California court have to pay any attention to what's in the Federal Constitution?

Student: Um ... Perhaps because of Article VI?

Professor: I assume you are referring to the portion of Article VI that says: "This Constitution ... shall be the supreme Law of the Land; and the Judges in every State shall be bound thereby, any Thing in the Constitution or Laws of any state to the Contrary notwithstanding."

Student: Yeah, that's it.

Professor: Well, that seems rather circular doesn't it? What if I showed you a different Constitution, also labeled "the Constitution of the United States." Suppose it has a provision that states: "The form of the government of the United States shall be a dictatorship." And suppose there is another provision: "This Constitution shall be the supreme law of the land; and everybody shall be bound by it, any thing in the constitution or laws of any state or other body to the contrary notwithstanding."

Tell me Ms. Smith, why is the Constitution printed in the front of your Constitutional Law casebook more authoritative than the "Dictatorship" Constitution?

Student: Umm....

And the conversation continues. "For every answer there is another question, until the exasperated students begin to feel like the point of the Socratic [M]ethod is to show how much smarter the professor is than they are."[6]

There is one additional aspect of the Socratic Method that may be very different than your previous classroom experiences prior to law school. Although law professors call their classes "lectures," they don't typically lecture in the sense of giving you information about what the reading or assignment actually means. Instead, the professor leaves you with many different possibilities of what a case or rule *might* mean. This drives law students crazy! Law students want to know the *right* answer. But often there is no right answer. Most frequently, the answer is: "it depends." Typically the answer depends on the *arguments* you can make about the rule as applied to the specific facts in front of you. If the facts change, then the outcome changes as well.

You will likely have law professors that use the Socratic Method, particularly during your first year. Proponents of the Socratic Method argue that it is not used to intimidate or "break down" new law students; instead it is used for the very reason Socrates developed it in the first place: to develop critical thinking skills in students and enable them to approach the law as intellectuals.

However, you will hear stories about professors who *do* abuse this method of teaching—and unfortunately, some of these stories are true. Further, although the Socratic Method may be a useful teaching methodology for some law students, research has shown that it actually enhances the learning of only a small percentage of students, i.e., those students who tend to learn by listening (aurally).[7] And for those students who learn differently (which is most of us), the Socratic Method—used alone—may not help us learn much at all. Some students who learn differently report that the Socratic Method prevents them from thinking clearly and absorbing the relevant information.

The good news is that there are more and more progressive law schools and law school professors that are adopting teaching methodologies *in addition* to the Socratic Method. These changes are good for all students, but they are particularly beneficial to students who approach learning differently than the traditional law student.

Consider the comments of Kelsey, a first year law student with ADD. She was shocked by her Property professor's use of the Socratic Method.

> I am petrified every time I'm there [in class]. And I know that's a horrible thing to say, but a lot of times people with ADD can only experience so many emotions and so many thoughts at the same time. And, so, I'm experiencing fear ... and ... anxiety ...

---

6. Inspired by Michael C. Dorf, *supra* n.5.
7. This learning style will be discussed further in Chapter 3.

It's hard because I can't believe I let someone get to me like that. And why does she get to me?

It's beyond [the traditional Socratic method].... I was yelled at one day for not being prepared when I was actually fully prepared. I actually didn't say the words that she wanted me to say it.

[She said:] ... "I can't believe you would come here unprepared. I can't believe you would ... not brief a paper like I told you." "You know I told you what you needed [to do] and you're not doing it.

... [F]or the rest of the day, you sit there and you think about it.

... So, when I go to that course, it's like, "[I]s she going to call on me? Am I not going to know the answer?"

Another student with ADD, Baker, described his initial reaction to the Socratic Method.

The first two weeks, I felt confident coming in that I was as smart as everybody else. I really didn't think that was going to be a problem. I still don't think that's a problem. I was definitely afraid of having to give an answer "on my feet." [T]here [were] a million different things they could ask you. And the social pressure around you. Like most people, I was terrified to go to class. The reading was fine. The material was fine. But going to class was horrible.

... I think it was the whole first year just stress in general. Some professors were tougher. And I looked back at my grades and I didn't do any better or worse really. So it was just a stressful environment.

And it's all new. And I don't understand that. I don't understand why when people are new at something you would grill them off the bat.

... That's kind of the problem in law school for me. Especially when it's "on you're feet" thinking. I'm just not that quick, I need to sit down and I write a lot. I write well. I worked through things as I write. I think slower than other people. And I don't know if that is a function of a learning disability or what, but I can't be put in pressured decisions....

Baker did make an important distinction, however. He recognized that things did get better during his second year.

[Law school] treat[s] second and third year students differently. It's not the "pressure cooker" it was. And, I can already tell I'm learning things. I'm remembering [more] because I'm [feeling] more positive in the classroom environment. Last year, I felt like I learned nothing. I mean, I look back and I couldn't even tell you what the basic elements of a contract are without having to look at my notes. It's the same thing with constitutional law and everything else.

The Socratic Method has been described as "mystifying and patriarchal, persisting because of the large classes and professors too lazy to adopt new teaching methods."[8] It has been found to be particularly ineffective for the teaching of women, minorities, and students who learn differently.[9] Yet this teaching methodology persists in the cultures of many law schools.[10]

The purpose of this section is to prepare you for the reality that law school may, at times, be difficult—particularly if you learn differently. But remember, the Socratic Method is just one part of law school. And although it will feel like a *big* part of law school initially, it becomes a much smaller part of your legal education during your second and third year.

C. But Then Again, Professors Aren't All That Important in Law School. YOU Are Ultimately Responsible for Your Own Learning!

Despite the fact that the classroom environment in law school may be challenging, the good news is that your law school professors are only a small part of your overall learning experience. Now I'm sure you're asking: "Why am I paying all this money for law school if the professors aren't really teaching me anything?"

One of the biggest mistakes I see students make in their first semester of law school is assuming that their professors will teach them everything they need to know to become good lawyers. And most first year law students believe they are in law school to learn the "law." Students are surprised that the focus of law school classes is not really on the substantive rules of law—particularly during the first year. Yes, you will cer-

---

8. Jennifer Jolly-Ryan, *Disabilities to Exceptional Abilities, Law Students with Disabilities, Nontraditional Learners, and the Law Teacher as Learner*, 6 Nev. L.J. 116, 124–125 (2005). *See also* Paula Gaber, *"Just Trying To Be Human in This Place:" The Legal Education of Twenty Women*, 10 Yale J. L. & Feminism 165 (1998) Alice K. Dueker, *Diversity and Learning: Imagining a Pedagogy Difference*, 19 N.Y.U. Rev. L. & Soc. Change 101 (1991–92); Paul L. Caron and Rafael Gely, *Taking Back the Law School Classroom: Using Technology to Foster Active Student Learning*, 54 J. Legal Educ. 551, 554 (2004).

9. Jolly-Ryan, *supra* n.8 at 125.

10. *Id.*

tainly learn the rules of Civil Procedure and discuss basic rules of law in Property. You will also learn a basic legal vocabulary and analytical framework in your courses. And if you're lucky, some of your professors will also teach you some important lawyering *skills* that you can apply to the actual work you will do eventually as a lawyer.

Although your professors will introduce you to cases, rules and skills, you will actually learn the details of each of those things *on your own*. There is a lot of learning that goes on in law school *outside* of the classroom. And my main point is this: ultimately, *you* are responsible for your own learning.

So one of your main tasks in the first few weeks of law school is to determine *how* you learn most effectively. And this is particularly important for you if you learn differently. Chapter 3 of this book will talk about different learning styles and, hopefully, it will give you some insight about the way in which you learn best.

Quite simply, law school seeks to help you become a legal thinker, one who is largely self-taught. And in order to teach yourself the law well, you need to know how you learn and retain information most effectively. And you need to become an active learner. If you approach law school like you approached college, you may be surprised at the dismal results. Therefore, use the first weeks of law school to become a motivated and proactive learner.

D. Friends or Competitors? Get Ready for Competition in Law School!

I am always amazed to witness how law students change during their first year of law school. Students start out friendly and collegial and they transform into competitive and (often) unhappy individuals. This has been a reality in law school for a long time: legal education thrives on competition. With my own students, I notice that they are initially friendly and hopeful, and generally happy individuals. But the intense competition in law school tends to alter their initial excitement and optimism. There have been several empirical studies that have illustrated how law school takes a negative toll on law students' emotional well-beings.[11] One of the

---

11. Lawrence Krieger found in one study that: "The incidence of clinically elevated anxiety, hostility, depression, and other symptoms among these students ranged from eight to fifteen times that of the general population." Lawrence Krieger, *Institutional Denial About the Dark Side of Law School, and Fresh Empirical Guidance for Constructively Breaking the Silence*, 52 J. LEGAL EDUC. 112, 114 (2002).

See also, e.g. K. M. Sheldon and Lawrence S. Krieger, *Personality and Social Psychology Bulletin, Understanding the Negative Legal Effects of Legal Education on Law Students*, http://psp.sagepub.com/cgi/content/abstract/33/6/883 (last visited 09/12/09) (finding that "law school has a corrosive effect on the well-being, values, and motivation of students, ostensibly because of its problematic institutional culture." *Id.*

most accurate quotes about peer relationships in law school is as follows: "Relationships forged in law school are like those forged in war: what you share with these people is unlike any experience any of you have had before."[12]

You will learn a great deal from your law school colleagues. Some aspects of your peer relationships will be very positive and other aspects will be negative. I *can* promise you it will be an experience you will never forget.

How does the law school curriculum breed such intense competition? Consider the following reality: law schools are filled with talented and dedicated students—all of whom have excelled in the past. Now place all of those talented, driven students into a completely performance-oriented environment. What do I mean by performance-oriented? I mean that in law school, you are judged solely based upon your *performance* on law school exams—particularly during your first year. There are no bumps in your grade for good attendance or stellar class participation. There is no extra credit for coming to office hours or just being a wonderful and insightful student. Your entire grade in a course is determined by your performance on either one or two exams (or writing projects):[13] a midterm examination and a final examination. You (and everyone else around you) will work all semester and study like crazy. And, strangely, you will go into each exam with little idea about whether or not you *really* understand the material. The exam will last for three or four hours (depending on the amount of credit assigned for the course) and you will attempt to spill out an entire semester's worth of material during that single exam period. And the exams are graded anonymously. You will receive a final score on the exam which will determine your grade in the class.

And if that weren't enough pressure on new law students, almost all law schools still use a mandatory curve during the first year (and often some variation of the curve in years 2 and 3 as well). A mandatory curve means that in any given class, law professors are only *allowed* to give a certain percentage or number of students an A, B or C. In addition, law professors are also required to give a certain number of grades *below* a particular letter grade—usually below a C or C–. In a class of eighty students, if only 10% of students can receive an A, this means that only a handful of students will get A's. Likewise, a certain percentage of students (likely

---

12. Corrine Cooper, *Letter to a Young Law Student*, 35 Tulsa L.J. 275, 276 (2000). *See also* the advice given to first year law students by Professor Barbara Glesner Fines, at http://www.law.umkc.edu/faculty/profiles/glesnerfines/bgf-home.html (*citing* Corrine Cooper, *Letter to a Young Law Student*, http://www.law.umkc.edu/faculty/profiles/glesnerfines/letter.htm (last visited 9/12/09)).

13. In your legal writing or first year skills class, your grade will be determined largely by one or two writing projects (more or less "take home" exams).

around 10%) *must* receive grades below a C–. You are graded against your peers and *not* against an objective "good" answer. In other words, the poorer your peers do on an exam, the better your chances of grabbing one of the top grades.

Why does legal education persist in keeping the curve despite its perverse effects? I believe that the legal job market, in part, keeps the curve in place in legal education. If law school were pass-fail, or if there were no exams at all, then competition between students would be minimal. Everyone would leave law school with their diplomas and be on their way. But the competition in law school is caused, in part, by the job market. There are fewer jobs than there are lawyers. In order for law firms (and other legal employers) to determine who they will hire, legal education has created a hierarchy. Some law firms or judges only interview students who are in the top 10% or 15% of their law school classes. This means that at least 85%–90% of all law students will not have the opportunity to interview for these more exclusive positions.[14] And everyone would *like* the opportunity to interview for these types of positions.

So after first semester grades come out each year, the relationships between students often change—for the worse. Certainly, some students choose wisely not to "buy into" the ranking game. But it is very hard to resist because everyone wants to do well in law school.

Your personal experience (and happiness) in law school may be related, in part, to how you react to the inherent competition in law school. Some students allow it to motivate them; others allow it to scare them. Some students let it anger them. Interestingly, each 1L class develops its own sense of competition; some 1L groups become very supportive communities and others become groups of intensively competitive individuals. You have *control* over how you deal with the competition. Law school competition will always be there but you do not have to buy into it. In other words, try to focus on *learning* in law school and not on simply getting the "A" in a class.[15]

And the reality of competition in law school is that it exists for *all* students—whether you learn traditionally or differently. But let me be completely honest. The competitive experience of law school may be even

---

14. This is know as "OCI" or "On Campus Interviewing." In the fall of your second year, many of the elite larger employers (those that know that they will hire twenty summer associates every year), come to campus to interview students. Because everyone wants to interview with them, they restrict who they will interview to the top students. And this same phenomenon occurs with government jobs, i.e., District Attorney Offices or Defender Offices. These are just as coveted as private law firm experiences.

15. I completed an empirical study on whether law students who thrived on competition actually did better than law students who focused on learning. *See, e.g.,* Leah M. Christensen, *Predicting Law School Success: A Study of Goal Orientations, Academic Achievement and the Declining Self-Efficacy of our Law Students,* 33 J OF L. & PSYCH. REV. 57, 57 (2009).

more difficult for you if you happen to learn differently. This next sub-section will address how law students who learn differently can feel particularly isolated in law school.

E. Isolation in Law School for Those Who Learn Differently

Although most law students experience feelings of isolation at some point during their years in law school, the results of my research suggest that law students with learning disabilities (or those who learn differently) may experience *additional* feelings of isolation that their traditionally-learning peers. In a small study at my former law school, I asked law students with ADD about their experiences in law school. One consistent theme throughout my interviews with these students was that law students with ADD experienced significant feelings of isolation in law school.

In the literature, learning disabled law students often have been characterized as a "hidden minority" in legal education for two main reasons. First, law students with ADD and other learning disabilities tend to underreport their learning disabilities; and second, learning disabilities are typically "hidden" or unseen by the outside world.[16]

Each of the participants in my study described a need to hide their learning disability. Only one of the law students I talked to formally sought accommodations for her learning disability (ADD) and she was very selective about which friends, if any, that she chose to tell. The literature suggests there are personal and social consequences to having learning disabilities in law school that even the best accommodations and rules cannot address.[17]

Consider the comments of these three students with ADD: Alexa, Kelsey and Baker.

---

16. Alfreda A. Sellers noted that:

Even though learning disabled law students have access to tremendous legal tools with which to demand equality of educational opportunity, they often feel constrained from using them. The source of this constraint within the law school environment and the failure of learning disabled law students to identify themselves as beneficiaries of extraordinary, but available resources, emerge from the same dominant discourse and dynamic that fosters racism, sexism and homophobia. Although not completely analogous, the threat of being cast as "other" by those who occupy the constructed positions of whole-bodiedness is similar to the threat felt by people of color and women who experience oppression due to dominant normative hierarchies.

Alfreda A. Sellers Diamond, *L.D. Law: The Learning Disabled Law Student as Part of a Diverse Learning Environment*, 22 S.U. L. Rev. 69, 80–81 (1994).

17. *Id.* at 83–84.

Alexa was a second year student and she described how she began law school feeling isolated. Alexa's learning disability was diagnosed in college. Although Alexa had requested accommodations for her learning disability, she was conflicted about this decision.[18]

> ... I didn't tell anyone my first year [about my disability] because I was embarrassed. And then, getting good grades makes me more embarrassed because I don't feel like [the accommodations are] warranted.[19]

> My first year, I told my study partners [about my learning disability] because I would get anxiety. They would be like, "Oh, I can't finish with the times that they are giving us." [They asked me:] "Where are you when you're going to take the test?" I was like, "No, I take extended time and I'm not in the room because I have all these things. I still didn't feel comfortable even with my study friends.[20]

> I'd say in law school it's been difficult. Very difficult.[21]

> Again, because I'm getting this [accommodated] testing. The grades that I'm getting, I don't feel like I deserve them. Like in college, ... I was getting good grades, but I was working extra hard for them. Or, if I didn't get a good grade, it was because of the disorder.[22]

> Now, because I am getting accommodated testing, I'm getting good grades because of the disorder. Then, if I don't do well, then I just don't know. It just doesn't—I would say it has been difficult. And, I'm just feeling like I don't know.[23]

In contrast to Alexa, Kelsey was a first year law student that did not request accommodations for her learning disability. Kelsey was diagnosed with ADD while she was in grade school. Kelsey made it clear that she did not want to be treated differently because of her ADD. But Kelsey also expressed feelings of isolation.

> I don't like to be set apart for [ADD] at all. I feel like you can use ADD to your advantage and actually have an advantage over other students.[24]

---

18. Alexa received 50% additional time on her exams and took exams in a separate location than her peers. She also received note-taking accommodations during her first year.

19. Transcript of Interview with Student 100 at 6 (on file with the author).

20. *Id.*

21. *Id.* at 9.

22. *Id.* at 10.

23. *Id.* at 6.

24. Transcript of Interview with Student 103 at 9 (on file with the author).

Well, because your mind is more creative generally. You have an infinite way of thinking about one thing and I think that usually people with ADD tend to have more energy ... I feel like if you can turn it around and make it into something positive and really learn to control it. You have more energy going into that one reading. A "normal" person will just maybe read [a case] casually. But to me, like if I'm reading [a case], ... it's my entire world for that moment. [S]o I think, sometimes, you can read it more [intensely]—and you can remember it more. [25]

... I very much feel isolated.... I don't really have very many friends here. I almost feel like I've intentionally "outcasted" myself in a way. Well, I guess I just—I don't want to study with them ... And I don't go out with them or anything like that ... I guess, I don't know, I have had a hard time making friends in law school which is really strange to say because I've never had a problem with it before. [26]

Finally, Baker was a second year law student and, like Kelsey, he did not want to be treated differently because of his ADD. Baker was diagnosed with his learning disability in high school. The competitive nature of law school took a toll on Baker's self-esteem.

To me ... I don't want accommodations for my "thing." I'll get the grades I get in the system [because of] the way it's designed. I don't want an accommodation. Part of that is because I fear that if I got the accommodation and I didn't do any better, then what is the consequence of that? I don't know, I haven't really thought about it.[27]

... If my skills aren't supported in law school in terms of grades, then that's fine. I'll walk out of here and say, "[law school] doesn't [acknowledge] my skills and that doesn't bother me. I'm not gunning for the top job and six figures right out of law school. Perhaps the reason that I'm not gunning for one of those jobs is because I can't get the grades to get one.[28]

There is no question that legal education needs to make some changes in how we assess and evaluate students. Our students should be much more to us than merely grades or class ranks. But until law schools become more humane environments, it may be up to students individually to protect themselves against the negative effects of competition in law

---

25. *Id.* at 10.
26. *Id.* at 9.
27. Transcript of Interview with Student 102 at 7 (on file with the author).
28. *Id.*

school. By knowing how you learn most effectively, and by having a study plan during your first year, you can succeed in law school.

This book is dedicated to all the brilliant law students who may have learning disabilities or who may just "think out of the box" and learn differently. For those of you who fit into this category, you will need to approach law school differently—but I wholeheartedly believe you can succeed. Let's begin the journey now.

Chapter 2

You Are Not Alone: The Increasing Number of Law Students with Learning Disabilities

Law schools are filled with students that learn in a variety of ways. Several decades ago, law schools had a more homogenous student population that consisted mainly of "traditional learners." By traditional learners, I mean the stereotypical law student from decades ago who was most likely a student coming right out of undergraduate school in his mid-twenties. A traditional learner responds well to traditional instructional techniques like a teacher lecturing in front of the room. A traditional learner can easily progress through a group curriculum. In contrast, non-traditional learners tend *not* to respond as well to more traditional teaching methodologies. Non-traditional learners can include adult learners, students with learning disabilities, or simply students who tend to learn best by processing information differently. Non-traditional students can learn effectively but they may need more creative teaching and learning methodologies to reach their learning potential.

The current reality of our law school populations is that they are far more diverse—in terms of gender, ethnicity and learning styles. Part of this new diversity includes having students that learn differently or non-traditionally. And this new reality in legal education means that law school pedagogy (the way in which we teach law students) is also slowly changing to meet the needs of our diverse student population. Some law students learn differently because of learning disabilities, either diagnosed or undiagnosed. Other law students may simply learn *differently* compared to others. However, an important point to consider is that most law professors teach in the way that *they* learned in law school. But the way that your law professors learned in law school may not work for you. In other words, there can be a mismatch between how law professors teach in law school and the way in which you learn.

It is difficult if not impossible to know how many students in law school have been diagnosed with learning disabilities. An actual number of law students with disabilities may never be known given that more and more law students with learning (and other) disabilities choose not to self-identify.[1] But we do know that the overall number of people with disabilities in our society is growing. Recent census data reports that there are approximately 54 million people with disabilities in America, or roughly one in five Americans.[2] We also know that more students with documented disabilities are attending college than ever before. In 1996, over nine percent of all college freshmen documented a disability.[3] Thirty-five percent of college freshmen reporting a disability have a learning disability.[4] With advances in knowledge about education, including knowledge about different learning styles and providing appropriate accommodations, more students are matriculating through undergraduate programs with a high degree of success. Many of those successful students with learning disabilities will attend law school and become lawyers.

Professor Robin Boyle asserts that the majority of law school classes are likely to include students with Attention Deficit Disorder (ADD).[5] Approximately five to eight percent of Americans have ADD which means that more than 10 million Americans are affected by ADD.[6] Further, many people, including law students, may not be aware that they have ADD or another learning disability, which means that law professors will not know this either.[7] In higher education, the number of students reporting that they have ADD is substantial.[8] In a survey conducted in the United States, of the 16.5 million undergraduate students in the United States, 6.4 % of the students reported having ADD.[9] This suggests that there are over one million students who know they have ADD and report it to the

---

1. Kevin H. Smith, *Disabilities, Law Schools, and Law Students: A Proactive and Holistic Approach*, 32 Akron L. Rev. 1 (1999).

2. Jolly-Ryan, *supra* chapter 1, n.8 at 121 (citing the ABA Commission on Mental and Physical Disability Law, Goal IX: A Report on the Status of the Participation of Persons with Disabilities in ABA Section, Division and Forum Leadership Positions (2005)).

3. *Id.* at 122 (citing Stephen B. Thomas, *College Students and Disability Law*, 33 J. of Special Educ. 248, 248 (2000)).

4. *Id.*

5. Robin A. Boyle, *Law Students With Attention Deficit Disorder: How to Reach Them, How to Teach Them*, 39 J. Marshall L. Rev. 349 (2006).

6. *Id.* at 350 (citing Edward M. Hallowell & John J. Ratey, Delivered from Distraction: Getting the Most Out of Life with Attention Deficit Disorder 8 (2005)).

7. *Id.*.

8. *Id.*

9. *Id.* (citing Nat'l Ctr. for Educ. Statistics, U.S. Dep't of Educ., Profile of Undergraduates in U.S. Postsecondary Institutions: 1999–2000 (Statistical Analysis Report) iii (2002), available at http://nces.ed.gov/pubs2002/2002168.PDF.). After significant attempts, I did not find any sources of statistics on how many law students have ADD).

institution.[10] Just as many students may have ADD and choose not report it, or are unaware that they are affected by the disability.[11]

Further, a recent American Bar Association law school enrollment survey revealed that as recently as 2002, law schools provided accommodations for both physical and learning disabilities for 2,655 law students out of a total of 132,885 students, or 1.9%.[12] Law students with learning disabilities are now the largest group of students with disabilities.[13] Although these students may learn differently than the traditionally-learning law student, they are a reality (and an important part of) legal education.

---

10. *Id.*

11. *Id.*

12. ABA Commission on Mental and Physical Disability Law, supra n.2 at 2.

13. M. Kay Runyan & Joseph F. Smith, Jr., *Identifying and Accommodating Learning Disabled Law School Students*, 41 J. LEGAL EDUC. 317, 317–21 (1991). By 1991, six percent of all disabled law students reported learning disabilities and were the largest group of disabled students.

Chapter 3

Succeeding in Law School by Knowing How *You* Learn Best: What Is Your Individual Learning Style?

Each of us has a different learning style (or a combination of learning styles). A "learning style" refers to how someone processes and retains new and difficult information. There is no single *right* way to learn—there are only different *ways* to learn. Professor Michael Hunter Schwartz advocates that law students need to become *expert* learners.[1] In other words, not only do you need to know how to learn generally, but you also need to know how you "personally learn best" and how you "prefer to learn."[2]

Traditionally-learning law students will have learning preferences just like non-traditional learners will prefer some methods of learning over others. An important point, however, is that law school tends to *favor* some learning styles over others. For example, a student who learns best by *listening* to her law professor lecture may find law school classes more meaningful than a student who prefers to *see* the concepts on PowerPoint slides or graphs. As we discussed in Chapter 1, the most common approach in law school teaching is the lecture format, combined with the Socratic Method. However, this method of teaching does not always work well for every law student *because not all students learn effectively within this lecture format*. Therefore, in order to maximize your learning in law school, you need to begin by understanding more about the way in which you learn.

A. The Basic Learning Styles

Your learning style refers to the way in which you like to approach new information. Each of us processes information in our own way, although we may share some learning patterns, preferences, and approaches.

---

1. Michael Hunter Schwartz, *Teaching Students to Be Self-Regulated Learners*, 2003 MICH. ST. DCL L. REV. 447 (Summer 2003).

2. *Id.*

There are five basic learning styles but most of us use a combination of more than one.[3] In the order from most common to least common, the learning styles are typically described as follows:

(1) *Verbal Learners.* These students absorb information most effectively through written text.[4] The majority of law students fall into this category.

(2) *Visual Learners.* These students tend to be more right-brain, holistic learners who absorb information as a whole, rather than in parts, and who process information best when it is presented using pictures and diagrams.[5] Students who are visual learners tend to learn most effectively by using visual aids because they remember best what they read or see.

(3) *Oral (or Auditory) Learners.* These students tend to work best when they 'talk out' their ideas.[6] In addition, these students develop their ideas or process information by participating in class discussions. Further, many students find that they learn effectively when they walk around their apartments or study rooms 'talking' out difficult concepts.

(4) *Aural Learners.* These students might learn best by listening to lectures, class discussions, study group discussions, or tapes.[7] The student who tapes his or her lecture to listen to it again may be an aural learner.

(5) *Tactile and Kinesthetic Learners.* These students tend to learn material by touching and experiencing what they need to absorb.[8] In the law school environment, these students tend to learn most effectively by writing and taking good notes, and through "learning by doing," which might include role-playing, simulations, clinical experiences, or hands-on research exercises.

There are many different "learning style" inventories that can assess how you learn most effectively. It may be beneficial to you to spend some time filling out one of these detailed questionnaires. One example of a simplified "learning styles" questionnaire can be found in the chart opposite. This chart asks a series of questions which relate to three of the most common learning styles: visual; auditory; and kinesthetic. For each

---

3. There are many excellent articles and books analyzing law students' learning styles. *See* Michael Hunter Schwartz, Expert Learning for Law Students. 2nd edition. (Carolina Academic Press, 2008); *see also* Vernellia R. Randall, *The Myers-Briggs Type Indicator, First Year Law Students and Performance*, 26 Cumb. L. Rev. 63, 68–74 (1995); M.H. Sam Jacobson, *A Primer on Learning Styles: Reaching Every Student*, 25 Seattle U. L. Rev. 139, 142–143 (2001).

4. Anthony S. Niedwiecki, *Lawyers and Learning: A Metacognitive Approach to Legal Education*, 13 Widener L. Rev. 33, 34 (2006), n.6 (*citing* Jacobson, *supra* n.3 at 151).

5. *Jacobson, supra* n.3 at 152.

6. *Id.* at 154.

7. *Id.* at 155

8. *Id.*

Learning Styles Questionnaire

1. When I try to **concentrate** …	I grow distracted by clutter or movement, and I notice things around me other people don't notice.	I get distracted by sounds, and I attempt to control the amount and type of noise around me.	I become distracted by commotion, and I tend to retreat inside myself.
2. When I **visualize** …	I see vivid, detailed pictures in my thoughts.	I think in voices and sounds.	I see images in my thoughts that involve movement.
3. When I **talk with others** …	I find it difficult to listen for very long.	I enjoy listening, or I get impatient to talk myself.	I gesture and communicate with my hands.
4. When I **contact people** …	I prefer face-to-face meetings.	I prefer speaking by telephone for serious conversations.	I prefer to interact while walking or participating in some activity.
5. When I **see an acquaintance** …	I forget names but remember faces, and I tend to replay where we met for the first time.	I know people's names and I can usually quote what we discussed.	I remember what we did together and I may almost "feel" our time together.
6. When I **relax** …	I watch TV, see a play, visit an exhibit, or go to a movie.	I listen to the radio, play music, read, or talk with a friend.	I play sports, make crafts, or build something with my hands.
7. When I **read** …	I like descriptive examples and I may pause to imagine the scene.	I enjoy the narrative most and I can almost "hear" the characters talk.	I prefer action-oriented stories, but I do not often read for pleasure.
8. When I **spell** …	I envision the word in my mind or imagine what the word looks like when written.	I sound out the word, sometimes aloud, and tend to recall rules about letter order.	I get a feel for the word by writing it out or pretending to type it.
9. When I **do something new** …	I seek out demonstrations, pictures, or diagrams.	I want verbal and written instructions, and to talk it over with someone else.	I jump right in to try it, keep trying, and try different approaches.
10. When I **assemble an object** …	I look at the picture first and then, maybe, read the directions.	I read the directions, or I talk aloud as I work.	I usually ignore the directions and figure it out as I go along.
11. When I **interpret someone's mood** …	I examine facial expressions.	I rely on listening to tone of voice.	I focus on body language.
12. When I **teach other people** …	I show them.	I tell them, write it out, or I ask them a series of questions.	I demonstrate how it is done and then ask them to try.
Total	Visual: _____	Auditory: _____	Tactile/Kinesthetic _____

question in the left-hand column, choose the response that best describes your learning preference. When you select an answer, give yourself a point for that column. The column with the highest total represents your primary processing style. The column with the second-most choices is your secondary style.[9]

If most of your responses fall within the first category, you may tend to be a visual learner. If most of your responses fall in the second column, you may prefer an auditory or oral learning style. And if most of your responses fall within the third category, you might prefer a tactile or kinesthetic learning style. Although this chart provides only a snapshot of an in-depth learning profile, the types of questions will allow you to begin thinking about your individual learning style.

After you have a sense of your learning style, consider how you might *use* your learning style to study more effectively in law school. For example, consider how the three different learning styles described above might affect how you read a case in preparation for class. If your primary learning style is visual, you might find yourself drawing pictures in the margins of the case as you read. Perhaps you *see* the facts of the case play out as if you are watching a movie.

In contrast, if your primary learning style is auditory, you may understand the text best when you *listen* to the words you read. Perhaps you carry on an internal conversation between yourself and the text, or you read the text aloud.

Or if your primary learning style is tactile/kinesthetic, you may find yourself using a highlighter to mark passages that are meaningful to you. You may also like to take notes or even walk around as you read so that you are both mentally and physically engaged in the learning task.

The main point of this exercise is to recognize that there are many different ways in which we learn. One key to academic success in law school is to understand your individual learning preferences so that you can maximize your learning in law school.

B. Applying Your Learning Style to Law School

In an ideal world, your professors in each of your law school classes would adapt their *teaching* styles to meet as many diverse learning styles as possible. However, you should be prepared to have several classes in law school where your professor teaches in a way that does not necessarily meet your individual learning style. Therefore, you must be prepared to take on some of the responsibility for your own learning in law

---

9. This learning inventory was taken from The Ageless Learner Website, under the link for "Learning Style Assessment," at http://agelesslearner.com/assess/learning style.html (last visited on May 5, 2009).

school. You will be more successful in law school if you know how *you* learn best. This is called "meta-cognition" and this involves "self-regulation of cognitive activities through monitoring and making appropriate adjustments" in one's learning.[10] In other words, you need to teach yourself *how* to learn.

If you know your learning style, you can adjust your approach to classroom learning and studying as you need to do so (depending on your professor). You can also challenge yourself to become more adept at learning in different ways, thereby becoming a more successful independent learner. For example, if you are a verbal learner, you probably will learn by reading your casebook and supplementary materials. If you are a visual learner, you will likely want to supplement your learning in the regular classroom by creating charts or other visual aids. You may make detailed, color-coded outlines or use other visual cues to assist your learning. If you are an oral learner, you may feel comfortable engaging in class discussions. You may also like to read aloud or become involved in several study groups so you can talk over the concepts in detail. If you are an auditory or aural learner, you will probably enjoy the lecture format of the law school classroom. You might consider asking your professor's permission to audiotape the lecture. Finally, if you are a tactile or kinesthetic learner, you may find yourself taking notes or using index cards, creating your own essay and multiple-choice questions. You may also find that you love law school most when you are working in a clinical program or engaged in experiential learning.

Remember that law school learning requires *more* than just memorization skills that may have worked for you before. You need to become more involved in your learning—devising a study plan that utilizes your learning strengths.

Of course, learning styles are also affected by personal characteristics such as intelligence and personality, which are least subject to change, and information processing (right brain/left brain functions), social interaction (motivation, values, and social milieu), and instructional preferences (e.g., light, temperature, sound, design), which can and do change.[11]

Although these specific issues of personal and social characteristics are beyond the scope of this book, they may indeed affect how you learn. For example, you will want to determine whether forming or joining a study group is a good use of your time. The answer depends on how you learn best. Some students become distracted if they study with others. Other students find it incredibly helpful. For example, an oral learner, who learns by *participating* in discussions, or an aural learner, who learns by

---

10. Niedwiecki, *supra* n.4 at 35.
11. Jacobson, *supra* n.3 at 146–147.

listening to discussions, may find study groups an ideal way to learn material. But this method may be less helpful for the verbal, visual, tactile, or kinesthetic learner. Deciding whether a study group is for you also depends on the social milieu in which you operate best and within which you are most comfortable. If you decide to form or join a study group, get to know your colleagues first and choose the group members with care. If they are of the same mindset and work ethic as you, you are more likely to have a successful study group experience.

Finally, knowing one's learning style is also integral to your ability to process the large volumes of information that you must digest in law school. Keep in mind that some courses give law professors more opportunities than others to meet the learning styles of their students, and often class size is an important factor in the number of active, experiential activities that will occur in a class. For example, you may find that you thrive in your Legal Research and Writing course, a required course in most law schools during the first year. These types of smaller classes that focus on learning skills (research and writing) in combination with substance can give professors more opportunities to teach to diverse learning styles. In addition, these types of classes often give students who learn differently the opportunity to learn in a variety of ways, such that the learning style of almost every student can be satisfied in these classes. For this reason, students who learn differently tend to excel in these types of hands-on, skills classes.[12] If you find that you do like these smaller, experiential classes, you may want to select as many of these classes as possible throughout law school.

C. Law Students with ADD: How Did They Learn Best in Law School?

In this last subsection to Chapter 3, I would like to share the *learning* experiences of three law students with ADD. As part of a study on law students with ADD, I asked three students to describe how they learned most effectively. What I discovered was that the two most successful students, Alexa and Kelsey, knew their individual learning styles and this knowledge helped them excel in law school. In contrast, the third student, Baker, did not have a good sense of how he learned. This may have contributed to Baker's challenges in law school. However, what *was* similar amongst these three students with ADD was that each of them acknowledged that they learned differently from their peers. This subsec-

---

12. These classes tend to be legal writing classes, law school clinical programs, trial advocacy, appellate advocacy, etc. In these classes, you focus on both doctrine and the skills of applying the doctrine to client-type situations.

tion will offer the comments of Alexa, Kelsey and Baker with regard to how they studied and learned in law school.

Alexa was a second year law student with ADD. At the time of the study, Alexa was in the top 5% of her law school class. Alexa appeared to understand very specifically how she learned and she organized her study materials to fit her unique learning style. Alexa described herself as a visual learner and she seemed to have learned this through trial and error during her first semester of law school. Alexa also seemed to exhibit a read/write learning style. Alexa described her learning style as follows:

> I learned it in college that, for me, that I just have to rewrite things over and over. And over again. That [is] how I would study in college.... I had all my handwritten notes and before an exam I would type them up. Or I would rewrite them. And I've been doing that now as well. That's like outlining is a great thing [for me]. Like where you have to rewrite it.[13]

> ... I wrote note cards because just reading it [only] doesn't help. And so then just writing it in the computer doesn't help. Its— I would love to say that I'm a hypochondriac or something because like I sometimes think I have OCD because like just certain colors. With this I'm going to color code everything. Where I become just extremely organized and I—for my appellate brief visually had everything in different colors.[14]

Kelsey was a first year student with ADD, and ended up in the top 30% of her class. Kelsey described her initial frustrations at figuring out how to study and learn in law school.

> Well, it was really hard for me at first [in law school]. And I did really horrible when I first did midterms.... I was trying so hard to read everything and remember everything about *every* case. It was just like killing me. So, I got my grades back from midterms and it was like, "Gosh, I'm [stupid]. I shouldn't be here."[15]

> And so, I had to go through and evaluate [what I was doing].... I talked to the academic advisor, and I just kind of stepped back and let them say, "O.K., what am I doing wrong?" [I] realized I was kind of focusing on the wrong details. So, I guess it kind of comes down to reading and how I was trying to read everything and remember everything ... I think it became a lot easier after

---

13. Transcript of Interview with Student 100 at 8–9 (on file with the author).
14. Transcript of Interview with Student 103 at 9 (on file with the author).
15. *Id.* at 4–5.

that. And, I did really well on my finals. But at the same time, my grades weren't as great because I totally failed midterms.[16]

Kelsey discovered her preferred learning style after midterms during her first semester of law school. In order to organize her reading and studying in law school, she devised a very intricate highlighting system where she would use ten different colors of highlighters to note particular aspects of any case. To work with her ADD, Kelsey described how she would create visual cues as she read in order to trigger her memory about a particular aspect of a case. Kelsey acknowledged that she was a visual learner.

> The colors give me a point of reference ... It makes my mind think, "O.K., I know what that is." I don't have to read it once I color it. Once I color "facts," I know what those facts are. Part of my process is [that when I] highlight them, [I'm] kind of saving them in my mind.[17]

> "Pink" are the rules.[18] Underlining in "pink" [marks] a commentary rule.[19] And, then, "purple" is court's reasoning. "Blue" is the court's holding and ... order. "Yellow" is a fact. I have other colors. I have a "light orange" [that] I use to represent a case that is cited in a case. And I use a "dark orange" for procedural history. And I use "red" for dicta. And ... a weird "green" color I use for my notes within a case.[20]

Kelsey also studied most effectively in a quiet setting, most often away from the law school. Kelsey described that she had to get in her study "zone." In addition, Kelsey knew that structure and organization were important to the success of her learning.

> Well, [I] ... have to get into this zone ... Because it's like you have to shut out everything else ... your whole world exists on what you're doing.

> ... So everything in your energy goes to that. Everything you're doing is trying to stay [in] that [zone] Otherwise, you're going

---

16. *Id.* at 5.
17. *Id.* at 7.
18. The "rule" refers to either the statutory law or case law that a court uses to determine the outcome of the case at hand. A court may cite several "rules" to determine the outcome of a case and a larger rule may be broken down into sub-rules, called "elements."
19. A court may discuss laws (or " commentary rules") within an opinion that help to provide a context for its reasoning, but are not the actual law that needs to be applied to the case at hand. *See e.g., Marchetti v. Parsons*, 638 A.2d. 1047 (R.I. 1994) (wherein the court presents the development of the claim of bystander negligent infliction of emotional distress in Rhode Island through discussion of prior holdings).
20. Transcript of Interview with Student 103 at 7 (on file with the author).

to see something and be more interested [in that] or you're going to sometimes just feel like you're everywhere

... Like stress can really [make] that "zone" hard to control.[21]

Baker was a second year law student at the time of this study. Baker had ADD and felt that this contributed to his struggles in law school. After his second year, Baker was in the bottom 15% of his law school class. Baker commented on the stressful environment of his first year. Baker was likely a kinesthetic learner; he stated that he needed to move around as he studied.

> I need to move around [when I study] and the library intimidates me. Seeing everybody else sitting at a desk in one place for six hours and not moving—it's an uncomfortable place for me. I like a place like the coffeehouse. Its odd, but I can focus where there are things going on and the light noise. I'd just be like, oh, looking around.[22]

> Yes. It's the [law school] environment. It's the whole law school environment.... But coming to school and seeing everybody sitting in the library until 1:00 a.m. at night, reading through case after case after case was just—I couldn't take it.

> ... [I]t's just the culture of law school and a lot of it is bred in the first year ... It's this hyper-intense environment of competition and competing with yourself, and trying to become a perfectionist and all that.[23]

Each of these students described above learned differently. Alexa was a read/write learner; Kelsey was a visual learner; and Baker was a kinesthetic learner. Why should *you* care about your learning style? When you acknowledge and validate your individual learning style, you will do better in law school. If you can identify and utilize the strengths inherent in how you learn, you will learn information more easily and more permanently. In the above-referenced examples, Alexa and Kelsey developed a sense of how they learned most effectively, and this contributed to their success in law school. In contrast, although Baker seemed to know that he needed movement and background noise in order to study well, he may not have understood that he was likely a kinesthetic learner.

As you begin your first semester of law school, determine if you have a specific learning style. Consider which classes seem easier for you and which ones feel more challenging. For those classes that are more challenging, consider how you will supplement your learning in those classes.

---

21. *Id.* at 6.
22. Transcript of Interview with Student 102 at 5 (on file with the author).
23. *Id.*

Perhaps you can buy review tapes or listen to lectures. Or maybe you can create note cards for each rule and diagram the rule with different colors. Perhaps you will create flowcharts to help you organize the information in a class.[24] The key is to begin early and to have a plan for using your learning style to maximize your academic success. The remaining chapters of this book will provide you with specific ways you can maximize your learning strengths in the law school classroom and on exams.

---

24. *See infra* Chapter 6, part B(6), *Organize Your Class Notes.*

Chapter 4

Legal Reading: The Key to Law School Success

Through my research, I have learned the importance of *how* law students read judicial opinions. Although many professors assume that students come to law school knowing how to read a case well—legal reading is very different than any other type of reading you have done before. The most successful law students read cases differently than law students who tend to struggle during their first year—regardless of whether they learn traditionally or non-traditionally. In an empirical study on legal reading, I found that traditionally-learning law students in the top 50% of their class read cases very differently than law students in the bottom 50% of their class. Further, in a second study on legal reading, I found that law students with ADD who were at the top of their class read cases in almost the same way as traditionally-learning law students who were higher-performing. Chapter 4 will discuss the results of the general study on legal reading and the correlation between how a student reads a case and her law school GPA. In Chapter 5, I will focus specifically on how three law students with ADD read a judicial opinion. My research has shown that regardless of learning styles or learning differences, legal reading is one of the *most* important skills to master in law school.

A. Legal Reading and Law School Success: Traditionally-Learning Law Students

You will spend thousands of hours in law school reading judicial opinions. Yet rarely will your law professors discuss *how* you should approach legal reading. Instead, law professors will assume that you are an excellent reader because you have obviously been successful as a student before getting into law school. However, legal reading is a particularly challenging task. In order for you to fully comprehend *legal* text, you need knowledge of legal terminology and an understanding of both case structure and legal theory.[1] One of my favorite quotes about legal reading comes from Scott Turow

---

1. Peter Dewitz, *Legal Education: A Problem of Learning From Text*, 23 N.Y.U. REV. L. & SOC. CHANGE 225, 226 (1997).

describing his first year at Harvard Law School. He compared reading cases to "something like stirring concrete with my eyelashes."[2]

Although many law students adapt quickly to legal reading, other students struggle with legal reading throughout law school — even if they are traditional learners. Sometimes struggling students simply take *longer* to read through the dense material found in a typical law school case. Other students read the cases quickly but they fail to take *out* of the case what the professor sees as the most important material or essence of the case. I believe that every law student can learn to be an effective legal reader — with or without learning differences. But like any other skill, you may need to practice *how* to read a legal case more effectively.

In 2007, I completed an empirical study that examined whether the way in which law students read a judicial opinion impacted their law school success.[3] Specifically, I questioned whether there was a correlation between the way in which first year law students in the top 50% and bottom 50% of their class read a judicial opinion and whether the students' use of particular reading strategies impacted their law school grades.[4] I found that even when students went through the same first-semester classes, the more successful law students read judicial opinions differently from those students who were less successful. Further, the study suggested there was a correlation between the reading strategies of the top law students and their first-semester grades.

Before you can improve your reading skills, however, you need to understand what happens in good readers' minds while they read. You probably do many of these things already. Good readers — whether they learn traditionally or non-traditionally — have developed *habits* when they read. We call these habits "strategies." Reading strategies help legal readers understand, connect to, and determine the importance of *what* they are reading. Let's first examine the three categories of reading strategies that are used most frequently.

B. Three Types of Reading Strategies

There are three main types of reading strategies: (1) default reading strategies; (2) problematizing reading strategies; and (3) rhetorical reading strategies.[5]

---

2. Mary A. Lundeberg, *Metacognitive Aspects of Reading Comprehension: Studying Understanding in Legal Case Analysis*, 22 Reading Res. Q. 407, 409 (1987) (*citing* Scott Turow, One L 30–31 (1978)).

3. Leah M. Christensen, *Legal Reading and Law School Success: An Empirical Study*, 30 Seattle U. L. Rev. 603, 603 (2007).

4. I categorized these students as traditionally-learning law students in the sense that they had not been diagnosed with a learning disability.

5. Dorothy Deegan (Evenson), one of the first researchers to examine how law

The first type of reading strategy is called a *default* reading strategy. Default reading strategies represent the basic strategies that any of us use to move through legal text, including paraphrasing, rereading, noting certain structural elements of text, underlining text and making margin notes.[6] The research has shown that when readers use default strategies, they move through the text in a linear progression.[7] Dorothy Deegan Evenson, an expert on legal reading, describes default reading strategies as follows:

> Typically, readers would restate or paraphrase portions of the information, often underlining and/or making margin notes. What differentiated these moves from the ones associated with [other] strategies was the unproblematic nature of the process. In other words, these verbalizations were not specifically initiated from or tied to explicit questions or hypotheses.[8]

Beginning readers tend to rely more heavily on default reading strategies because these strategies are both accessible and familiar. If you are new to legal reading, it makes sense for you to begin reading by underlining or highlighting the opinion because these are the same types of reading strategies that you used earlier in your academic careers.

In the reading study, readers used default reading strategies when they moved through the text in a linear progression.[9] For example, readers used default strategies when they "paraphrased" or "underlined" text. Default strategies also included "making margin notes," "noting aspects of structure" and "highlighting" text.

The following example illustrates a student using default reading strategies as the student read through the case for the first time. For the purposes of my study, I had the students perform a "think aloud," where the study participants would read a portion of the opinion out loud, and then stop and reflect upon what they were thinking at that point in their reading. The regular text is the student's thoughts or "think aloud." The highlights and margin comments indicate which reading strategy the student was using.

---

students read legal text, used the results of her reading study to construct three categories or types of reading strategies: problematizing strategies, default strategies, and rhetorical strategies. Dorothy H. Deegan, *Exploring Individual Differences Among Novices Reading in a Specific Domain: The Case of Law,* 30 Reading Res. Q. 154 (1995), at 161. In the present study, I adopted these categories to define and analyze the way in which my students read a judicial opinion.

6. Dewitz, *supra* n.1 at 228–229; Deegan, *supra* n.5 at 161.

7. Deegan, *supra* n.5, at 160.

8. *Id.* at 161.

9. Deegan, *supra* n.5, at 160–161.

Ok. So it is a disciplinary proceeding action, —— noting important detail
and the main issue is the attorney's failure to dis-
close material information that was known to ⎤— noting aspect of structure
him. Um—and it was directly adverse to his —— paraphrasing
client's position. He didn't advise the client
paraphrasing —⎡ and he didn't advise the court and so there was
a public reprimand and admonishment. Um— —— noting factual detail
skimming —— just briefly skimming the, um, keynotes, the —— noting aspect of structure
Attorney and Client, failure to disclose au-
paraphrasing —⎡ thority in the Rules of Professional Conduct
there would be Rule 1.4 and 3.3. I'm skimming —— skimming
with that.[10]

These twelve moves represented the use of default reading strategies.[11]

The second type of reading strategy is called a *problematizing* reading strategy.[12] Problematizing reading strategies contain techniques to help readers solve *problems* within the text. "Readers use problem formation strategies to set expectations for a text. They ask themselves questions, make predictions, and hypothesize about developing meaning."[13] Prior research in reading has found that problematizing strategies involve "strategic behavior" on the part of the reader, in that the reader's behavior can be described as purposeful.[14] Various studies have associated the use of problematizing strategies with high performing student readers and expert/lawyer readers.[15] These readers asked questions; they talked back to the text, made predictions, hypothesized about meaning, and connected with the overall purpose of their reading.[16]

---

10. Transcript of Interview with Student 105 at 1 (on file with the author).

11. Deegan, *supra* n.5 at 161 (citing R.J. Spiro, B. Bertram & W. Brewer, eds., *Constructive Processes in Prose Comprehension and Recall*, in THEORETICAL ISSUES IN READING COMPREHENSION 1, 256 (1980)). Deegan relied on Spiro's theory that "the default assignment process … probably forms the basis for a large part of construction in comprehension." *Id.*

12. Deegan, *supra* n.5, at 161. In the present study, I adopted these categories to define and analyze the way in which my students read a judicial opinion *See also* Michael Pressley & Peter Afflerbach, *Verbal Protocols of Reading: The Nature of Constructively Responsive Reading* 1–14, 119–40 (1995).

13. Dewitz, *supra* n.1, at 228–229 (describing his definition of Deegan's problematizing strategies).

14. Deegan, *supra* n.5, at 160.

15. See Deegan, *supra* n.5, at 163–165; LAUREL CURRIE OATES & ANNE ENQUIST, LEGAL WRITING HANDBOOK: ANALYSIS, RESEARCH, AND WRITING 37 (4th ed., Aspen Publishers, 2006) at 159; Lundeberg, *supra* n.2 at 417.

16. Oates, *supra* n.15, at 159–160.

The following provides an example of a law student reading using problematizing strategies. Once again, the regular text in the paragraph below represents the student's thoughts about the case. The highlights and margin comments indicate the particular reading strategy used by the student. And the italicized text is the actual text of the case.

connecting with prior text —— So now I'm just going to go back to where they started talking about the facts. Because I'm more concerned about the videotape as I think —— hypothesizing

that's going to be an issue. *Prior to the client's initial hearing, and before the client met with or hired a lawyer, the client was advised by videotape*

evaluating —— *of his rights.* So this is curious. Um—I guess

voicing confusion —— it's so unclear to me. Apparently at the first ap- —— synthesizing
pearance, the client viewed the videotape and
pled guilty. But I guess it's a little unclear and —— evaluating

distinguishing —— apparently he wasn't represented at that time.[17]

Note how the student is actively working through the text—grappling with the potential legal issues in the opinion.

Finally, the third type of reading strategy is called a *rhetorical* reading strategy.[18] While using rhetorical reading strategies, readers move through the text in an evaluative manner or in way that synthesizes what is being read with the reader's own experiences.[19] Rhetorical strategies "represented points where the reader engaged in the kind of practices where the reader took a step beyond the text itself. They [were] concerned with constructing a rhetorical situation for the text, trying to account for the author's purpose, context and effect on the audience."[20]

In the study, law students used rhetorical reading strategies when they examined text in an "evaluative" way or when they moved outside of the text "into the realm of [...] personal knowledge."[21] In my study, I categorized the following moves as rhetorical: "evaluating," "connecting with prior experience," "contextualizing" and "connecting with purpose."[22]

---

17. Transcript of Interview with Student 109 at 3 (on file with the author).

18. Deegan, *supra* n.75, at 161.

19. *Id.*

20. *Id.* (citing C. Haas & L. Flower, *Rhetorical Reading Strategies and the Construction of Meaning*, 39 COLLEGE COMPOSITION AND COMMUNICATION 167, 176 (1988)).

21. *Id.* at 161.

22. *Id.*

This last example illustrates a law student using rhetorical reading strategies. Note in particular how the reader evaluated the case and actively read the case to prepare for a client interview.[23]

These examples illustrated the three types of reading strategies used by law students in the study: (1) default reading strategies; (2) problematizing reading strategies; and (3) rhetorical reading strategies. The next section of this chapter will explore the study background and results in more detail.

C. The Legal Reading Study: Background and Results

My study examined the way 24 first-year law students read a legal case using these three types of reading strategies.[25] These students were traditionally-learning law students and each of them volunteered to participate in the study. Specifically, I asked the law students to read a judicial opinion authored by the Indiana Supreme Court, *In Re Thonert*, 733 N.E.2d 932 (Ind. 2000).[26] The students were instructed to read the text of the case

---

23. I asked the study participants to read the case with a specific purpose in mind: prepare for a client interview. When students used this purpose in their reading, I coded their move as "connecting with purpose" which is a rhetorical reading strategy.

24. Transcript of Interview with Student 105 at 4 (on file with the author).

25. This first legal reading study involved students who had not been diagnosed with a learning disability. For the purposes of comparison, I am categorizing these law students as "traditionally-learning" law students. In the second study, the students had been diagnosed with a learning disability. Accordingly, I categorized those students as "non-traditional" learners.

26. The opinion, *In Re Thonert*, was a *per curiam* decision by the Indiana Supreme Court reviewing a disciplinary proceeding against an attorney. *In Re Thonert*, 733 N.E. 2d. 932, 932 (Ind. 2000).

aloud, stop every sentence or two and tell me what they were thinking. In psychological research, this type of activity is called a 'think aloud.' I recorded the students as they read and had the recordings transcribed.

Before I had the students read the opinion, I instructed the students to read the case with a particular purpose in mind:

> **Read the following legal text assuming that you are a practicing attorney and that you are reading the opinion to prepare for a meeting with a client who has a case that is similar to the facts of case you are reading.**

I gave them this specific purpose because I wanted to find out whether reading with the purpose of preparing for a client meeting changed the way in which students read the case.[27]

The introductory portion of *In Re Thonert* is printed below.[28] You may want to skim the case yourself to see how *you* read the judicial opinion before you consider the study results.

---

733 N.E.2d 932

Supreme Court of Indiana.
In the Matter of Richard J. THONERT.

No. 02S00-9902-DI-151.
Aug. 22, 2000.

Disciplinary proceeding was brought against attorney, in which Disciplinary Commission and attorney entered Statement of Circumstances and Conditional agreement for Discipline. The Supreme Court held that attorney's failure to disclose to appellate tribunal controlling authority which was known to him, and had not been disclosed by opposing counsel, that was directly adverse to his client's position, and to advise client of the adverse authority, warranted public reprimand and admonishment.

So ordered.

* * *

PER CURIAM.

The respondent in this attorney disciplinary matter is charged with failing to disclose to an appellate tribunal controlling authority known to him, not disclosed by opposing counsel, that was directly adverse to his client's position. He also failed to advise his client of the adverse authority when his client was contemplating his legal options.

This matter is presented to this Court upon the Disciplinary Commission's and the respondent's *Statement of Circumstances and Condi-*

---

27. I did not give the students any particular facts to suggest their client's issue. I left the client's legal problem purposefully vague.

28. The full text of the opinion can be found in Appendix A at the back of this book.

tional Agreement for Discipline, entered pursuant to Ind.Admission and Discipline Rule 23(11)(c), in resolution of this matter. That agreement is before us now for approval. We note that our jurisdiction of this matter derives from the respondent's admission to the practice of law in this state in 1974.

The parties agree that the respondent represented a client charged with operating a motor vehicle while intoxicated. Prior to the client's initial hearing and before the client met with or hired the respondent, the client was advised by videotape of his rights. He pleaded guilty to the charge, and the matter was set for sentencing hearing. Prior to that hearing, the client met with the respondent to discuss the possibility of withdrawing his guilty plea. During their meeting, the respondent told the client of another criminal case, *Snowe v. State,* 533 N.E.2d 613 (Ind.Ct.App.1989), in which the respondent had prevailed on appeal for the defendant. He provided a copy of the Indiana Court of Appeals decision to his new client. The respondent agreed to represent the client for $5,000, which the client paid.

Snowe also involved a prerecorded videotaped televised advisement of rights, but the record in that case failed to indicate whether the defendant had ever viewed the tape advising him of his rights. Further, the opinion held that a trial court judge cannot rely solely on displaying a videotape advisement of rights, but instead must also determine whether the defendant knows of and understands his rights, the nature of the charge or charges against him, the full import of the rights waiver in his guilty plea, and the sentencing possibilities for the charges against him. *Snowe,* 533 N.E.2d at 617.

At the client's initial hearing, it was established that he had viewed the videotape, that the videotape advised him of his rights and the sentencing possibilities under the charges filed against him, that he understood the charge against him and his rights as explained in the videotape, and that he voluntarily waived those rights and pleaded guilty.

On May 30, 1996, the respondent entered an appearance on behalf of the client and filed a motion to withdraw the guilty plea. The trial court denied the motion without hearing. The respondent appealed that ruling, alleging that his client had a right to withdraw the plea because, due to the absence of counsel at the time he entered it and the fact that the record did not reflect that the trial court properly examined the client as to waiver of his rights, the client had not made it knowingly, intelligently, or voluntarily. The respondent further argued that the client had a right to a hearing on his motion to withdraw the plea.

The respondent represented the defendant in *Fletcher v. State,* 649 N.E.2d 1022 (Ind.1995). In that case, this Court addressed the questions that the respondent raised in his client's case. The ruling in *Fletcher* was adverse to the arguments that the respondent offered on appeal of his client's case. The respondent had served as counsel of record for defendant Fletcher in the appeal before this Court. This Court's ruling in *Fletcher* was issued on May 1, 1995, over one year before the respondent filed his appeal on behalf of the client. In his appellate brief filed on behalf of the client, the respondent failed to cite to *Fletcher* or argue that its holding was not controlling authority in the client's case. The respondent also failed to argue that the holding in *Fletcher* should be changed or extended. Although he advised his client of the *Snowe* case, he failed to advise him of *Fletcher* or explain any impact *Fletcher* might have on his case. Opposing counsel had not previously disclosed *Fletcher* to the Court of Appeals.[29]

    * * *

The results of the study were very interesting. I found that there were significant differences between how the Higher Performing students (HP)[30] and the Lower Performing Students (LP) read the text.[31] The HP students spent more time engaged in problematizing and rhetorical strategies, and significantly less time engaged in default reading strategies. In contrast, the LP students spent the majority of their time using default strategies, and only a small percentage of their time using problematizing and rhetorical reading strategies.

Consider the following graph, which illustrates the results of the study.

Table 1: Results of the Christensen Study

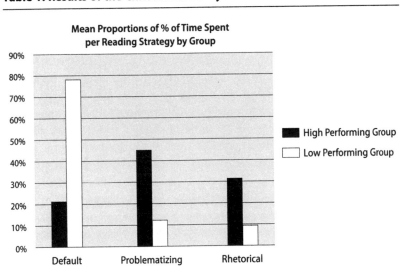

---

    29. *In re Thonert* 733 N.E.2d 932, 932–933 (Ind. 2000)

    30. The Higher Performing Students (HP) were in the Top 50% of their law school class.

    31. The Lower Performing Students (LP) were in the Bottom 50% of their law school class. None of the LP students had been diagnosed with a learning disability. Accordingly, for the purposes of the reading study, I classified them generally as traditionally-learning law students.

The HP students spent only 20% of their reading time engaged in default strategies. In contrast, the HP students spent 46% of their reading time engaged in problematizing strategies and 33% in rhetorical strategies. Accordingly, the HP readers spent almost 80% of their reading time using problematizing and rhetorical reading strategies.

In contrast, the LP students spent the majority of their reading time, i.e., almost 77%, using default strategies. LP students spent only 13% of their reading time engaged in problematizing strategies and 10% of their reading time using rhetorical reading strategies.

These results showed that although the most successful law students used all three types of reading strategies, they spent much more of their reading time engaged in high-level, analytical reading, i.e., problematizing and rhetorical reading strategies. In contrast, LP students failed to utilize the higher-level reading strategies to the same extent; instead, LP students spent most of their reading time using default reading strategies.

The other significant finding in this study was a statistical correlation between the way in which the law students read, i.e., their use of reading strategies, and their law school GPA.[32] Notably, there was no correlation between undergraduate GPA (UGPA) and LSAT scores with the use of any particular reading strategy. In other words, when students entered law school with high UGPA and strong LSAT scores, these scores did not correlate to high grades in law school.

However, there *was* a correlation between law students' use of problematizing and rhetorical reading strategies and law school grades. In other words, the more time a student spent using problematizing and rhetorical reading strategies, the higher the student's law school, first-semester GPA. Therefore, in my study, the way in which a student read a judicial opinion was a more accurate predictor of law school success than the student's undergraduate GPA or LSAT scores.

These results are important to all law students—but they are particularly important to law students who learn differently: even if you didn't come to law school with high undergraduate grades or a high LSAT score, you can still achieve success in law school by learning how to read like the most successful law students. The next section of this chapter will discuss in greater detail how the HP law students read differently than the LP students.

---

32. Pearson *r* correlations were used to determine the correlation, if any, between grades, LSAT scores, and reading strategies. Law school GPA was correlated with the use of problematizing (.646), rhetoric (.632) and default strategies (−.710), all at the .001 level. There were insignificant correlations between the use of reading strategies and UGPA and LSAT scores.

D. What Did the Successful Law Students Do Differently?

The HP law students read differently in four distinct ways. First, the most successful law students "connected with the purpose" of the case reading more frequently. Second, the most successful law students established the "context" of the case before they began to read. Third, the most successful law students worked actively to "resolve their confusion" before they moved on to another section of the case. Fourth, and finally, the most successful law students did not overuse any one reading strategy—instead, they utilized all three types of reading strategies as they moved through the text.

This section will explore more specifically how the HP readers approached case reading.

1. The HP Law Students Connected with a Purpose

The HP law students who connected with the purpose of preparing for a client meeting were more engaged and active in their case reading than the law students who read without noting a specific purpose. The HP students as a group connected to the purpose of their reading more frequently than the LP students. I asked each of the students in the study to read the judicial opinion as if they were a practicing lawyer who was preparing for a client meeting. Those students who internalized this purpose seemed to do several things very differently as they read: (1) first, they read the facts of the opinion more closely (to determine whether their client's case might be analogous to the facts of the opinion); second, they noted the defendant's punishment (to inform their client of potential consequences); and third, the students noted the procedural posture of the case more accurately (understanding that the court was reviewing a mutual agreement).

Consider the following examples from the reading transcripts of two law students as they connected to the purpose of the reading, i.e., reading the case to prepare for a client meeting. For these examples, the bolded text illustrates the students' responses and the italicized text is the language from the actual opinion.

A female in the HP group (who was in the top 3% of her law school class) began her case reading by taking note of her overall purpose.

> **"All right. I am a practicing attorney and I'm reading the opinion to prepare for a meeting with a client and they have a case that is similar to the facts that I am reading."**[33]

---

33. Transcript of Interview with Student 134 (on file with the author).

About mid-way through the facts of the opinion, she once again related her reading to her purpose, i.e., analyzing the case to counsel her client:

"So going back to *Fletcher v. State*.... So *Fletcher*, if we're basing our arguments on Fletcher, that is not good for our client's case."[34]

This student connected with purpose consistently throughout her reading, assuming the role of an attorney as she moved through the text.

In contrast, here's an example of a student in the LP group who failed to connect with the given purpose during any part of his case reading. As a result, this student was more distracted as he read and he appeared to be overwhelmed by the details of the text.

On May 30, 1996, the respondent entered an appearance on behalf of the client and filed a motion to withdraw the guilty plea. **So I'm going to write that in my facts. "30, May." I don't like all the numbers next to each other so I put "May" after.** *The respondent entered an appearance on behalf of the client and filed a motion to withdraw. Attempt to withdraw guilty plea. The trial court denied the motion without hearing.* **Ok. So—I'm going to put that up in procedural history. I'm going to put it above the appellate court. Trial court denied motion. And I'm going to make a line connecting them. Ok. Now I'm thinking what I'd like to purchase on Ebay. I actually stopped drafting my briefs on the computer because I would become distracted by Ebay. Ok.[35]**

Reading the case as if he were a practicing attorney (or assuming any other active role) may have helped this student focus more on the details of the case. After his first semester of law school, this student was in the bottom 10% of his law school class.[36]

2. Successful Law Students Established the Context of Case

The second factor that influenced the way top law students read a case was that the HP students paid close attention to the context of the case both before and during their case reading. By in large, students in the HP group *contextualized* the opinion more frequently than LP students. Specifically, the HP law students noted which court wrote the decision, the year of the decision, and the historical/legal significance of the decision as they read the case.

---

34. *Id.* at p. 2.

35. Transcript of Interview with Student 100 at 6 (on file with the author).

36. Certainly there could be several reasons why this student struggled in law school. It is certainly possible that this student may have had an undiagnosed learning disability. However, this student struggled *at least* in part because of the way in which he read his cases.

Table 2: Amount of Time Spent Contextualizing

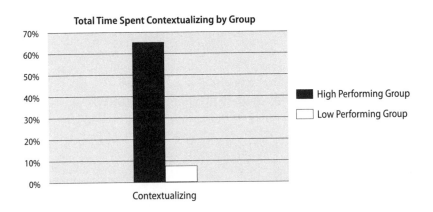

Total Time Spent Contextualizing by Group

- ■ High Performing Group
- ☐ Low Performing Group

Contextualizing

Table 2 illustrates that the HP students as a group noted the context of the case close to 68 times during their reading protocols (almost 5 times per student); in contrast, the LP students as a group noted the context of the opinion only 8 times total (or less than 1 time per student).

For example, the HP students noted that the case was decided by the Indiana Supreme Court; that the case was a recent decision; and that it was a *Per Curiam* decision.[37]

In reviewing the student protocols, I noticed that when law students took the time to understand the context of the case *before* they began to read, they improved their overall comprehension of the case. The case had context. The students understood whether or not it had precedential value as compared to other cases.

Consider the following examples taken from the student protocols as they related to the context of the opinion.

A female in the HP group (in the top 10% of her class at the end of her first semester) began her reading by noting the context of the case.

> **All right this case is in Indiana and it comes from the north-eastern quarter** *in the matter of Victor H. S. 02S009902 VI 151. The Supreme Court of Indiana.* **So this would be the highest court.**[38]

Similarly, another female participant (also in the top 10% of her class) began her reading as follows:

---

37. A *Per Curiam* decision is a ruling issued by an appellate court with multiple judges in which the decision rendered was made by the court acting as a whole, anonymously, as compared to a more typical judicial opinion which is authored by a named judge or justice. *Per Curiam* decisions tend to be brief in length, and usually deal with relatively non-controversial issues. The designation is stated at the beginning of the opinion.

38. Transcript of Interview with Student 103 (on file with the author).

> Ok. This case is from the Supreme Court of Indiana. August 22, 2000. *It's in the matter of Richard J. Thonert. Disciplinary proceeding was brought against attorney in which disciplinary commission and attorney entered statement of circumstances and conditional agreement for discipline.* It sounds a little juicy. Attorney on trial.[39]

In contrast, a male in the LP group jumped right into the text of the opinion without noting anything about the date, type or subject matter of the opinion. Instead, this student spent his time highlighting and noting the structural components of the opinion as opposed to the deeper substantive issues. As this student read, he became very confused about what was actually happening in the case.

> The first thing is I would take out—I would take out my green marker, which means [holding] and I very rarely use it; it only means holding and I would mark—the Supreme Court would get a thick line and then I would try to break up the different phrases of that sentence so that it would be easier to pick up with the explanation, but it's all in one sentence and it's kind of confusingly written. So the Supreme Court, and then one line is: *Held that attorney's failure to disclose appellate tribunal controlling authority, which was known to him* and then I would be done at this comment. I would put a thick line through and because connecting word—*had not been disclosed by opposing counsel* and I'd stop at that comment again. *That was directly adverse to his client's position.* I'd stop at that comment again.[40]

This student continued to skim and mark the case as he read it—spending a great deal of time highlighting the text. However, the student's actions seemed to overshadow his real understanding of the case. At the conclusion of his case reading, the student was confused as to what the attorney did wrong. Although it was fairly clear in the opinion that the attorney would be sanctioned for his breach of the rules of professional responsibility, the student may not have grasped this important conclusion of the court. He ended his case reading as follows:

> Right now I'm thinking to myself, I don't know exactly what happened here. I know that they didn't tell. Something has not been disclosed to the client. I'm not exactly positive what that thing is. I'm still not sure what this adverse authority or counsel is.[41]

Although this student seemed to work very hard to understand the text—highlighting and noting details in the text, the student failed to

---

39. Transcript of Interview with Student 102 (on file with the author).
40. Transcript of Interview with Student 114 (on file with the author).
41. *Id.*

grasp a larger sense of what the case was about. This student may have improved his comprehension of the case by taking a few moments before diving into the text to note the context of the case, including the type of opinion, the procedural posture of the case and the court that rendered the opinion. Establishing the context of any case you read is a simple but important technique to use whenever you begin to read a new case.

3. Successful Law Students Resolved Their Confusion Before They Moved on to the Next Paragraph in the Case

Another interesting difference between the HP and LP students was how they handled their confusion as they read. Almost every student in the study was confused at some point in time during their reading. This happens to practically everyone when they read an unfamiliar case. But what I noticed in particular is that the HP students dealt with their confusion very differently than the LP students. The HP students resolved their confusion early on. In other words, when the HP students got stuck, they would page back and figure out the answer to their question before moving on to the next paragraph. In contrast, the LP students tended to leave their questions hanging. Instead of figuring out the answers, the LP students simply moved on through the text hoping that the opinion would eventually make sense in the end.

Let's turn to a specific example. A male participant in the LP group began his reading protocol by making an incorrect assumption about the subject matter of the case. Although the introductory portion of the opinion was indeed confusing (the headnotes[42] characterized the case as involving an attorney-client issue), the opinion clarified early on that the legal issue in the case was actually an attorney disciplinary issue. Like many of the students who read the *In Re Thonert* case for the first time, this LP student began his case reading thinking that the central issue dealt with the attorney-client privilege.

> This is an issue of—I'm seeing this as an attorney-client privilege. Maybe professional conduct rules kind of a case? The second note here is—the keynote is Attorney and Client.[43]

As the student read a few more paragraphs, he questioned whether the case really dealt with the attorney-client privilege. The student had

---

42. A headnote is a short synopsis and/or excerpt from a court's written opinion on a specific point of law. The headnote is created by the publisher of the case, for example, Westlaw, and aids the reader in understanding isolated segments of the court's opinion. Additionally, headnotes from all decisions (published by Westlaw) are organized by a key number system that assist people in doing research.

43. Transcript of Interview with Student 113 at 1 (on file with the author).

a hunch that the case was really about the attorney's breach of the rules of professional conduct. However, instead of going back to re-read the text to confirm this hunch, the student simply kept reading on hoping that his confusion would eventually resolve. However, this didn't happen. The student ended his reading protocol just as confused as he began it. Consider the end of his reading protocol.

> *It is therefore, ordered that the respondent, Richard J. Thonert, is hereby reprimanded and admonished for his violations of Professional Conduct.* **That is—it's not clear to me quite what the outcome is at this point other than to say that whatever the agreement the parties have reached and discipline that's called for from that agreement is what the appellate court agrees should happen. Okay, I'm going to read on.** *The Clerk of this court is directed to provide notice of this order ... and to provide the Clerk of the United States Court of Appeals for the Seventh Circuit. The Clerk of each of the United States District Courts in this state and the Clerks of the United States Bankruptcy Court in this state with the last known address of respondent as reflected in the records of the Clerk. Costs are assessed against the respondent.* **So with regard to the actual punishment, I'm assuming that there was some actual public reprimand. What that is I am not exactly sure. It's also as the punishment costs are assessed to the attorney. And that was it.** [44]

In reviewing this student's think aloud, I found that he really struggled with being able to choose between relevant and irrelevant information within the text. This student seemed to believe that all the details in the text were equally important. In addition, this student spent 68.65% of his reading time using default reading strategies and he paraphrased the text most of the time. The student evaluated the text only 2 times during his reading protocol and he failed to connect with the purpose of the text at all. In short, the student never gained a full understanding of what was occurring in the case. And it became clear to me that the way in which this student read cases affected his law school performance overall. This law student's GPA was in the bottom 2% of his class after the first semester of law school. Further, this student *knew* that his reading strategies were not working for him. He felt very frustrated after his first semester of law school. In a follow-up interview, the student described his method of reading cases as follows:

Student: Ah—Ideally, I try and read cases twice. Realistically that doesn't happen as often as I'd like it to. My goal is through the first reading to get to understand what the case is about. Who the main players are? To basically—

---

44. *Id.*

> to understand the case and to get an idea of what I would
> need to put together in a basic brief. If I can't read for
> the second time, ... I try and skim through and pick
> out perfect details ...
>
> Interviewer: Has this been successful for you?
> Student: Arguably no. No.
> Interviewer: Where do you feel you get stuck?
> Student: Just it's very time consuming. I feel like I'm a slow reader
> and even to read it once and to go back through even
> to skim it for the details that I'm looking for, I feel that
> I'm not getting through the material as quickly as I
> would like to and to grasp as much as I would like. To
> retain as much. The retention.[45]

This student needed to figure out how to read cases more efficiently and effectively. It is quite possible that this student may have had a learning disability or may have simply needed to learn additional reading strategies to help him read faster and retain more information. There is no doubt that this student was spending a great deal of time and effort reading cases for class, but he was not extracting the *right* information out of the cases. In other words, the student was not seeing the deeper legal arguments within the court's opinion. It is quite possible that using different reading strategies would have improved this student's classroom and exam performance.

In contrast, consider the following example which illustrates how a student in the HP group resolved his confusion. Note how this student really stuck with the legal text until he understood the key facts and concepts. This HP student evaluated the text and related what he read back to his own personal experience (a rhetorical reading strategy). Further, he was actively engaged in "talk[ing] back to the text."[46] As a result, this student appeared to have a better comprehension of the court's decision overall.

> **Boy, that first paragraph was a little thick for me. It sounds like
> there is a lot going on. It sounds like neither party was forthcoming
> with a controlled issue.** *Failure to disclose to appellate tribunal
> controlling authority, which was known to him.* **So he had knowl-
> edge and didn't disclose it. It sounds like he is in trouble. There
> are about four different keynotes. All of them are titled attor-
> ney and client. I'm just going to read two of them. Because if I
> read too many of them it sort of taints my reading. And I'd
> rather just — so this is keynote.**[47]

---

45. *Id.* at 6.

46. Elizabeth Fajans & Mary Falk, *Against the Tyranny of the Paraphrase: Talking Back to Texts*, 78 CORNELL L. REV. 163, 163 (1993).

47. Transcript of Interview with Student 102 at 1 (on file with the author).

Note how this HP student was actively involved in the text. His reading continued.

> Ok. So here, this is probably the third or fourth time that I read this sentence. And now, it's finally clear what's going on. So Thonert, he is a pro se for the respondent because he is an attorney himself and it's an attorney disciplinary action. He was involved in an appeal and he had information that's pertinent in his client's case. The opposing counsel didn't reveal it. So, he had an ethical duty to review it. That's the issue. It's probably— I'm just going to speculate about the matter—how big of a wrap are we going to give this guy because he didn't adhere to ethical standards to the profession. And I'm going to assume that they're talking about the facts. This accusation that he didn't disclose information, that it was known, and that the only consideration the court could find is what is the appropriate punishment. Oh, here is another top to it. He also failed to advise his client of the adverse authority when his client was contemplating his legal options. . . . So here is a case in which omissions of the lawyer are represented.[48]

This student re-read various parts of the case to make sure he understood the facts before moving on. In addition, although this student took the same amount of time overall to read the opinion as the LP student above, his effort paid off. This HP student finished the opinion having an excellent understanding of the case. Further, this student ended up in the top 10% of his law school class at the end of the first semester.

4. The Overuse of Default Strategies

Finally, I noted that LP students as a group relied too heavily on default reading strategies which included things like highlighting text, paraphrasing, or writing notes in the margin. In contrast, the HP law students as a group used a variety of reading strategies throughout their reading protocols. Table 3 illustrates the amount of time each group spent using default reading strategies.

The LP law students (as a group) spent almost 78% of their reading time using default reading strategies. Although we all use default reading strategies at some point in time when reading new material, never going *beyond* default reading strategies does not work in law school. Law professors want you to go deeper into the case. The students in the LP group approached the case as if there were simply 'filling in the blanks'

---

48. *Id.* at 2.

Table 3: HP and LP Students Using Default Strategies

of a standard case brief: facts, issue, holding, and reasoning. Although you certainly need to be able to articulate the facts, issue and holding of any case, you also need to understand how the case relates to the other cases you've read in the class. For what proposition does the case stand? How does the case change the law? Using problematizing and rhetorical strategies in *addition to* default reading strategies will allow you to go deeper into the court's analysis.

Consider the following example of a female LP student at the beginning of her reading protocol:

> Ok. I have my headnotes in my computer and I'll probably read over them again so that I understand what important rules or professional conduct that they are talking about. *And when the attorney failed*—why is he going against the rules of professional conduct? So I'll probably read over those again and make sure I've got them in my head and then I'll go onto the case. *The respondent in this attorney disciplinary matter is charged with failing to disclose to an appellate tribunal controlling authority known to him not disclosed by opposing counsel, but was directly adverse to his client's position.* So I would underline that what he was charged with and then in the margin I would put—I would just write the words "charge." "Charged." And then I'd put "failure to disclose." And I wouldn't write out the whole thing because I'm going to go back. I'm just putting in the margin so that I have kind of like reference points and I go back to the case. I don't have to reread the entire paragraph. I've got the whole margins to tell me that kind of pinpoint to me what that paragraph is about. So when I go back

into my computer I will—I will do the briefing of the case, but I will do that at the end after I've read the entire case. So I just put notes in the margin so that when I go to brief the case I can just refer back to these margins to find the stuff I need. *He also failed to advise his client of the adverse authority when his client was contemplating his legal options. He failed to advise his client of adverse authority.* I would underline that. On legal options. So that's a paragraph of what he was charged with. So that's where I put "charge with failure to disclose" in the margin.

Notice that this LP student spent most of her time paraphrasing the text as she read. Although she clearly had a system for reading the case, it was unclear whether her system improved her comprehension of the case. This student spent 85% of her reading time using default reading strategies; only 2.91% of her time using problematizing strategies and 11.65% of her time using rhetorical strategies. Although she was able to recognize the distinct parts of the case, i.e., facts, issue, holding, and reasoning, she failed to hypothesize, synthesize facts with rules in the case, evaluate the court's result or connect with the underlying purpose of the reading. In this sense, the student missed many of the nuances of the court's decision.

The next example shows how a male student in the LP group over-relied on the use of "highlighting." This student had a very intricate system of using different colored highlighters to represent the structural components of a case. Although highlighting can be helpful as a way of designating important text, a successful law student needs to do more than simply filling up the page with highlighted text. A representative portion of this student's reading protocol is as follows:

So this is getting confusing because they are talking about different clients over and over and they are not saying last names. They could be much more helpful. But this is going to get a green line again because it's a ruling. So the ruling in *Fletcher* was adverse to the argument that the respondent offered on appeal to the client's case. That is in green. *The respondent had served as counsel of record for the defendant in Fletcher in the appeal before this Court. The court ruling in Fletcher was issued on May 1, 1995.* So now I'm going to use a big yellow highlighter for May 1, 1995 and I'm going to put a line through the court's ruling of *Fletcher* that was issued on that date and that way I can look on this page and there is only a few spots where there is big yellow line and only two of them are numbered, so it is very easy for me to see that this was a year apart.

Although this student used other reading strategies as he read, he highlighted almost every paragraph of the decision. Once again, although highlighting is both common and helpful, law professors want you to go beyond simply noting important text. Minimally, we want you to put the text into your *own* words. If you only highlight the text (and don't take the next step of rewriting the text in your own words), you are taking a shortcut that may backfire in the end.

What can you learn from these reading protocols? The HP students developed their own opinions about the law. Further, successful law students (and lawyers) questioned the decisions they read; they evaluated the results of any case, and they considered the implications of any rule as applied to the facts. Reading the law is far more than simply making notes or highlighting text. As law professors, we want you to read the law critically and efficiently.

Although there will be many things you can do to enhance your success in law school, becoming an efficient and capable legal reader is probably the most important skill to develop during your first year. If you are concerned about your reading, you may want to get help sooner rather than later. The best thing you can do is make an appointment with your Academic Support Program. Typically, the professors that work in the Academic Support Program will have specific exercises to assess your reading problems. In addition, they may have ways that you can improve your reading speed, accuracy, vocabulary, etc.

There is no doubt, however, that legal reading is very important to *any* new law student's success. Paying attention to the way in which you read will allow you not only to become a better law student, but a better lawyer as well.

Chapter 5

Legal Reading for Law Students with ADD: Did They Read Any Differently?

After I completed the first legal reading study, I wanted to explore whether law students with ADD read the law differently than tradition-ally-learning law students.[1] Although I knew that law students with ADD did not represent the full spectrum of law students with learning disabilities (or those without), I wanted to examine (at least) whether law students with learning disabilities approached case reading uniquely. In other words, did successful law students with ADD read a case similarly to higher-performing law students without ADD? Or did law students with ADD approach legal text differently?

In the second study, I found that law students with ADD read a judicial opinion in almost the same manner as law students without ADD. Specifically, I found that the most successful law students with ADD read the case just like the HP law students in the first study. Likewise, I found that struggling law students (both with ADD and without ADD) read a judicial opinion in the same way. In other words, the way in which these first year students read the law—whether the students had ADD or not—either contributed to or inhibited their law school success in the same way. The results of this second study confirmed for me *that the way in which you read legal text does affect your overall success in law school*—regardless of whether you learn traditionally or think outside the box. This chapter will describe the results of the second reading study as they relate to law students with ADD.[2]

The second reading study focused on three law students. Two of the students in the study were very successful in law school. Alexa,[3] a second-

---

1. Leah M. Christensen, *Legal Reading and Success in Law School: The Reading Strategies of Law Students with Attention Deficit Disorder*, 12 THE SCHOLAR: ST. MARY'S LAW REVIEW ON MINORITY ISSUES 177 (2010). Once again, I used "traditionally-learning" and "non-traditional learner" very broadly to define the differences between law students with ADD and those without.

2. In this study, Alexa and Baker were second year students, and Kelsey was a first-year student.

3. The names of these students have been changed to protect their anonymity.

year law student with ADD, was in the top 5% of her law school class at the end of her second year. Kelsey, a first-year law student with ADD, was in the top 30% of her law school class at the end of her first year. In contrast, the third student in the study, Baker, had just completed his second year of law school and was in the bottom 15% of his law school class. Table 4 shows the students' grade point averages and incoming LSAT scores.

Table 4. Study Participants

Participant	Disability	UGPA	LSAT	LGPA	Law School Class
Alexa	ADD	3.64	155	3.69 (top 5%)	2L
Kelsey	ADD	2.89	155	2.94 (top 30%)	1L
Baker	ADD	3.44	148	2.51 (bottom 15%)	2L

In this study, I had the law students read the same case as in the prior study, *In Re Thonert*. I also asked the law students to assume the same purpose for reading the case (of preparing for a client meeting).[4] Once again, I examined the students' reading moves based upon three categories of reading strategies: (1) default reading strategies; (2) problematizing reading strategies; and (3) rhetorical reading strategies.

The results of the study were notable. Alexa and Kelsey, both successful law students, read the text very similarly to the HP students in the first study. In contrast, Baker, the second year law student in the bottom 15% of his class, read the case very similarly to the LP students in the first study.

Specifically, Alexa spent 21% of her reading time using default reading strategies; 26% of her time using problematizing reading strategies; and 56% of her time engaged in rhetorical reading strategies.[5]

Kelsey's reading protocol showed similar results. Kelsey spent 32% of her time using default reading strategies; 42% of her time using problematizing strategies; and 26% of her reading time using rhetorical reading strategies.[6]

In contrast, Baker spent most of his reading time, 67%, using default reading strategies; 14% of his time using problematizing reading strategies; and 17% of his reading time using rhetorical reading strategies.[7]

---

4. *See generally*, Christensen, *supra* n.1. The purpose was: "Read the following legal text assuming that you are a practicing attorney and that you are reading the opinion to prepare for a meeting with a client who has a case that is similar to the facts of the case you are reading."

5. *Id.*

6. I suspect that Kelsey spent more time than Alexa using default reading strategies because Kelsey was a first-year law student still getting used to legal reading. Alexa was a second year law student at the time of this study which meant that she had that additional year to become more comfortable with case reading.

7. Christensen, *supra* n.1.

Table 5 provides a graphical comparison of how Alexa, Kelsey and Baker read the judicial opinion.

Table 5. Law Students with ADD: % of Reading Time Spent per Reading Strategy

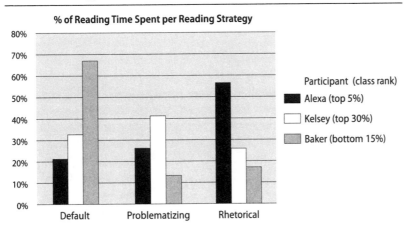

Note how Alexa and Kelsey spent their reading time using problematizing and rhetorical reading strategies, and they spent far less time using default strategies. Alexa spent only 21% of her reading time using default reading strategies; Kelsey spent 32% of her reading time using default reading strategies. In contrast, Baker spent close to 70% of his total reading time engaged in default reading strategies.

Once again, these study results suggest an important relationship between the use of problematizing and rhetorical strategies and increased law student success, and an inverse relationship between a student's use of default reading strategies and law school success. In other words, those students who used more problematizing and rhetorical reading strategies were more successful in law school.

In addition, this second study seemed to suggest something else: the fact that Alexa and Kelsey had ADD did not seem to dramatically alter the way in which they read the opinion—at least objectively. Alexa and Kelsey read the judicial opinion using the same percentages of reading strategies as the HP law students without ADD. And Baker appeared to read the case in almost the same way as the LP law students without ADD.

Consider Table 6, on the next page, which compares the three students with ADD with the HP and LP students without ADD (from the first study). The same information is shown graphically in Table 7. Note in particular that both Baker and the LP students spent the majority of their reading time using default reading strategies. In contrast, Alexa and Kelsey read similarly to the HP students in the first study. Like the HP stu-

Table 6. Comparison % of Reading Time Spent Using Different Reading Strategies Between Students with ADD and Non-ADD Law Students

Participant	Class Rank	Default	Problematizing	Rhetorical
Alexa (ADD)	Top 5%	21.05%	26.32%	56.23%
Kelsey (ADD)	Top 30%	32.43%	41.89%	25.68%
HP (Non-ADD)	**Top 50%**	**21.43%**	**45.70%**	**32.87%**
LP (Non-ADD)	**Bottom 50%**	**77.48%**	**12.54%**	**9.55%**
Baker (ADD)	Bottom 15%	67.19%	14.06%	17.19%

Table 7. Alexa, Kelsey, and Baker as Compared to Higher- and Lower-Performing Law Students Without ADD

dents, Alexa and Kelsey spent most of their reading time using problematizing and rhetorical reading strategies.

The next section of this chapter will address more specifically how Alexa, Kelsey and Baker read this judicial opinion.

A. Alexa's Case Reading

Alexa used many of the reading strategies adopted by the most successful law students. For example, when Alexa first approached the opinion, she placed the case in context by noting the name of the court. Alexa re-read the text frequently as she moved through the opinion to make sure she understood each paragraph before moving on. In addition, Alexa read in a very non-linear fashion—she rarely began at one place and moved directly through the text. Instead, Alexa was flexible about the order and way in which she read. Initially, Alexa would make hypotheses about the court's reasoning and she would read to confirm or deny her original hypothesis. If she hypothesized correctly, she would move on to the next section. If her original hypothesis was incorrect, she would page back and reread that section of the text.

The following is an excerpt from Alexa's think aloud. Note how Alexa questions and hypothesizes shortly after she begins reading the decision. Alexa is actively engaged in her reading of the case.

> *In the matter of Richard T. Thonert, Supreme Court of Indiana, April 22, 2000.*
> **I don't like reading the head notes. I find them confusing. What is this case about? Attorney discipline?**
> *Disciplinary proceeding was brought against attorney in which disciplinary commission and attorney entered statement of circumstances and conditional agreement per discipline..*
> **Ok. So this must actually be a PR case.**
> *The respondent in this attorney disciplinary matter is charged with failing to disclose to an appellate tribunal controlling authority known to him not disclosed by opposing counsel that was directly adverse to his client's position ...*
> **So, this is a disciplinary matter, so it goes straight to the Supreme Court of Indiana. I am assuming that's what happened. I would think so.**
> *This matter is presented to this court upon the disciplinary commissions and ...*
> **I just need to reread that. Ok.[8]**

Like a real lawyer, Alexa re-read different sections of the case as she needed to in order to fully comprehend the case. Alexa also connected to the purpose of the case reading as follows:

> **Ok. So looking at [the opinion]. I'm going to have a meeting with a client who has similar facts, and my client is an attorney who withheld information or precedent in front of an appellate court. So, I would have to advise him that if the facts are similar that he would also be found to violate rules 1.4 and 3.3. Ok. Straightforward decision. I agree with the court. Good decision.[9]**

Alexa also evaluated the case, like a lawyer, expressing her opinion that the court's decision was correct. In other studies on legal reading, Alexa's strategies of hypothesizing, connecting to purpose, reading actively and evaluating correlated to success in law school.[10] Alexa engaged in a conversation with the text—and in so doing, she improved her overall understanding of the case. Alexa was able to extract the essence of the case—

---

8. *Id.*
9. *Id.*
10. *Id.*

focusing on the relevant information in the case and leaving the irrelevant details behind. I believe that Alexa's active reading contributed to her law school success overall.

B. Kelsey's Case Reading

Kelsey also used many of the reading strategies of the most successful law students, including contextualizing, questioning and re-reading. Like Alexa, Kelsey was actively engaged in the text. Kelsey placed the case in context, i.e., noting the case was decided by a state court. Kelsey also worked to resolve her confusion as she read by initially creating a hypothesis and then reading further on in the text to either confirm or deny her hypothesis.

Consider the following excerpt from Kelsey's think aloud.

> *In the matter of Richard J. Thonert the Supreme Court of Indiana ...*
> **It's a state jurisdiction case. I don't really know what it's trying to say. I usually don't read ... headnotes in their entirety. So I'll come back to those if I need help. I'm going to start with the case. So, the attorney disciplinary matter.**
> *The attorney was charged with failing to disclose to a tribunal controlling authority known to him.*
> **So this guy has something to do with a disciplinary procedure. I [like to] highlight what happened. This attorney and what is happening is the story of this case.**
> *He failed to give known authority and he also failed to advise his client of the adverse authority when his client was contemplating his legal options.*
> **So that probably means he misrepresented the information to his client. And, in his client's favor.**[11]

Kelsey also used another effective reading strategy: she put the language of the case into her own words. This strategy helped Kelsey more clearly understand what was happening in the case. Notably, Kelsey spent a fair amount of time highlighting within the opinion.[12] As Kelsey explained during her interview, she used highlighting as a technique to help her "trigger" her memory when she looked back on the case before class.[13] In addition, Kelsey created mental pictures or "cues" as she read.

---

11. *Id.*

12. She spent 14.86% of her total reading time noting that she was highlighting text.

13. Kelsey's reliance on "highlighting" the text, typically a default reading strategy, may also explain why Kelsey spent a higher percentage of her reading time using default reading strategies as compared to Alexa, i.e., 32.43% versus 21.05%, respectively.

She would often comment to herself about what she was reading—and she often expressed her personal opinion about what happened in the case. Each of these techniques helped Kelsey stay engaged with her case reading.

A further example from Kelsey's think aloud is as follows:

> *The respondent appealed that ruling alleging that his client had a right to withdraw the plea because due to absence of counsel at the time he entered it and the fact that the record did not reflect that but the trial court properly examined the client.*
> **Ok. So that's a relief. So this is a case about a "stupid" attorney.... The Respondent represented the defendant in *Fletcher v. State*, so this seems like we're actually getting more relevant about that it was actually [the same] attorney in that case. The support, the address, the same court, [and the same] questions that the Respondent raised in his client's case.**[14]

Clearly, Kelsey felt comfortable expressing her own opinions about the case, i.e., commenting about the "stupid" attorney. This was actually an effective technique that Kelsey developed over time. In her interview, she described how creating a story about the case helped her despite her struggles with ADD. Whereas many first year law students might simply defer to a professor's interpretation of the case, Kelsey was willing to assume a more active role in relation to the outcome of the case. She had a strong opinion about whether the court was correct or incorrect. Again, these reading strategies, i.e., agreeing or disagreeing with the court, engaging actively with the text, are reading strategies used by both successful law students and successful lawyers.[15]

C. Baker's Case Reading

Finally, the third student with ADD, Baker, had a more difficult time making sense out of the opinion. Baker's reading was more like the LP students from the first study. Like the LP students in the first study, Baker used primarily default reading strategies, i.e., 67.19% of his reading time. Further, in contrast to Alexa and Kelsey, Baker never connected to the purpose of the reading (of preparing for a client meeting) nor did he assume any other role as he read. Baker read to decode the text, i.e., he read to simply understand the basic meaning of the words. As a result, Baker never got to consider the deeper analysis that lay within the judicial decision. The following is an excerpt from Baker's think aloud.

---

14. Christensen, *supra* n.1.
15. *Id.*

In the Matter of Richard J. Thonert ... The Supreme Court of Indiana, August of 2000.

So I'd start from the beginning and I'll read through the case notes and start. So here we go. Ok. That first paragraph. "It's so ordered" at the bottom, and basically two long sentences with a lot of words and I really don't know what I read, so I'm going to have to read it again. I'm grabbing for something to mark it up in case; I see a word or something that I want to latch onto. Ok. It looks like the attorney did something wrong and he didn't disclose some information he knew to opposing counsel and the appellate tribunal.

...

So, "*Per Curiam.*" That is—I don't even know what that means. "*Per Curiam.*" I can't remember. I can't think of it right now. I have to look it up in my dictionary.... Anyway. I think originally I said this was about one attorney's failure to turn over something to another attorney.[16]

Note how Baker struggled with the legal vocabulary in the opinion. Specifically, Baker struggled to understand the significance of a "*per curiam*" decision. Failing to understand the meaning of the words he read inhibited Baker's overall comprehension of the text.[17]

In addition, Baker took much longer to complete the overall reading task than either Alexa or Kelsey.[18] Because many of the words were unfamiliar to Baker, he had to re-read the text frequently during his reading protocol. While re-reading can be a helpful reading strategy, it was clear that Baker read too slowly to keep up with the volume of reading in law school.

Here is a further example from Baker's think aloud.

I'm going to read this through and then read it again. That's what I usually do. I read through it first and then go back and read it again. On 933, the first whole paragraph on the right hand side says that the "*client had not made it knowingly, intelligently or voluntary.*" Those terms are going to be I can't really think—The footnote and I'm going right through it again. I'd probably read it again and then go back through it. Ok. *Indiana Professional Conduct Rule.* I'm highlighting probably some kind of regulation for this case. It takes place I think in Indiana. Let

---

16. Student Transcript 102 at 1 (on file with the author).

17. The best way to deal with vocabulary issues is to look up any unfamiliar words as soon as possible during your first semester of law school. You want to obtain a strong legal vocabulary early on in law school so it doesn't impede your reading.

18. Baker spent over 55 minutes completing the 'think aloud.' Alexa spent approximately 35 minutes completing the 'think aloud,' and Kelsey spent approximately 39 minutes completing the 'think aloud.'

me see here. I can't remember. Yeah. And so it's probably important and I'll read it over again.[19]

Baker was working hard to move through the text but his case reading was not efficient and this lead to significant frustration on his part. Baker needed some individual instruction to improve his legal reading. Although law professors (and students) often assume that everyone begins law school able to read efficiently and effectively, this is not always the case.

If you suspect that you may have some problems with your legal reading, it is wise to get help as soon as possible. Consider making an appointment with your Academic Support Program or your Student Services Office. Admitting that you may need help with legal reading in no way suggests that you are not destined to become a lawyer. Legal reading is simply a *skill* that you need to master in order to become a successful law student and lawyer. Therefore, you want to develop this skill as soon as possible in your legal career.

What conclusions might we draw from the legal reading studies described above? First, the results suggest that Alexa and Kelsey, like the HP students from the first study, were more successful in law school because they used a higher percentage of problematizing and rhetorical reading strategies. The studies also suggest that there is far more to legal reading than simply reading a judicial opinion quickly. In the second study, all three law students with ADD re-read the text frequently. But the real issue became one of reading *effectively*—not just reading quickly. *Effective* legal readers know what to pay attention to and what to let go of—in other words, they know what details are relevant to the decision and what details are irrelevant. Most importantly, effective legal reading will allow you to go beyond the mere words in any opinion into the analysis and reasoning of the court. To be a successful law student (and lawyer), you must also become an effective legal reader. Although Alexa and Kelsey had mastered case reading, Baker struggled with case reading into his second year of law school.

D. When Might You Need Additional Reading Help?

Reading legal text well occurs when you can use "a number of interrelated skills" when you read, and "when the reader chooses among these skills wisely in light of the purpose of the reading being tackled."[20] If you find yourself taking a very long time to read your assignments (and your reading speed does not improve within the first month of

---

19. Christensen, *supra* n.1.

20. Ruth Ann McKinney, Reading Like a Lawyer: Time-Saving Strategies for Reading Like an Expert, 267 (Carolina Academic Press 2005).

law school), you may need to get some additional help with your legal reading.

The research has shown that poor readers make more oral reading errors[21] that can affect the meaning of texts than good readers.[22] This danger is particularly acute in law school: if you are misreading or skipping words as you read, you are at risk of miscomprehending whatever you are reading and this will only hurt you in law school.

Further, if you have been diagnosed with a learning disability, you may be more prone to reading problems.[23] And it may not be enough that you are a careful and accurate reader—you must also be an efficient reader so that you can devote your mental energies toward reading comprehension. Reading research illustrates that good readers store words and word parts in their memories as visual orthographic images.[24] Such storage allows readers to bypass the decoding stage to quickly retrieve words from memory. For skilled readers, this process takes place within 250 milliseconds of encountering most words.[25] This automaticity allows readers to devote their focus toward comprehension.[26] In contrast, slower reading poses two major threats to comprehension. First, slower readers must dedicate their mental efforts toward decoding (figuring out the meaning of the text), leaving limited cognitive resources for meaning-making.[27] Secondly, slow reading taxes short-term memory, as it is more difficult to retain the long and complicated sentences often found in higher level texts at slow reading rates than at rapid speeds.[28]

This can be particularly problematic in law school reading. In light of the typical law school workload, this choppy and hesitant reading poses a very real and practical challenge. If you are assigned 60 pages of reading per week in *each* course, this reading load is substantial for even the most effective legal reader. However, this amount of reading will likely be overwhelming for a law student with a slow reading rate. An average college student's reading rate is around 263 words per minute.[29] If your reading speed is less than 250 words per minute in law school, you may need to get some additional help to improve your reading speed.[30]

---

21. "Oral reading errors" are errors that readers make while reading out loud.

22. Lauren Capotosto, *Decoding and Fluency Problems of Poor College Readers*, http://www.collegetransition.org/promising/rtp8decodingandfluency.doc (last visited on 9/5/09).

23. You may be processing information differently and/or seeing the text differently.

24. Capotosto, *supra* n.22 at 1.

25. *Id.*

26. *Id.*

27. *Id.*

28. *Id.*

29. *Id.*

30. McKinney, *supra* n.20 at 268.

How can you determine your average reading speed? Adopting the advice from Professor Ruth Ann McKinney, choose anything around the house that you'd like to read (although not likely law-related because that will be too difficult).[31] Also avoid newspaper articles where the text is printed in columns. And read something you haven't read before.

Read for five minutes and accurately time yourself (or have a friend do so).[32] Mark where you started and where you stopped in the text. Calculate how many words you read in total and divide by five. This number is your average number of words per minute. If you are reading less than 250 words per minute, you likely need to speed up your reading in general.

Luckily, there are likely resources available to you if your law school is associated with a university campus.[33] Most campuses have reading centers and reading specialists that can help you. If you do not have access to a formal reading center, consider using a good book with exercises to help improve your reading speed.[34] You can improve your reading speed markedly by doing simple exercises over a period of a few months. As your speed increases, this will open up more time in your reading to do all those things that the most successful law students accomplish in their case reading. If you are no longer stumbling over words and phrases, you can take the time to consider and evaluate the court's opinion.

The good news is that legal reading is a skill you can develop over time. You don't need to withdraw from law school if you are a slow reader or if you have some reading issues. But you do need to be honest with yourself and work to develop the legal reading skill set that will *help* you in law school—not hold you back.

---

31. *Id.*
32. *Id.*
33. *Id.*
34. *Id.*

Chapter 6

Going Beyond the Traditional Case Brief

Now that we've discussed the importance of legal reading, it is time to discuss how you can use case briefing to help you get more out of your casebook reading in law school. During your first week in law school, you will likely be given a template for a traditional case brief. In addition, you will be told that you need to brief every case in order to prepare well for your law school classes. However, you are not always told *why* you need to brief your cases. This chapter will explain the *why* of case briefing and give you some tips to get the most out of briefing your cases.

First and foremost, you should know that case briefing is based *in part* on a template for legal analysis called IRAC. You may have already been introduced to this formula.[1] IRAC is a formula for the way you will frame a legal argument in law school. "IRAC" is an acronym for Issue, Rule, Analysis and Conclusion.

The "I" in IRAC stands for *Issue* and this part of the formula identifies the questions (or legal issues) raised by a fact pattern. Any one or sometimes several of the legal arguments discussed in a case may give rise to a legal issue. How do you *find* "issues?" Some will jump out at you, even on the first read of the case. Sometimes the court states the issue specifically. For other legal issues, you will need to work harder to uncover them by asking yourself *why* each fact is present and then *testing* that fact against the rules that are articulated in the case. Any time you read and brief a judicial opinion, you will need to identify the legal issues.

Next comes "R" in IRAC which stands for the *Rule*. Your job is to determine which rule or rules govern the court's decision. Typically you want to write a succinct, clear rule statement of the precise law that governs the issue that you stated above. You will recognize the rule because there is usually a specific rule statement or a legal citation in a case that the court uses to identify the rule.

The "A" in IRAC stands for the *Application* or *Analysis* of the issue and this is often the most important part of the formula. In the context of case

---

1. The IRAC paradigm is particularly helpful to writing coherent exam answers and in formulating legal arguments for your legal writing classes. In Chapters 13 and 16 in Part II of this book, we will work with IRAC very specifically.

briefing, you will be looking for the court's *reasoning* here. In an exam context, the "A" is your opportunity to say *why* the facts either meet or don't meet the elements of the rules you stated. (More on this part of the "A" later). Sometimes, there are good arguments to be made on both sides of a legal issue and the court will discuss both before coming to a conclusion. Certain facts may point to the satisfaction of a particular element, while other facts indicate that element is not met. In the "A" section of a case brief, you want to describe how the court argues and supports its position with regard to the legal issues raised by the parties.

Finally, the "C" in IRAC stands for the Conclusion. The Conclusion is the wrap-up where you will resolve the issues or questions you have raised earlier. In the context of case briefing, the Conclusion is typically the conclusion of the court. What was the court's final decision? Did it agree with one party over another? What happened to the case? Did it go back for another trial or was a claim dismissed? Try to figure out not only the legal conclusion but also the *procedural* disposition of the court, i.e., what did the court do with the case?

You will likely receive a copy of a traditional case brief which contains several sections which are enumerated below. See if you can identify the IRAC formula within the components of the case brief provided below.

Title (e.g., Patty v. Smitty)
Citation (e.g., 500 U.S. 100 (1987))

Facts: Summarize the facts of the case. Focus on the facts that you need to understand the holding and reasoning of the case.

Procedural Posture: Most of the cases that you'll read in law school will be appellate court decisions. In this section, list what happened at the lower court level. Although you don't have to go into too much detail, you do need to understand how the case came to the present court. One or two sentences are sufficient for this section.

Issue(s): What is/are the legal question(s) facing the court? Form the issue questions in a way that they can be answered by **yes** or **no**. Often you can find the issue statement within the initial paragraphs of the opinion.

Holding: How did the court answer the issue question(s)? First, answer this question with either a yes or no, and then provide a short statement as to why the court so held.

Reasoning: This is the most important section of your case brief. Here you want to list in more detail the reasoning of the court in reaching its decision. Be detailed in this section but try not to simply rewrite the opinion. Restate the reasoning in your own words. List what the law was before this case was decided and how the law has changed after this decision. **Important note: Law professors tend to focus on the reasoning of a case in class discussions.**

Concurring/dissenting opinions: Make a note as to the basic arguments of any concurring/dissenting opinions but this section should be fairly short.

Although this template is a good start to help you extract the necessary information out of a case, it may not go far enough. Before you begin briefing all of your cases using this template, I would like you to consider how case briefing helps you work through your case reading.

A. Case Briefing Provides a Cognitive Schema

As discussed in Chapters 4 and 5, legal reading is very difficult. The vocabulary is unfamiliar and the structure of a judicial opinion is strange. Legal text is unique in both its form and content; it is its own special genre. The case brief serves as an effective cognitive "schema" to provide you with a framework within which to analyze a legal opinion.

What is a schema? "A schema is a cluster of information that we hold in our mind about a subject."[2] In simple terms, a schema is stored knowledge. During reading, comprehension occurs when the reader can match the text information to a pre-existing schema.[3] The new information is compared against the old.[4] The existing schema fills in the gaps in the text and allows for many kinds of inferences.[5]

Schemas are "critical building blocks of the human cognitive process."[6] They permit us to process the never-ending amount of information we encounter each day.[7] Categories and schemas affect not only what information receives our attention, but how we categorize it and what we remember about it.[8] Without prior experience in the law, you have no

---

2. RUTH ANN McKINNEY, READING LIKE A LAWYER: TIME-SAVING STRATEGIES FOR READING LIKE AN EXPERT, 17 (Carolina Academic Press 2005). *See also*, Leah M. Christensen, *The Psychology of Case Briefing: A Powerful Cognitive Schema,"* 29 CAMP. L. REV. 5, 5-6 (2006).

3. Christensen, *supra* n.2 at 11 (*citing* Peter Dewitz, *Reading Law: Three Suggestions for Legal Education*, 27 U. TOL L. REV. 657, 660 (1996)).

4. *Id.*

5. *Id.*

6. Christensen, *supra* n.2 at 11 (*citing* Ronald Chen & Jon Hanson, *Categorically Biased: The Influence of Knowledge Structures on Law and Legal Theory*, 77 S. CAL. L. REV. 1103, 1131 (2004)).

7. *Id.*

8. *Id.* at 11-12.

schemata to deal with legal reading, and your ability to read and analyze the law is often inefficient and overwhelming.[9]

Case briefing gives you the framework within which to enter into the discourse of law. A case brief is nothing more than a schema. Especially in the first semester of law school, case briefs can help you preserve your thoughts and observations as you begin to organize the content of the cases you read. By going through the process of drafting a case brief, you will free up your short term memory which will allow you to think about what the case actually means.[10]

Note, however, that you are not likely to receive feedback on your case briefs. Your case briefs are for your own benefit; law professors do not ask you to hand them in. Therefore, you will need to evaluate whether you are briefing correctly largely on your own. If you would like additional help on case briefing, you can go to the instructors and professors in your Academic Support Program. This is precisely the type of feedback that they can give you early on in law school.

Most law students prepare their case briefs on their laptop computer. As illustrated above, a typical brief contains the following components: case heading; parties' names; procedural history; facts; issues or questions presented; holding; reasoning/rationale; and perhaps a separate section for the reader's own thoughts.[11]

Law students are particularly diligent during their first semester of law school and they figure out how to "fill in" the parts of a case brief fairly quickly. However, all too often, students stop at that point. In fact, many law students stop briefing cases altogether because they consider it too time-consuming. Consider the words of a first year law student:

Interviewer: Do you use case briefs as a study strategy?
Student: No, I used it in the first week. I had a hard time writing out the holdings. I actually have a hard time when I'm writing out the brief. Not concentrating … It's time consuming and inefficient.[12]

By giving up case briefing so soon in her law school career, this student may have missed out on the benefits of the case brief as a cognitive

---

9. Christensen, *supra* n.2 at 12 (*citing* McKinney, *supra* n.2, at 18-19). Further, traditional law school teaching usually concentrates on only one learning style; it does not address the varied cognitive styles represented in each entering class. Students who have different cognitive styles than the typical "Socratic" method will have to learn legal reasoning on their own.

10. *Id.* at 13 (*citing* McKinney, *supra* n.2 at 23).

11. Note that most traditional case briefs do not have a section for your own thoughts. I believe that you should add this section. Evaluating the case and forming your own opinion about the result allows you to more actively participate in the case reading/briefing.

12. Transcript of Interview with Student 102 at 10 (on file with the author).

schema. Although a brief will help you organize a judicial opinion, it also serves as a way to help you think critically and creatively about the law. This is a key aspect of case briefing that often goes unrecognized by most students. Further, those students who continue to brief their cases into their second year of law school may have an academic edge over those students who have stopped briefing cases.

One student in the top 5% of her class after the first semester of law school disclosed that she still briefs every case before class. Although she highlights text and writes in the margins during her initial read-through of the case, she briefs the case during her second reading. She appeared to recognize that the process of briefing a case enhanced her overall case analysis.

Interviewer: Tell me a little bit about what reading strategies you use [in general]?

Student: Um, typically I start by reading the case once through. I highlight what I think is the issue, rule of reasoning, procedural history all in the margin. I highlight it and then put the "R" next to it. I read it through that one time and depending when it's due for class, I'll either brief it right after that or wait until the next day. When I brief it is when I really understand it. I understand it the first time through, but when I brief it, it really solidifies in my head.[13]

....

Interviewer: Do you still brief cases after you read them?

Student: Yeah. Everything. Well, there are rare occasions where I don't need to or I'm too lazy. But, yeah, I still brief pretty much everything including the notes after the case and everything. Um, just because that's my way of understanding it. That's my "learning." When I write it down is when it solidified in my head. So, I'll read it through the first time carefully and then, based upon what I highlighted, I usually do end up rereading the whole case. I don't just read what I've highlighted because it's not always correct. Or I miss something. So, I go through and write down everything that I think is important, mostly the reasoning and rule of law. I don't spend a lot of time on the facts.

Interviewer: Have you felt that these strategies have been successful for you?

Student: Yeah. Extremely successful. Because when I read it through— I mean for me, that's pretty passive. I mean, yeah, I'm trying to mark out what the issue and the holding is and everything, but I won't remember it the next day. Now, if I brief it, then I do remember it the next day. And, plus, its right in front

---

13. Transcript of Interview with Student 111 at 7 (on file with the author).

> of me. I don't like paging through the case and trying to find where I put my "H." So, I like having it all in front of me and I think it's been really successful. I mean I always — I won't say never. But I hardly ever feel lost in class, and if anything, I might do it too thoroughly, because I just know everything.[14]

This student possessed a sophisticated understanding of both how she learned most effectively and the underlying benefits of case briefing. She understood that she did not learn the case until she "briefed" it. Law professors often forget to discuss case briefing after the first week of law school. Yet I've found that the way in which law students use their case briefs evolves over the course of their law school career. When asked to describe how her case briefing strategies changed throughout the course of her first year of law school, the above-student responded:

> My briefing has gotten a lot better. I mean it's — before I just did-n't know — when I started law school, I did not know what was important at all. Because of the certain tone of judicial opinions, I think when you first start out you think everything is important and it sounds so above your head. So you're like, well, if I don't understand this, it must be important. But, now I can just pick out right away — this has nothing to do with what we're talking about or this is definitely what this court finds to be the most important issue that the case turns on or the most important fact … And I definitely can pick out the rule of law so much faster.[15]

This student, like so many of my first year students, began to develop her own cognitive schema about the law. As her legal vocabulary increased and her understanding of an opinion's unique structure became more refined, her case analysis also improved.

B. Taking Your Case Briefs Beyond Your Yellow Highlighter

By the end of the first semester of law school, most students choose to "book brief" their cases by underlining or highlighting components of a legal opinion. This is a good start, but it is rarely enough. You might think you are saving time by simply marking your casebooks with a highlighter. However, using the highlighter to move through the assigned reading rarely accomplishes what a new legal reader needs at this point in your law school career.[16]

---

14. Christensen, *supra* n.2 at 15-16.
15. Transcript of Interview with Student 111 at 8 (on file with the author).
16. Christensen, *supra* n.2 at 16 *(citing,* McKinney, *supra* note 2, at 176.)

One first-year student who was still struggling with case analysis after first semester admitted she spent a great deal of time highlighting cases as she read. She used a color-coded system of highlighting, using a different color to represent the different structural components of a judicial opinion.

Interviewer: Tell me a little bit about what reading strategies you use?

Student: [I] summarize as I go. Like, reread, because there is a lot of stuff in here that I just don't get the first time. I understand the words, but I have no idea what the meaning is so I have to read it two or three times and underline.

        ....

Interviewer: So you highlight?

Student: Oh, I highlight a lot. I underline. I tend to write a lot of words in the margins in pencil.... If it's a rule of law, I'll highlight in a certain color. So I use orange for a rule of law. The reason I use different colors a lot of time is just because I'll use all one and I stop looking at it.[17]

If possible, try not to fall into this habit. Blindly highlighting your casebook or simply briefing on your computer without doing something more will hold you back. If you only highlight text in your casebook, you are simply marking what has been written by the author.[18] You are failing to engage in your own analysis or evaluation. Even the best highlighting only "capture[s] the author's words."[19] Effective case analysis requires more than simply highlighting the author's language. One of the most important functions of a good case brief schema is to force you to consider your *own* thoughts and reactions to the case.[20]

Further, while most students would agree that case briefing helps them prepare for class, it does more than that. Not only does writing a case brief help you understand the case, it is also a way of "chunking" information to free up working memory so you can think about the main idea of a case. In other words, a case brief is not simply an end in and of itself.

C. Case Briefing Promotes "Chunking"

Law professors want you to think about the "chunks" of information you have written in your briefs so you can analyze the case on your own

---

17. Transcript of Interview with Student 112 at p. 6 (on file with the author).

18. Christensen, *supra* n.2 at 17 (*citing* McKinney, *supra* n.2, at 176).

19. *Id.*

20. Your model case brief should contain a section for the student's own thoughts and/or conclusions.

and see how it fits into the context of the course. This is where your learning truly occurs. In addition, this is a key facet of case analysis. Experts in any field have ways of chunking information into rational groups.[21] Once clumped in a rational group, the same amount of information takes up less storage space in working memory, thus freeing more space in working memory for the challenging task of actually thinking about the material.[22] The ability to recall more information is, therefore, a function of the size and information content of the individual chunks.[23]

Case briefing is the beginning of your journey toward a fuller understanding of the nuances and flexibility of legal text. How can you make this happen? The remaining section of this chapter will provide an example of how to expand your traditional case brief to get more out of your case reading.

D. A First Year Student's Example Case Brief

I would like to provide you with an example of an actual first year law student's case brief. This student sought out comments from my writing assistant about whether he provided enough detail in his brief to really aid him in understanding the case. My writing assistant provided detailed comments back to the student on how he might improve his case briefing.

Note how the student used the traditional case brief template. Although the student was on the right track, he needed to go a bit farther into the reasoning and details of the case. The student's case brief with my research assistant's comments are provided on the next page. Read the student's case brief critically to determine what, if anything, you would do differently. This section ends with some very useful advice given to the student by my writing assistant (from her perspective as a third year law student).

---

21. Christensen, *supra* n.2 at 18 (*citing* McKinney, *supra* n.2, at 174). Cognitive scientists understand that knowledge is structured in memory like cohesive groups of concepts or "chunking." In turn this "chunking" of knowledge makes information meaningful. Information, including facts, figures, and beliefs, is organized into clusters of knowledge. "The concept of knowledge, as distinguished from information, implies understanding." Paula Lustbader, *Construction Sites, Building Types, and Bridging Gaps: A Cognitive Theory of the Learning Progression of Law Students*, 33 Willamette L. Rev. 315, 320 (1997).

22. Christensen, *supra* n.2 at 18 (*citing* McKinney, *supra* n.2, at 175).

23. Christensen, *supra* n.2 at 18 (*citing* Gary L. Blasi, *What Lawyers Know: Lawyering Expertise, Cognitive Science, and the Functions of Theory*, 45 J. Legal Educ. 313, 344 (1995)). Blasi cites the following example "Most people who glance at the following string of symbols will have some difficulty remembering it: WYSIWYG/P6/ QWERTY/AS400. To a person with limited knowledge of computers, this is a string of twenty-three individual symbols, possibly bearing an encrypted message. But a more computer-literate person will quickly recognize this string of symbols as four discrete chunks, each representing a known concept or object, and will easily remember it." *Id.* at 343.

Sample First-Year Case Brief with Comments

United States v. Jewell
(US Court of Appeals, 1976)

Parties: Π/respondent- US; Δ/appellant- Stoner

Procedural History:

Π sued Δ for smuggling drugs.
Judgment for Π.
Δ appealed.

> T.A. Comment: Generally speaking, you may want to include a little more specific information for your procedural history (in this case specifically, it's not really necessary). But, it will help you tremendously in all areas of the law to understand what really happened—and a good majority of the tricky legal terms/concepts will appear in the procedure sections.

Facts:

- Δ drove into the US in an automobile and claims to have "<u>unknowingly</u>" transported illegal drugs

> Isn't this really the "issue" in the case? If you put this down as a "fact" on an exam, it would likely be marked wrong. The fact is only what actually happened—D drove across the border with drugs in his glove compartment. His claim of "unknowingly" transported illegal drugs is really the defendant's argument or legal issue.

- Question of whether defendant "knew" he was transporting illegal drugs

> Make sure to distinguish what is a fact and what is an issue. They are very different things.

- Jury found that Δ had positive knowledge of marijuana,

> This is a case on appeal, which doesn't have a jury. The appellate court is looking at this from a court record. You may want to distinguish procedural facts (of the appellate court) from these underlying facts (which is what happened at the lower court level).

- (Deliberate ignorance)

> This part of "deliberate ignorance" is good—were you asking yourself why the jury found that he behaved knowingly, and therefore violated the statute? Good.

Legal Issue:

- Can deliberately turning a blind eye to illegal activity that you know is likely to be going on be construed as "knowledge"?

> I would restate this to be clearer. The issue looks correct but you want it to read smoothly.

Rule:

- Deliberate ignorance = positive knowledge (high probability).

> This is a good rule statement for the purpose of being prepared for class, but think about using your brief to help you with future exam-writing as well. Write out a more formal rule statement.

My Reasoning:

- According to the facts, Δ had entertained the knowledge, in high probability that marijuana was in his automobile. If Δ knew that he was transporting illegal, but instead covered his eyes, then defendant has knowledge.

> Why? Make sure to create that analytical bridge for your reader, even if you think the point seems obvious.

Courts Reasoning:

- The defendant knew of the high probability that he was smuggling drugs and therefore, based on the rule, certain "knowledge" can be imputed to the defendant and he is therefore guilty.

> Be more specific in pointing to which facts demonstrate that he knew of the high probability that he was transporting drugs.

Disposition: Affirmed

In your first semester, the process of case briefing has two (if not more) important purposes. First, it will help you test your ability to recognize and isolate the different elements of IRAC by having to compartmentalize them in a written format. Additionally, it will give you an outlet to practice writing out your rule statements and your analysis. This practice will be very valuable when it comes time to write an exam. Make sure that your case brief uses as many facts from the case at hand as possible and ask yourself why a particular fact is significant to the outcome of a case. It is likely, especially in the beginning—your case brief will not hit on the issues discussed in class. Don't be discouraged by this! You may have simply articulated things in a different way or gotten to the correct conclusion by taking a different road. Either way, make sure to seek out some one-on-one time with your professor to discuss case briefing. You may want to ask that they comment on your analysis, clarity of your writing, and organizational structure. If you don't take a proactive approach to getting feedback on your briefs, you may miss an opportunity to improve your skill set.

E. Going Beyond the Traditional Case Brief

After you receive your traditional case brief template, consider revising the template to incorporate more of the types of questions that your law professors want you to consider as you read through a case for class.[24] The following example provides a revised case brief format that poses the types of questions you should be able to answer if you have read the case well.

1. **CONTEXTUALIZE THE CASE**[25]
    Where is the case from?
        What court wrote the opinion?
        What year was the opinion written?
        How will this case act as precedent to your issue?
    Why are you reading the case?
        What is your purpose for reading the case?
        What should you focus on?

2. **OVERVIEW**
    Briefly skim the synopsis of the case.
        What is the subject matter?

---

24. Note how many of these questions in this case brief are the types of questions the Higher Performing law students noted in their think-alouds as a part of the reading study described in Chapters 4 and 5.

25. Christensen, *supra* n.2 at 24–25 (citing Mary A. Lundeberg, *Metacognitive Aspects of Reading Comprehension: Studying Understanding in Legal Case Analysis*, 22 READING RES. Q. 430–432 (1987)). This example is based in part on Lundeberg's suggestions about revising the typical brief format.

What are the keynotes?

What are the main issues?

3. READ THE CASE.

What's the procedural posture?

What is the summary of legal proceedings?

What are the issues in dispute?

Outline the Facts.

Who are the parties and what do they want?

Create a picture of the facts.

Identify the key issues.

What issues is the court deciding and/or reviewing?

What did the court decide?.

Identify the holding and the rule/s applied by the court.

Why did the court so hold?

What occurred in the case procedurally? Is the judgment reversed or affirmed, or is the motion denied?

4. REREAD TO GET THE BIG PICTURE

Make sure you understand all the legal terms.

Distinguish relevant from irrelevant facts.

Using the issue and holding, note which facts are legally relevant to the court's decision.

Understand the court's rationale. Can you write it out in your own words?

What is the court's reasoning? What is dicta?

What rules is the court applying? What is the policy behind the rules?

5. EVALUATE THE CASE

Do you agree with the decision?

Was it well-written? Well-reasoned?

Why are you reading the case, i.e., why is it in your casebook?

Why did the court come to this conclusion?

6. MAKE NOTES

Summarize the case in your own words.

In the margin or in a separate case brief, use your own words to summarize the case, its facts, the law, and the law as applied to the facts. Why is the case important? Is the judge correct? What influenced the judge's decision? Were facts or law more important to the outcome? How will this decision serve as precedent for future cases?

Hopefully, if you adopt this revised case brief template, you will begin to understand that there are many facets to case analysis. It is all too easy to read a case only to plug its components into the corresponding section of the case brief. You cannot stop there. Case briefing is only the *beginning* of case analysis, not the end. If your case analysis never develops beyond identifying the structural components of a case, your full understanding of any case will be limited. As law professors, we want you to have your own opinions about cases and about the law.

One successful first-year student in the top 10% of her law school class understood this concept well. In an interview, I asked her to consider what advice she would give to a beginning law student about to start his or her first semester:

> We're often taught to believe that because there is a holding in a case, there is a right answer. And I really don't believe that you can do well in law school if you just accept that. I think you should always be open and never discount your reaction because if you feel it, then you can make an argument for it. Don't back down just because the holding is a position that the majority of the court took. Use your own thoughts and ideas, and intuition.[26]

Remember that when you brief a case, you need to go beyond merely paraphrasing the text.[27] Try to become open to more than one argument in the judicial opinion. Good lawyers and law students question the decisions they read; they evaluate the results of the case, and they consider the implications of any rule. This is precisely what law professors *test* in exams. We want you to read the law creatively, as well as critically. A good case brief can help you accomplish this task more effectively.

---

26. Transcript of Interview with Student 102 at 11 (on file with the author).

27. Because this is a book about law students who learn differently, I wanted to provide an additional way of revising the traditional case brief. Professor J.J. Brown, of Stetson College of Law, has created what he calls a 3D "holographic" case brief for the 21st century. Professor Brown developed a way that casebook cases can be analyzed in multi-dimensional aspects similar to a holographic projection. The method, entitled the Advocacy Template, gives students a way to look beyond the printed pages to uncover "the story" behind the litigation in an appellate decision. An example of Professor Brown's template can be founded in Appendix B.

Chapter 7

How to Prepare for Class: What Does Your Professor *Really* Want from You?

Your main task in your first-year classes is to read a series of cases that discuss a specific rule of law. From the cases, you will distill a legal rule or holding. The professor expects you to read and understand the cases *before* you come to class. The actual classroom experience will not tend to focus upon the facts, issue, and holding of the case (although you will likely cover these basics in the first part of class). Instead, after an introductory discussion of the case, your professor will pose a hypothetical. A hypothetical is a new factual situation that will contain a similar legal issue. Your job is to apply the rule (from the first case) to the new factual situation and determine the likely outcome. If your professor uses the Socratic Method, the professor will choose a student from the class and hold a "conversation" with the student focusing on this new hypothetical. The purpose of this conversation is to point out the nuances of the court's reasoning and to consider how the case might apply to this new set of facts.

In law school, we assume that you have read and understood the cases before you come to class. The classroom experience *applies* that information and reasoning. The purpose of law school classes is to expand upon that information; to test the credibility of the court's reasoning; to discuss the policy implications of the court's decision, etc. You can prepare for class most effectively by thinking about the difference between what the professor wants you to do *before* class as compared to what the professor expects you to do *in* class. This next section will provide you with a list of suggestions to help you through the three stages of the law school classroom experience: (1) what to do *before* class; (2) what to do *in* class; and (3) what to do *after* class.

A. Things to Do Before Class

1. Before You Begin Reading, Determine *Why* You Are Reading the Case!

As you sit down to prepare for your first several assignments, one of your tasks is to figure out *why* your professor is having you read that case. As we've already discussed, good reading entails active, careful reading of the cases in your textbooks. This is easier said than done. You need to consider *why* you are reading the case. Why did the casebook author select *that* particular case to illustrate a particular rule or concept?

Before you dive into reading the case, take a moment to check the table of contents of your casebook. Try to understand what topic or subject matter the case covers. Is the author trying to illustrate a particular rule of causation? The table of contents will give you a good idea of what rule the case is meant to illustrate. In addition, check your syllabus. Your professor may have given you a hint about why he or she is having you read *that* case at that particular time in the course. If you can begin your class preparation with some idea of the *context* of a case—both in terms of why you're reading the case at this time in the course and the context of the case itself— you've given yourself a leg up on what you will be asked in class.[1] After you understand the basics of the case, try to focus on the part of the case that discusses the rule or theory most relevant to that section in the book.

2. Go to Class!

First and foremost, make sure you attend class. Have your homework done *before* class. If you cannot complete the full reading assignment, you want to minimally skim the reading and/or use a commercial outline to get a sense of the basics of the cases.

3. Schedule Your Study Time

You will need to schedule your study time. Be prepared to feel like you should spend every minute of your day studying the law. And you could try to do that but you'd burn out in a week. Taking regular breaks helps you learn by giving your mind, eyes and body a rest. Then you can return to your work refreshed and able to comprehend more information.

You need to schedule your study time for another reason as well. If you learn differently, you may find that you become too immersed in a

---

1. Remember that knowing the context of the case was something that the most successful law students did as they read a case.

single course or a particular reading assignment.[2] Perhaps you are spending too much time on one subject and failing to get to the assignments in another class.

There is something to be said about scheduling law school like you would organize a work day for your job. Consider that law school *is* your job right now. You should assume you will work reasonably hard during your first year at your new job. Therefore, you should schedule 50 hours a week of study time (in addition to class time). Plot out exactly how much time you will spend on each reading assignment. If you have three classes to prepare for in one evening, then you need to assess realistically how much time you have. If you have 6 hours in that evening, you should schedule two hours per class. This allows you to attack your studying very purposefully and carefully so that you can cover as much of the reading as possible in your allotted time.

4. Use Commercial Outlines and Study Guides Strategically

Commercial law school outlines[3] tend to be comprehensive guides that cover the cases and legal rules applicable to a given course. Commercial outlines can be helpful to students because they present the 'big picture.' In some first-year courses, like Torts for example, it can take several weeks to cover all the elements of negligence. By referring to a commercial outline (or another type of study aid), you can gain a helpful perspective about how the individual pieces of the law fit into the larger whole. Commercial outlines and other study materials present material in a condensed, highly structured fashion, and they are often designed to parallel the materials presented in popular casebooks.

There are many different types of study aids which include commercial outlines, treatises, or hornbooks. During my first year of law school, my professors told us *not* to buy any study aids. I dutifully listened to their advice and used only my casebook and class notes to create my outlines during the first year. On my exams, I very carefully regurgitated all

---

2. For law students who learn differently, your reading and studying ability may not be efficient enough initially to get through all of the material. This is precisely why you need to spread your study time out so you make sure to *at least* cover the main components of each class. This may also be where study aids can be very helpful to you.

3. There are a whole host of supplementary materials available. You can choose from outlines, flashcards, nutshells (short mini-books that give concise explanations), etc. There are also the "Examples and Explanations" series or a "Question and Answer" series, as well as longer treatises (more descriptive statements of the law) and hornbooks (typically written by the casebook author to provide background information in the law). I have also suggested that students use bar review materials and/or tapes, particularly if they are auditory learners. You will want to choose a study aid that matches with your learning style. Try a few out. You do *not* need to buy them all.

the cases we discussed in class. But I missed seeing the forest through the trees. I failed to understand the bigger picture of how the individual cases formed larger concepts or doctrines, and I lost points because I missed this larger perspective. During my second year of law school, I used commercial outlines. The outlines allowed me to do two things: first, I was able to preview the cases before I read them in my casebook; second, the outlines allowed me to see the big picture of how the cases fit into the full context of the course.

Commercial outlines or other study aids, however, cannot substitute for your course materials. You need to go to class (because your professor will test you on the material you've covered in class). Study aids *can* be an important resource to help you prepare for classes and exams. Anything you do to improve your understanding of the basics of the case gives you 'context' to help your case reading. Study aids also provide you with various hypotheticals or examples of how the rules apply to real-life situations. These examples are important to your classroom (and exam) preparation. Although you will discuss the basics of the cases and their holdings in class, most of your class time will be spent discussing the application of the case rules to new hypotheticals. If you've already considered possible examples as you've prepared for class, you will be one step ahead of your peers. And you will be better prepared for your exams as well.

Table 7 will help you become familiar with the different types of study aids available to you. Your school library will likely have many of these, so you may want to see what your library carries before you spend extra money on study aids. Note also that different study aids may work more effectively for different types of learning styles. Keep your learning style in mind when you choose a study aid.

Table 7. Study Aids

Type of Study Aid	Description	Strengths	Drawbacks	When to use this type of aid	Example of this type of aid
Canned Briefs	Provide you with a one-page case brief similar to what you will need to prepare for class. Includes the rule, facts, parties' arguments, and court's holding and reasoning in a concise format.	Good resource for first semester as a 1L when you will struggle more with legal reading.	Cannot use INSTEAD of reading cases. May give you a false sense of security about your understanding of the case. Professors tend to dislike pre-prepared briefs.	After you've read a case or towards the end of the semester for review. Learning Styles: Visual, Read-Write	High Court Case Summaries
Hornbooks or Treatises	Longer, text-based books that very thoroughly explain a concept in the law. Contain narrative explanations with some examples.	In-depth coverage; detailed explanations. Professors tend to prefer these.	Lengthy, expensive and boring. Often provide too much information and minute detail.	Can use throughout the semester. Learning Styles: Visual, Read-Write, Auditory/Oral Examples and Explanations	Prosser and Keeton Dobbs on Torts

Type of Study Aid	Description	Strengths	Drawbacks	When to use this type of aid	Example of this type of aid
Commercial Outlines	Cover all the material presented in a course in an outline format. Will have black letter law broken down into elements; include examples and brief explanations of key concepts and cases.	Can be very useful to see the 'big' picture; help to synthesize the different concepts introduced in a course. May come with practice essay and multiple choice questions.	Less detailed than class notes and will not follow the structure of your class. Use only to supplement class notes; do not use a commercial outline in place of creating your own outline.	Use throughout the semester. Start by glancing at the large-scale outline in this supplement before you begin classes to learn the vocabulary, general rules, and elements most pertinent to the course. Revisit the outline throughout course to help you put concepts together. Use at the end of the course to supplement your outlining. Learning Styles: Visual, Kinesthetic (doing practice exams, problems); Read/Write	Gilberts (uses charts, graphs, flow charts, etc.) Emanuels Legalines Roadmap
Audio recordings	Recorded lectures on a particular subject. A spoken version of a commercial outline.	Flexible; can use in your car, at the gym, in iPod. Some also come with a corresponding workbook of examples.	Can be expensive (but can purchase used). Suited primarily for one specific type of learning style (auditory/oral).	Use any time during semester; good for synthesizing at end of semester; use before you get to a concept in class for general overview. Learning Styles: Auditory/Oral; Kinesthetic (can move around while listening)	Flemings PMBR Bar Review
Exam Preparation Materials	Geared toward helping you prepare for final exams; use flow charts; checklists; tree diagrams, and capsule summaries	Concise; incorporate visuals for all different learning styles.	May not provide in depth coverage of issues and/or courses.	Geared toward exam preparation toward the end of the semester versus class preparation Learning Styles: Visual; Read/Write; Kinesthetic	CrunchTime PMBR Finals—Law School Exams Series Law In a Flash-Flashcards
Bar Preparation Materials	Examine black letter law for multi-state bar subjects	Concise and fairly general; provide good "big picture" review of specific courses/subject matters	Examine concepts more than cases; may not follow your course outlines.	Geared toward bar exam preparation; big picture. Learning Styles: Visual (charts, flow charts); Auditory (tapes, computer cd's); Kinesthetic (review questions)	PMBR Bar Charts Flash Cards

5. Create Your Own Case Briefs When You Can

As we discussed in Chapter 6, case briefing is a way to help you figure out what's going on in the case more quickly. Doing a separate case brief for your cases is very important in the early weeks of law school. As you progress through law school, many students find that they simply do not have enough time to create separate case briefs for every case in an assignment. If you are not creating separate case briefs, you need to *minimally* make notes in the margins of the case *in your own words*. Take the concepts that you've read and internalize them into concepts that you understand. At the very least, write out portions of the case in your own words.[4]

6. Read the Case Notes in Your Casebook

Along the lines of knowing *why* you're reading the cases—you should also make time to read the case notes *following* the major cases (or a series of cases) in your casebook.[5] Sometimes it's good to skim the cases notes *before* you read the actual case. The case notes, like the table of contents, can give you a sense of why the case is important and how the rule has been applied more recently.

In addition, it is possible that your professor will actually spend class time discussing the case notes. After the professor has gotten through the basic aspects of the case, the professor will begin asking you how the particular rule of law from the case will apply to a different fact situation or hypothetical. The case notes and problems will help you prepare for this important aspect of the class.

---

4. There are canned briefs (briefs already written for you) likely available on most of the major cases you read. These are not necessarily bad study aids—*if* you use them appropriately. Canned briefs can be a useful way of getting oriented quickly to a case—particularly to an older case whose language is unfamiliar. Canned briefs give you a basic summary of the facts of the case, the procedural posture and the court's holding. Once you've read the canned brief, you can then read the actual case having had the additional background and context. Canned briefs can be a good place to begin if you find you're having trouble getting through your course material.

5. The case notes are questions at the end of a case that are meant to make you think about the principles. These questions can sometimes be frustrating to students because they are often ambiguous and difficult to address given your present knowledge of the material. However, they also replicate the types of questions that may be on an essay exam. Try to take the time to go through some of these examples. This teaches you to apply the rules to a new set of facts—which is what you will be asked to do on an exam.

B. Things to Do in Class

1. Arrive on Time

Law professors want you to arrive to class on time. If you are prone to being late, set your clock back! Some law professors will ban you from class if you arrive more than 5 minutes late. Perhaps in your undergraduate courses you could slink in late in a large lecture—that's almost impossible in law school.

2. Sit Strategically in the Classroom

Consider where you will learn most effectively in the classroom. Is it close to the professor? Do you need to be by the door to take a break during class? Do you need to minimize noise from other students? Do you need to position yourself away from your friends so you can prevent yourself from being distracted by comments and/or jokes? We all have our own learning styles. Try to do what is best for your learning style. If you tend to get distracted, you may want to stay up towards the front of the classroom. In law school, you want to do everything possible to create an environment that is conducive to learning.

3. Use Your Laptop for Notes Only!

Laptop computers can be a very distracting element in the classroom. Although you might believe you can multi-task, the truth is that you cannot learn as effectively when you are multi-tasking. As you begin law school, you need your full concentration. Give yourself the opportunity to fully engage in your classes.

4. Take Effective Notes

After the first week of law school, you will develop your own style of taking notes in class. Initially, you'll probably feel like you want to write down everything that goes on in class. Your notes will resemble a transcript of everything your professor discussed and everything your classmates said in response to the professor's questions. You will learn to be more discerning in what you write down. Many times the answer your classmate gives may *not* be the right answer.

One key strategy is to write down the *questions* your professor asks during the class. As you go back through your notes after class, you will start to get a sense of what your professor thinks is important about the case.

In addition, evaluate what you hear in class—both from your peers and your professor. You won't agree with everything discussed in class—but if you don't agree—be able to articulate *why* you disagree.

Another effective strategy for taking notes is to create an electronic template for your class notes. Consider the template at the bottom of this section. A template will allow you to take notes consistently throughout the semester and save them in a single document for each class, which will make them easier to review.[6] After every two or three classes, review your notes—reorganize them and revise them. This will make outlining easier as the semester progresses.[7]

Note Taking Template

Class:
Date/Time:
Reading Assignment:

Main Lecture/Note Taking Area

In this section, record the lecture as meaningfully as possible. Try *not* to just script or write down *everything* your professor says.

Questions

The *Questions* section is likely the most *important* aspect of your note taking. Write down the professor's questions about a particular case or concept. This gives you a sense of what the professor sees as important in the case. Try to write down a good answer for the question as well. In addition, consider writing down good questions by other students if it helps your understanding.

Summaries

The Summaries section can be filled in when you review your notes between classes. Try to summarize key points from that lecture in a sentence or two. Also note additional questions you may have or additional readings.

---

6. It is essential to devise a good back-up system for your computer files. Many students have computer problems at some point during law school. Use flashdrives, send to your email account, etc. Devise a way to protect your data. You won't have extra time to recreate it!

7. Outlining, a way to distill a law school course down to its essential elements, will be discussed in Chapter 9.

5. Review Class Notes

Because of the large volume of material you will learn each semester, you need to review your class notes regularly. You cannot cram all that information into your brain during finals. And if you learn differently, it may be impossible for you to cram for finals. Therefore, take time to review class material. You should also highlight or note questions that you still had even after you reviewed the material. These will be concepts you'll want to review with your professor.

If you get to class five minutes early, review your notes from the last class. Ideally, your professor will recap the highlights of the last class at the beginning of the new class, but this is not always the case. Reviewing material from the prior class will help you transition and make connections with the new cases. Learning the law is not a series of discrete lectures and elements; everything builds upon a rule or skill that you have mastered previously. By conducting a five minute review before each class, you are ensuring that you have mastered one concept before moving on to a new one.

6. Organize Your Class Notes

After every 1–2 weeks, organize your class notes by using a method that works with your learning style. You might try using flowcharts, graphic organizers or spatial learning strategies. In talking to successful law students with ADD, each student had his or her own way of organizing class material based upon their learning style. Some students liked to learn by using audio tapes. Other students were more visual learners. Many of these students used graphic organizers. Graphic Organizers (or spatial learning strategies) provide a visual and holistic representation of facts and concepts and their relationships within an organized frame. Students who learn differently find that graphic organizers give them an effective tool for enhancing their thinking and learning. Specifically, they can help you represent abstract or implicit concepts in more concrete and explicit forms.

Examples of graphic organizers include charts, maps and flowcharts. Sometimes you will see graphic organizers referred to as "Mindmapping."[8] These graphics rely on the use of arrows or geometric shapes and spatial arrangements to describe the text content and to structure key conceptual relationships.

---

8. "A Mindmap is a thinking tool that reflects externally what goes on inside your head," Tony Buzan, *Maximize the Power of Your Brain*, http://www.youtube.com/watch?v=MlabrWv25qQ, (last visited September 19, 2009). For information on software that can be purchased to assist in creating a mind map, *see*, Mind Technologies, http://www.visual-mind.com/concept_edu.html.

Here is a typical graphic organizer that uses a combination of "Mindmapping" and a flowchart.[9]

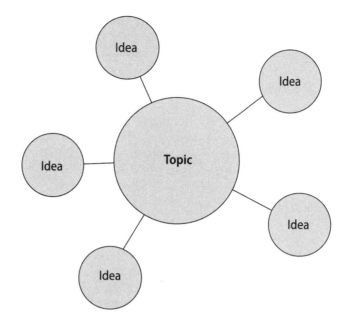

Here is a graphic organizer called a web flow chart.[10]

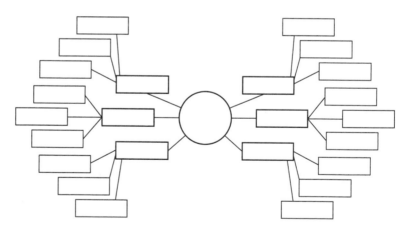

Traditional law school outlines have you look at your courses in a linear fashion and in the context of narrative text. Graphic organizers allow you to create visual images of the handful of core principles that link

---

9. ASCD, http://www.ascd.org/ASCD/images/publications/books/marzano2-001a_fig6.2.gif (last visited September 19, 2009).

10. *Printables for Teachers,* http://www.resources-teachers.com/img/graphic-organizers.jpg (last visited September 19, 2009).

seemingly unrelated bits of information.[11] Further, by converting the material you discuss in class to something visual, you begin the process of absorbing it, processing the information and retaining. It is as much the process of *making* a flow chart or a graphic organizer that helps learning as much as it is the end product.

Consider the example of a First Amendment flow chart.[12]

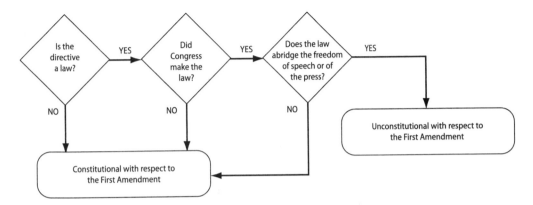

If you are willing to spend a little time on the web, you can find a software program that will help you create a variety of graphic organizers.[13] If you learn visually, then a picture is truly worth a thousand words. If you have a different learning style, then search for a method that allows you to learn most efficiently and effectively.

7. Study Groups

Outside of class time, you will also have the option of joining a study group. A study group is just that—a small group of students that meets together to discuss and review concepts from your classes. Members of study groups often share class notes and/or outlines. Study groups often work together to go over old exams. Many students find study groups helpful *if* you happen to pair up with students who learn in the same way that you do.

What makes for a good study group experience? In addition to finding students with similar learning styles, choose people with similar per-

---

11. Adapted from Study Guides and Strategies, The University of St. Thomas, St. Paul, MN.

12. From http://www.krusch.com/real/flow2.html (last visited July 15, 2009).

13. For more information visit: Write Design Online, http://www.write designonline.com/organizers/ (last visited September 19, 2009; Houghton Mifflin Harcourt, *Education Place,* http://www.eduplace.com/ss/maps/ (last visited September 19, 2009; Graphic.org, *Graphic Organizers, http://www.graphic.org/goindex.html* (last visited September 19, 2009).

sonality styles as well. For example, you want to avoid "moochers" if you are not a "moocher." Set objectives each week. Assign specific tasks for each member of the group. Use practice exam questions; invent your own multiple choice questions and/or use flashcards. All of these activities replicate the law school exam experience.

Note that you do not *have* to join a study group to succeed in law school. In fact, many law students with unique learning styles find that study groups are more bothersome than helpful. For example, if you need to learn the material by making your own flowcharts, then a study group that simply "talks out" problems may not be a good use of your study time. If you are having trouble simply getting through your course material, focus on *that* aspect of law school before joining a study group. In fact, any extra time you have may be better spent working one on one with the professors in your Academic Support Program.

Chapter 8

Obtaining Accommodations for Your Learning Disability

Once diagnosed with a learning disability, you will need to consider whether you want to request reasonable accommodations for your disability. There are several considerations that may factor into your decision. For example, you may not be ready to share this piece of information about yourself. Your diagnosis is personal—and there are some students who are reluctant to proceed with applying for disability accommodations during law school. Instead, these students tend to compensate for their learning differences in law school. For example, a student might study at home or work with a professor directly to get extra assistance.

That being said, sometimes merely *compensating* for learning differences will not work well enough in the law school context. Consider Baker's experience in the prior chapters of this book. Baker worked extremely hard with respect to the amount of time he read and studied in preparation for his classes—but his ADD significantly affected his reading and test-taking abilities in law school. I strongly believe that Baker could have improved his academic achievement in if he had learned and applied different study strategies during his first year.

Remember that the purpose behind disability accommodations is to *level the playing field*. Try not to think of receiving accommodations as something extra. If you have a learning disability, there is likely a neurological difference within your brain and any accommodations you receive simply allow you to function at the same level as law students who do not have a learning disability. Receiving disability accommodations equalizes the playing field—it does not give you an advantage.[1]

If you find that you have tried to compensate for your learning differences but those differences are significantly impeding your learning in law school—you need to get help as soon as possible. Likewise, if you sus-

---

1. Not everyone understands what it means to have a learning disability. You will undoubtedly face students or even law school professors who are ignorant about the origin of learning disabilities and who may assume that you are feigning your condition to get 'extra' exam time. Try your best to ignore these individuals. Do not let these prejudices affect your decision of whether or not to apply for disability accommodations.

pect that you may have a learning disability but have never been tested—now is the time! Make an appointment with the professionals in your Academic Support Program. These educators are very knowledgeable about learning strategies and disabilities. If you already know you have a learning disability, you may want to go directly to the Student Services or Disability Office at your school.

It is important to remember, however, that simply obtaining a *diagnosis* for your learning disability does not guarantee that you will meet the eligibility requirements for "reasonable accommodations" under the law. There is a legal standard that must be met before any law school is required to provide you with disability accommodations. The remainder of this chapter will provide you with the legal background for the accommodations process and it will discuss the necessary tests and documents that must support an accommodations application.

A. Requirements for Obtaining Disability Accommodations under the ADA and the Rehabilitation Act

The principal law governing individuals with disabilities is the Americans with Disabilities Act (ADA).[2] The purpose of the ADA is to prohibit discrimination against a qualified individual with a disability on the basis of that disability.[3] Title II of the ADA prohibits discrimination by public entities in the provision of services, programs, and activities; and Title III prohibits discrimination by private entities that operate places of public accommodation.[4] Law schools are covered by both Title II and Title III by virtue of their educational relationships with students.[5]

Prior to the enactment of the ADA, individuals with disabilities were able to bring suit under the Rehabilitation Act of 1973 (generally referred to as "The Rehabilitation Act" or "Section 504"), which was intended to empower individuals with physical and mental disabilities "to maximize employment, economic self-sufficiency, independence, and inclusion and integration into society."[6] The Rehabilitation Act prohibits discrimination by entities receiving federal funding against an otherwise qualified individual with a disability solely on the basis of that disability.[7]

---

2. Suzanne E. Rowe, *Reasonable Accommodations for Unreasonable Requests: The Americans with Disabilities Act in Legal Writing Courses*, 12 Legal Writing: J. Legal Writing Inst. 3, 3 (2006).

3. *Id.* at 8.

4. 42 U.S.C.A. § 12182, *see also* Rowe, *supra* n.2 at 8.

5. Rowe, *supra* n.2 at 9.

6. 29 U.S.C.A. § 701, *see also* Rowe, *supra* n.2 at 8.

7. 29 U.S.C. § 794(a), *see also* Rowe, *supra* n.2 at 8–9.

Because law schools receive federal funding, they are covered by the Rehabilitation Act as well as the ADA and students can assert their rights under both the Rehabilitation Act and the ADA.[8]

However, the ADA draws extensively from the Rehabilitation Act.[9] Congress intended for the standards in the two acts to complement each other, despite the use of updated terminology in the ADA.[10] The ADA and its regulations interpret the terms "disabilities" in the ADA and "handicaps" in the Rehabilitation Act as substantively equivalent.[11] Because the requirements of the ADA and the Rehabilitation Act are almost the same, courts use cases decided under the two statutes to support each other almost interchangeably.

B. Can You Prove You Are a Qualified Individual with a Disability?

As a student considering whether to apply for disability accommodations, one of the first questions you need to ask yourself is if you are a *qualified* individual with a disability. Both the ADA and the Rehabilitation Act protect only individuals with disabilities who are otherwise *qualified* for the service that they seek.[12] The ADA defines a qualified individual with a disability as:

> an individual with a disability who, with or without reasonable modifications to rules, polices, or practices, the removal of architectural, communication, or transportation barriers, or the provision of auxiliary aids and services, meets the essential eligibility requirements for the receipt of services or the participation in programs or activities provided by a public entity.[13]

The Rehabilitation Act similarly protects only an "otherwise qualified individual with a disability."[14] Your first step toward showing that you are a qualified individual with a *disability* is to show that you have a disability recognized under the ADA. The ADA defines a disability as "a physical or mental impairment that substantially limits one or more of

---

8. Rowe, *supra* n.2 at 9 (*citing Bonnie Poitras Tucker & Joseph F. Smith, Jr., Accommodating Law Faculty with Disabilities*, 46 J. Leg. Educ. 157, 158 n.8 (1996)).

9. Rowe, *supra* n.2 at 9 (citing *Stern v. U. of Osteopathic Med. & Health Scis.*, 220 F.3d 906, 908 (8th Cir. 2000)).

10. *Id.* (Congress used "individuals with disabilities" in the ADA, rather than "handicapped individuals," to reflect the terminology current in 1990 and to respect the preferences of those who have disabilities.)

11. *Id.*

12. *Id.* at 10.

13. *Id.*

14. *Id.*

the major life activities of such individual; a record of such an impairment; or being regarded as having such an impairment."[15] A physical or mental impairment includes "specific learning disabilities" as well as physiological disorders and conditions, disfigurement, anatomical loss, and mental retardation.[16] However, "[m]erely having an impairment does not make one disabled for purposes of the ADA. Claimants also need to demonstrate that the impairment limits a major life activity."[17]

Major life activities include learning, reading, and working, as well as more basic activities such as walking, seeing, hearing, speaking, and breathing.[18] A disability under the ADA is an impairment that "*substantially limits*" one of these activities by preventing or significantly restricting an individual's ability to perform the activity.[19] The issue is the impairment's effect on a specific individual's ability to perform a major life activity, not merely the diagnosis of impairment.[20]

In the law school context, for example, a student who has been diagnosed with dyslexia but who self-accommodates sufficiently to be unimpaired in learning does not have a disability under the ADA. Another student with the same diagnosis who is significantly restricted in learning *does* have a disability under the ADA.[21] If you find that your learning, studying or reading is significantly affected by your learning disability—your impairment has arguably limited a major life activity. Your law school will ultimately make this determination. Therefore, if you choose to proceed with applying for accommodations, your first step is to notify your law school that you are an individual with a disability. Your second step is to begin the process of documenting how your disability significantly impacts your learning in law school.

C. What Is the Required Documentation to Support an Application?

As you begin the application process, you will need to prove the existence of your learning disability through documentation that meets three criteria: (1) the documentation must be sufficiently recent; (2) it must address the disability at issue; and (3) it must have been prepared by a qualified evaluator.[22] Documentation is "sufficiently recent" if you

---

15. *Id*. at 11.
16. *Id*.
17. *Id*.
18. *Id*. at 12.
19. *Id*.
20. *Id*.
21. *Id*.
22. *Id*. at 13.

have had tests with regard to your learning disability conducted within the past three years.[23] However, if you have had a definitive diagnosis of a learning disability earlier in your educational career, it may be sufficient for a qualified evaluator to simply review these prior tests and apply the diagnosis to the new academic pursuits you are undertaking in law school.[24]

It will be your job to provide the necessary documentation for your application for disability accommodations. In other words, you have the *burden of proof*. First and foremost, you need to find out what your school requires. Early on in the process, you should make an appointment with your school's Student Services or Disability Office. Each academic institution has its own process, forms, and required information. An example of a law school's typical application forms can be found in Appendix C in this book.

1. The Psycho-Educational Evaluation

The most important document to support your accommodations application is the psycho-educational evaluation. This is a report that is created by a psychologist that documents your disability and describes how your learning disability impacts your life. The psycho-educational evaluation is an assessment of your functioning in three primary areas: 1) learning aptitude or cognitive ability; 2) academic achievement; and 3) psychological adjustment.[25] The purpose of a Psycho-educational Evaluation is to determine if a learning or other disability significantly impacts your academic performance.

A learning disability is diagnosed when the assessment results reveal a significant discrepancy between a student's scores on achievement tests (in reading, mathematics, and/or written language) and his/her educational expectancy range (based upon age, educational background, and intelligence.)[26]

Psycho-educational evaluations, however, require a significant investment of both time and money. A qualified psychologist will need to conduct a series of tests over several days. Depending upon the type and number of potential learning disabilities for which you are being tested, the cost of this type of evaluation can range from $1,500 to $3,000. You

---

23. *Id.* at 13 (*citing* Suzanne E. Rowe, *The ADA in Legal Writing Courses*, AALS Sec. Newsltr., Leg. Writing, Reasoning, & Research 1 (Spring 2004) (available at http://faculty.law.lsu.edu/aals)).

24. *Id.* at 13.

25. Dr. M.L. Burgee, *What Is Psychoeducational Evaluation,* http://www.iser.com/psychoed-evaluations.html (last visited September 26, 2009.)

26. *Id.* A psycho-educational evaluation can provide another benefit to you as well: it will likely give you a good indication of how you learn best (i.e., your learning style). Once you are empowered with that knowledge, you can continue to make adjustments in your law school studying to maximize your learning potential.

should expect approximately two to three days of testing in total—and each test will take approximately 3 hours.[27]

As stated above, there are three principal areas of testing: (1) learning aptitude; (2) academic skill development; and (3) personality/adjustment factors. The types of tests associated with each of these three areas are described briefly below.

1. *Learning Aptitude Tests:* Learning Aptitude Tests include intelligence (IQ) tests and cognitive processing tests. Cognitive processing tests investigate your ability on measures of verbal-linguistic skills (long-term memory, abstract reasoning, vocabulary development, comprehension, and auditory short-term memory) as well as non-verbal skills (visual organization and memory, nonverbal reasoning, planning ability, visual motor coordination, spatial visualization ability, and short-term visual memory). Supplemental cognitive (aptitude) tests may also be given to further investigate any problem areas based on in-take information and observations (e.g., attention, organization, visual-auditory associative memory, processing speed, auditory processing, long-term retrieval, visuo-spatial memory and fluid reasoning, etc.).[28]

2. *Tests of Academic Skill Development.* These tests will investigate your skills in the areas of reading, written language, and mathematics. Within each of these academic domains, you will be tested on measures of basic skill development and higher level application and reasoning skills. For example, reading tests assess word decoding, phonetic skills, word identification, fluency/rate and comprehension.[29]

3. *Tests of Personality/Adjustment Factors.* These types of tests will investigate your functioning with regard to the development of your academic coping strategies. Your functioning in this regard can be affected by self-esteem, anxiety, internal pressure, motivational levels, etc..You will also be screened for emotional distress (e.g., anxiety, depression) during this portion of the test.

An example of a typical psychoeducational evaluation for a law student is provided, in part, below. A full sample is provided in the Appendix B at the end of the book.

---

27. Evaluators typically only complete one test per "testing" day. Since each test takes between two and three hours, you will only take one test per session.

28. The most common types of learning aptitude tests are Wechsler Adult Intelligence III (including IQ, Index and scaled scores); Woodcock-Johnson Psycho-educational Battery, Revised Part I: Tests of Cognitive Ability; Stanford-Binet Intelligence Scale (4th Ed.); Kaufman Adolescent and Adult Intelligence Test; Detroit Test of Learning Aptitude-A (DTLA-A).

29. Common examples of these types of tests would be the Woodcock-Johnson Psychoeducation Battery, Revised Part II: Tests of Achievement; Wechsler Individual Achievement Test (WIAT); Scholastic Abilities Test for Adults (SATA); and the Nelson-Denny Reading Test (timed and untimed; given in conjunction with one of the above to further document reading abilities and reading rate.

Sample of Psychoeducational Evaluation

Brenda M. Peterson, Ph.D.

Name: Sam Sample
Date of Birth: 5-23-83
Age: 24
Testing Dates: 7-15, 7-17 and 7-25, 2009
Date of Report: 8-1-09

PRIMARY REFERRAL CONCERNS

Sam is a 24 year old male who has just completed his first year of law school at Baxter Law. He reported that his first year of law school did not go well and that he is in the bottom third of his class. According to Sam, his grades do not reflect his ability and understanding. He reported that there is a significant difference between what he knows and how he tests. Sam explained that he has trouble organizing his thoughts on timed tests. In addition, he miswrites words and misspells words frequently. He believes that his work on timed tests is disorganized. In comparison, Sam seems to do well in writing classes where he had more time to edit his work and improve his structure and organization. Sam also reports that it takes him a very long time to read the material as he must reread the material several times to retain it. In order to learn the material effectively, Sam takes notes as he reads and uses index cards. Sam has never been tested for learning disabilities or attention deficit disorder in the past and has never received accommodations in school. This summer, Sam is working as a law clerk in a civil litigation firm.

Before entering law school, Sam worked as a paralegal in the legal department of a law firm.

BACKGROUND INFORMATION

Developmental/Family: Sam was the product of a full-term pregnancy with no significant complications during the pregnancy or the delivery. Sam's development proceeded normally, and there are no developmental delays reported that would impair Sam's academic progress. There is a family history for the presence of learning disorders and ADHD on the maternal side, with Sam's uncle and grandfather both displaying symptoms of short attention span and learning difficulties in the area of reading. Sam's uncle has self-medicated with drug use and dropped out of college due to these difficulties. Both of Sam's parents were good students. Sam's mother completed college and his father runs a successful family business. Sam resides with his parents and his younger sister who is a high achiever academically.

Health/Medical: When Sam was 4-years-old, his tonsils and adenoids were removed to alleviate chronic problems with breathing, allergies, colds, and infections. This surgery helped, but Sam continued to suffer from allergies and has taken medication throughout his life for this condition. He has been receiving allergy shots for over two years, and currently receives one shot each month to manage his symptoms.

A few final thoughts regarding the psycho-educational evaluation. It is important that any report generated by the psychologist explain what tests were done and the results of those tests *very specifically.* The most helpful (and persuasive) psycho-educational reports are very detailed—both in terms of the diagnosis given and the recommended accommodations described by your evaluator.

Finally, any testing that you have done must be done by a *qualified* psychologist or evaluator. Whether a psychologist or evaluator is '*qualified*' will depend upon in part on the learning disability for which you are being tested.[30] Your best resource for finding a qualified evaluator is your school's Disability Office. Most schools have a disability office where they can refer students to a qualified evaluator with whom the school is familiar. Using your law school's recommendation for a particular psychologist or evaluator will have an added advantage: the professional has likely worked with law students before and he or she will be familiar with the unique demands of law school.[31] A psychologist who has worked with law students before should also be more familiar with the types of accommodations that law schools typically allow.

D. What Accommodations Are You Likely to Receive?

Once you provide your law school with your Psycho-educational Evaluation that both documents your learning disability (and illustrates that your disability significantly affects your learning in law school), *and* you have formally requested accommodations, the burden then shifts to your school to determine what accommodations would be most appropriate in your situation.[32]

The process of agreeing upon which accommodations will be most helpful to you will likely differ depending on your law school. Each law school tends to have a different philosophy with regard to granting disability requests. Some law schools will grant accommodations willingly while other law schools may have more rigid standards and will grant very few requests.

However, if you have provided the appropriate documentation and met the legal standard for obtaining disability accommodations, your school is required to provide you with reasonable disability accommodations. However, the key word is *reasonable* accommodations. Law schools are

---

30. Rowe, *supra* n.2 at 14 (*citing Guckenberg v. Boston University*, 974 F. Supp. 106, 136–137 (D.Mass., 1997)).

31. Typically, a qualified evaluator will be a licensed psychologist with a Ph.D.

32. Rowe, *supra* n.2 at 15.

not required to provide disability accommodations that would fundamentally alter the law school academic program at the school or place an undue financial burden on the school. A law school is not required to lower its academic standards or fundamentally change a course.[33] For example, if your law school typically gives essay exams, then you cannot request to submit an outline of an answer in an exam instead of a writing a full essay answer in a course. You *could* request additional time to complete the essay exam but you could not ask the school to alter its assessment standards in such a significant way.[34]

What sorts of accommodations are typically available as reasonable accommodations in law school? Law schools review accommodation applications on a case-by-case basis and your school will likely consider the recommendations made by your psychologist in your Psycho-educational evaluation. The Disability Office will also look closely at your skills and deficiencies, and make recommendations based upon that information as well.

It will be very important for you to develop a good relationship with your law school Disability Office. The following is a list of the most typical accommodations that students request divided into the following three categories: (1) in-class accommodation requests; (2) academic scheduling requests; and (3) law school exam requests.

1. Requests for In-Class Disability Accommodations

a. ***Requests to Avoid Participating Orally in Class***: Although many students ask to be relieved of the typical law school class requirement of "participating orally," this accommodation request is rarely granted. Class participation is considered to be a fundamental part of the law school curriculum. Therefore, law schools are reluctant to grant this accommodation request. However, as an alternative, some students have successfully arranged with their professors to schedule their class participation beforehand. In

---

33. *Id.* at 16. For example, the Office of Civil Rights held that Villanova University School of Law was not required to modify essential aspects of its program in order to accommodate a student with disabilities who requested, among other accommodations: (1) having "complex examination questions broken down clearly into their various parts in outline for or numbers subsections," and (2) "being allowed to generate comprehensive detained outline instead of essays on her examinations." The school denied the students request arguing, "both complex exam questions and essay answers were essential to the academic program." Fulfilling the student's accommodation requests would fundamentally alter the academic program. The ADA does not require schools to modify a course of study to accommodate its students. Additionally, schools are not required to provide accommodation that "would place an undue administrative or financial burden."

34. Rowe, *supra* note 2 at 17.

other words, the student knows ahead of time which days the student will be called upon and, therefore, the student can come to class prepared. In this sense, the student still participates in class but the student also has some forewarning and control over when she is called upon in class.

b. *Note-Taking in Class*: Some students request the aid of a note-taker. A note-taker is often another student in the class who has the job (and is paid) to take notes and provide a copy of his class notes to the student with accommodations. (The note-taker does not know to whom the notes are given so anonymity of the student who is receiving accommodations is preserved).[35] Note-taking is commonly allowed as a reasonable accommodation.

c. *Front Row Seating*: It is also common for a law student with a learning disability to request a front row seat. This may be helpful for students with ADD and ADHD. This request is commonly granted.

d. *Tape Recording Lectures*: Law students may request this accommodation particularly if they have trouble processing information in an auditory form (i.e., the professor speaking in class). Interestingly, however, some law schools deny this accommodation because law professors are reluctant to allow students to record their class lectures. Not all law professors object to tape recording classes, and therefore, you should request this accommodation if you believe it will help you in class.

2. Requests for Alternate Scheduling in Law School

a. *Reduced Course Load*: It can be very helpful for students with learning disabilities to request a lighter course load, particularly during the first year of law school. In other words, instead of taking five classes during a semester, you might request a course load of four classes. If your law school has a part-time program, this may be another option to help you manage the volume of reading and studying in law school. These requests for course reduction are frequently granted.

3. Requests for Examination Accommodations

a. *Requests for More Time on Law School Exams*: One fairly common disability accommodation is for students to request more time on their law school examinations. The most common time

---

35. Having a note-taker can be especially helpful for students with ADA or ADHD, who can use the notes to fill in gaps due to loss of attention.

extension tends to be "time-and-a-half." In other words, if an exam is typically three hours, a student receiving a "time and one-half" accommodation will receive four and one-half hours. Any break that a student needs to take during that lengthy exam period will likely be factored into the total allotment of time.

b. *Requests for More Time on Writing Assignments*: All law students are required to take some form of a legal writing class. Some students with learning disabilities try to request additional time on writing assignments as a reasonable accommodation. However, this accommodation request is not often granted. Because law students typically have several weeks within which to complete an assignment, law students with learning differences may be expected to work within this time frame.

c. *Requests for Private or Semi-Private Rooms*: A fairly common accommodation request is for a student to ask to take their law school exam in a private room (or with a small group of students). Generally, law school examinations are taken in large classrooms— just like the classrooms used during typical classes. For many students with learning disabilities, private or semi-private examination rooms can be very helpful—particularly for those students with ADD or ADHD (who can become very distracted by noise, etc.) Requests for private rooms are commonly granted.

Finally, it is important to remember that the Americans With Disabilities Act (ADA) also applies to state bar exams and multi-state examination just as it does to law school. Therefore, be sure to check the website of your particular state bar association to learn the specific requirements for obtaining disability accommodations for the bar exam. Sometimes these requirements can be very detailed, so you will want to give yourself plenty of time to apply for testing accommodations even as early as your second year of law school.

Chapter 9

Advice from Law Students Who Learn Differently

This section will offer the perspectives of three law students who learn differently. Each of the students was in their third year of law school at the time of the interview. The first two students had been diagnosed with a learning disability. The first student, Mary,[1] knew she had a learning disability (ADD) prior to law school. She was diagnosed during her first year of college. Mary seemed to use this knowledge to her advantage by pursuing accommodations for her disability in law school right away. This seemed to work well for Mary in terms of her academic success. She studied very diligently and kept up with her work. She participated in several outside student groups and internships. At the beginning of her third year of law school, Mary was in the top 5% of her law school class.

The second law student, Laura, was diagnosed with a learning disability (ADHD) during her second year of law school. Laura suspected she had a disability earlier in her undergraduate studies but she was able to compensate for her learning differences in college. During her first year of law school, however, Laura found that she could not keep up the volume of reading. Further, Laura knew that she understood the material from her classes, but she struggled to put all that information together coherently on her exams. She felt unfocused and disorganized. Consequently, Laura did not test well in her first year exams despite her hard work; she felt her grades suffered as a result. Laura was tested for a learning disability at the beginning of her second year of law school and she was diagnosed with ADHD. At the time of this interview, Laura was in the top 50% of her law school class.

The third law student, Andrew, did not have a diagnosed learning disability although Andrew definitely felt that he learned differently. Andrew excelled in one-on-one situations. He worked for several law professors at school and also worked as a law clerk in a law firm. However, Andrew never felt completely at ease in law school. He enjoyed the practice of law far more than the classroom experience in law school. At the time of this interview, Andrew was in the top 30% of his law school class.

---

1. The actual names of the students have been changed to protect their anonymity.

All three of these law students faced different challenges in law school and each of them learned very differently. Yet each of these students also achieved their own success in law school as well. While Mary experienced a great deal of academic success in law school, Laura and Andrew carved out their own success in other ways. Laura excelled in clinical programs and legal writing, and she worked successfully at several externships. Andrew worked for a law firm and held several research positions with law school professors. All three of these students became successful law students and I have no doubt they will become successful lawyers as well.

Here is their advice to you about navigating through the journey of law school when you are a student with a learning disability—or a student who simply learns differently.

Mary, 3L (Diagnosed with ADD)

Q: What is your learning disability and when was it diagnosed?

A: I was diagnosed with severe attention deficit disorder when I was 19 years old. No one ever mentioned that I should be tested until then.

Q: What has been the most challenging aspect of learning in law school for you?

A: The biggest problem I face is trying to keep up with the sheer amount of reading that there is to do. I have a very hard time sitting for long periods of time and staying focused, which law school requires (particularly during your first year). I find that I am usually unable to pay attention throughout an entire lecture, so I am forced to spend a lot of time outside of class teaching myself the material.

Q: Describe what the process was like to obtain reasonable accommodations (if you have done so?) What surprised you most about this process? Has it helped, i.e., have the reasonable accommodations assisted you, and if so, in what way?

A: Getting accommodations for law school was not as difficult as I anticipated. I provided my disability testing results and all of my records from the Disability Resource Center at my undergraduate university, and I was provided with virtually the same accommodations (note takers, additional time on exams, alternate testing environment, etc).

However, I have not been able to utilize all of these accommodations, specifically the note takers. Although they (the Disability Office) say it is supposed to remain anonymous who you are taking notes for, my first year I began to notice that the word was getting out that I had note takers. I felt very uncomfortable getting my notes from colleagues in my classes because if I ended up doing better than they did in the class, there were a lot of whispers about how unfair it was. I did not use note takers after my first year.

In order to get accommodations for the Bar exam, you need to have disability testing done within the past five years. I am about to get re-tested for this reason, which is going to cost me $1,500. Apparently getting accommodations for the bar, particularly if your disability is ADD, is a difficult process that often does not go in your favor. I hope that it is not as hard as I anticipate.

Q: How do you study most effectively?

A: Throughout the semester, I make sure to keep up with the reading. For me, getting behind is not an option, because I have a hard time with the amount of material as it is. For exams, I have worked with the same study partner since my first semester. First, on our own, we go through [the material] and make flash cards from our notes. After that, we quiz each other on that material. Then we go through all of the past exams for whatever class/professor that we have (and other professors if that helps). Finally, we usually do one or two timed exams based on the past exams. This has been a very successful method for both of us, as we are both in the top five percent of our class.

Q: What classes have been the best for you? What classes have been most difficult for you?

A: The classes that I have done the best in are classes that are in the subject area of what I want to practice, Criminal Law. I got the High Grade Award in Evidence and Advanced Criminal Law: Vice Law. I also got a 4.0 in Criminal Procedure, Civil Procedure II, Constitutional Law I, and (shockingly) Business Associations. Business Associations was definitely one of my most difficult classes because there is an absolute ton of material to learn and I am a bit biased against corporate law. I think I did so well because I was well aware of the difficulty of this class so I studied accordingly. Property and Contracts were my least favorite and most difficult classes. I had a great professor for Property, but I hated the material and found it really hard to understand it because it is based in ancient tradition instead of logic! I did not like Contracts because I had a terrible professor and thus was struggling a lot on my own to learn it.

Q: Do you think your learning disability will affect your work as a lawyer? How?

A: I think that my ADD has the potential to affect me as an attorney. For example, I currently intern for the Public Defender's Office, which is what I hope to pursue upon graduation. The misdemeanor attorneys usually have between 70 and 100 cases open at any time, so keeping track of what needs to be done at all times will be very hard for me. I have always thought I would be fine if I just had a really good assistant to stay on top of the details! But, even without that, I have learned how to manage my disability enough to know what I need to do, which includes always staying extremely organized and writing everything down (preferably not on little post-its, because I lose those as well!!).

Q: **What do you wish you had known before law school?**

A: I wish I had known that I should NEVER reveal to my colleagues that I receive accommodations for my disability. During my first semester, I started working with a study group. They would come up with hypotheticals, tell us to work on it for a few minutes, and then discuss it. I found I could not keep up with them so I told them about my disability, requesting that we come up with the hypos beforehand so that I could better prepare. Once they found out about my learning disability – and more importantly my accommodations – they spread the news around to anyone who would listen and started saying a lot of bad things about me. I was actually called in to speak with Student Services because people had complained after first semester exams that it was not fair that I received accommodations. It was an absolute nightmare. Law students are competitive and jealous, so when I did well, people equated that entirely with my accommodations and I felt terrible. I actually lost several "friends" over it.

I also wish I had known just how broke I was going to be, and how hard it would end up being to make ends meet. The stress of being financially insecure has definitely affected my disposition and my ability to stay focused in school.

Q: **What advice would you give to other law students who have (or may have) learning disabilities (or who simply think outside of the box)?**

A: First of all, don't share your situation with anyone you do not need to. Arrange for tutors if you have to, as most schools will provide free assistance if you need it. Do not be afraid to ask your colleagues for help, but revealing the nature of your disability is unnecessary and ultimately detrimental in my experience. Utilize your professor's office hours and get the extra explanations you need—no one will think less of you for needing help. Meet with financial aid staff to set up a budget. My ADD makes keeping track of things very difficult and I have gotten into serious financial trouble while in law school. Invest in the supplements as study aids for classes. Try to always keep up with your reading—and brief every case your first year to learn how to do it correctly, but don't worry if you have to use a book brief [writing directly into your casebook] every once in a while your second year. Make sure to get as much work experience through internships as you can to boost your resume. Even though Law Review is such a pain, if you are invited on or make a write-on competition, it is very helpful and you will learn a lot; it is worth the effort.

Don't listen to people talk about how much they study and let it intimidate you – most of the time they are lying, or spending half of their "study" time on Facebook. Don't talk to people after exams about their answers because (1) it will only stress you out thinking you missed things; (2) you can't change anything at that point; and (3) you probably caught issues that they didn't!

Finally, remember that there is life going on outside of law school and try to participate in it. Don't let your disability hold you back because you are just as capable as anyone else if you figure out what works for you.

Laura, 3L (Diagnosed with ADHD)

Q: **What is your learning disability and when was it diagnosed?**

A. The summer after my 1L year, I decided to undergo a psychoeducational evaluation. I was diagnosed with ADHD and a processing problem related to a slower reading speed.

Q: **What has been the most challenging aspect of learning in law school for you?**

A: Two things: (1) keeping up with the reading; and (2) organizing all of the information for each class. As law students, we have piles of books to read each semester. I've struggled with keeping up with my reading, and staying focused for the hours needed to sit and read the material.

Q: **Has your learning disability affected you in law school? If yes, how?**

A: Yes. I process information very slowly. This means that it takes me longer than the average student to read the assigned cases and prompts (factual hypotheticals) in an exam. My slower reading speed, in addition to my ADHD, makes the normal rigors of reading law school assignments even more difficult. In addition, it makes taking the high-pressure, timed exams in law school particularly difficult for me. However, I have learned to be more self-aware of my strengths and weaknesses about how I learn. This self-awareness has allowed me to develop techniques for briefing cases, studying, and outlining class material that work for me.

Q: **Describe what the process was like to obtain reasonable accommodations (if you have done so?)**

A. Unlike a lot of people who have their learning disability diagnosed at a young age or during their undergraduate years, I did not make the decision to obtain a psychoeducational evaluation until after my first year of law school.

While obtaining my undergraduate degree, I suspected that I had a diagnosable learning disability. My hunch was supported by certain behavioral traits I had and academic struggles in subjects that required certain processing skills (math and language). Throughout my first year of law school, I performed in the bottom third of my class despite my hard work, and long hours spent studying. And, I truly believed that I had achieved a good understanding of the material. My gut told me that my grades were not a proper reflection my actual comprehension of the material. I suspected that I had a learning disability that was affecting my performance.

After my second semester grades during my first year, I decided that it was finally time to obtain a psychoeducational evaluation. I tried, but was unable to find an evaluator. I decided to call my law school to speak with the administrator who handled accommodations. My law school was able to recommend a person to do my evaluation who was familiar with law students and the unique aspects of law student learning. The examination was expensive and time consuming (3-days), but worth it. With an official psychoeducational evaluation and a proper diagnosis, I was ready to complete my school accommodations packet. I submitted my completed accommodations packet to my school and the school began to consider it. Shortly thereafter, I received my law school's decision and they approved the accommodations recommended by the evaluator. Aside from the high cost of the formal evaluation, the process was far more simple than I had anticipated. And the accommodations have definitely helped!

Q: What surprised you most about this process? Has it helped, i.e., have the reasonable accommodations assisted you, and if so, in what way?

A: What surprised me the most about obtaining accommodations in law school was my school's willingness to work to find accommodations that suited my individual needs. I don't think all law schools are like that. Obtaining accommodations for my learning disability gave me the opportunity to learn on a level playing field with my peers. Due to my slow reading and processing speed, I was able to receive time-and-a-half for my law school exams. I was also permitted to take exams in a small group as opposed to a large lecture hall. These accommodations gave me the opportunity to read and understand my exam questions at a pace where I could focus and truly show my knowledge of the material. Overall, my accommodations took out the "panic" that I experienced on every exam during my first year.

Q: How do you study most effectively?

A: There are a hundred ways to study for law school. Just walk into a bookstore and you will see a stack of books claiming to have the secret to acing law school. Since I began law school (and especially since my diagnosis), I've really had to re-think how I study. Since I've started law school, I've tried many differed study techniques. Some

I've found helpful and I have continued to use them, while others I've found did not fit my learning style. There is no one way to study in law school. Each student should seek out which technique works best for him or her.

Q: What classes have been the best for you? What classes have been most difficult for you?

A: In addition to my regular lectures I've taken an oral argument class, various writing courses, and I've been involved with our school's legal clinics. I tend to work better in courses where the material or the professor engages me during the class. Law professors that take a fresh approach to teaching law school (and use something other than traditional casebooks) make my classes far more manageable. I do find that the more traditional courses that rely upon lectures and heavy reading in casebooks are the most challenging for me. However, no matter what course I've taken—I've had to find a way to work within that course material.

Q: Do you think your learning disability will affect your work as a lawyer? How?

A: As a person who learns and processing information differently, I will face certain challenges as an attorney. However, just as I have been able to adjust the way I study and work in law school, I will have the same opportunity to adjust in the work place. As a summer law clerk, I've gotten a taste of life as a lawyer. I've found that the challenges we will face as lawyers are more varied than those we face as law students. Law school tests exam-taking skills in timed environments. While life as an attorney will be both serious and challenging, I will not be asked to simply complete a series of multiple-choice questions. Instead, I will work with real people and real problems—and I've learned that I am very good at that. Those skills, however, are rarely tested in law school.

Q: What do you wish you had known before law school?

A: I wish I had obtained my psychoeducational evaluation prior to starting law school. Although I was able to compensate for my learning differences during college, I was not able to compensate for the unique rigors of law school. I suspected that I had a learning disability going into law school and I put my law school career at risk by not seeking a proper diagnosis until it had already affected my first year grades.

Q: What advice would you give to other law students who have (or may have) learning disabilities (or who simply think outside of the box)?

A: Know your academic strengths and weaknesses. Take the time to find out how you learn, read, study, and outline. Never lose sight that one day you will be an actual attorney. Take the three years you have in law school to hone your skills so that you can become the best attorney you can be—no matter how you learn. If you know that you learn differently and you suspect that you may have a diagnosable learning disability, you need to schedule a test. And if you do receive accommodations for your learning disability—remember that it only levels the playing field. There is nothing that can replace hard work and determination in law school (and beyond).

Andrew 3L (Learns Differently but No Learning Disability Diagnosis)

Q: In what way do you feel that you process information differently than most other law students?

A: I think it takes me a lot longer to understand and remember the rules if I don't get it on both a conceptual level and on a practical level. It seems that a lot of my friends can just memorize a rule and then plug in the facts without questioning the underlying purpose or the implications of the rule. If I don't know why the rule is there and how it is applied in a real life situation, I won't remember it very well and that slows me down.

Q: What has been the most challenging aspect of learning in law school for you?

A: The volume of work has been most difficult for me but for a specific reason. If I get behind (which I think is inevitable at some point), I lose my point of orientation in the course and I don't feel caught up until I've read every word that's been assigned. In my first year, I just ended up getting more and more behind because I wouldn't read case #5 until I'd read case #4, etc. I was working all the time, but I felt I was never up to speed and prepared for class the way I would have liked to have been. Now, in my last year, if I get behind—I fight that need to start at the beginning of my reading. Instead, I force myself to begin with the current assignment. And I'll try to work backwards so that by the end of the semester, I've caught up on everything. This also allows me to stay current so I can get the most out of class time.

Also, I absolutely hate getting called on in class. Sometimes, the anticipation of getting called on will distract me from paying attention to what the professor is actually saying.

Q: How do you study most effectively?

A: I do best when studying by myself. I've found that I really can't have distractions around me and still absorb what I need to. As I read, I have to write down key points to really understand what I've read and to maintain my focus, so I don't start thinking about everything else that's going on. I always have to prepare the day before the actual class. If not, I get stressed out that I won't finish the assignment on time and can't concentrate on the reading. In terms of what method helps me most, I've found that flashcards are most effective. I can break all the course material into bite size pieces and that way I don't get overwhelmed. Then, I do practice exams galore at least 2 or 3 weeks before the test, if not earlier. I practice outlining my answers first, then I practice writing them out in a timed situation.

Q: **What classes have been the best for you? What classes have been most difficult for you?**

A: The classes in which I've gotten my best grades are Torts (4.0) and Civil Procedure (3.7). I think I did fairly well in these classes because my professors gave us a ton of practice exams and gave me a lot of feedback on the practice exams I showed them in office hours. I think that I actually got the most out of my Evidence class because it taught me how to dissect a statute properly. After that class I had a new take on how to process the information I was getting in all my other classes. Contracts was my worst grade and also the worst class I've had overall. I would get very frustrated because I would read a case and think I understood what the court was saying, and then we'd get into class and the professor would discuss something totally different. I never got a good sense of how to do a 'contracts' analysis. So, although I thought I had the concepts down, for the purposes of an exam, I did not.

Q: **Do you think the fact that you learn differently will affect you as a lawyer?**

A: I think that the way that I process information will definitely affect me as a lawyer. I have to understand each individual puzzle piece and the puzzle as a whole before I've really learned something. In law school, this can be a detriment due to the time constraints of daily reading and time constraints on exams. However, I think this quality also makes me very detail-oriented in my analysis of issues, and I think that will be helpful to me in practice. I do worry sometimes, though, about how it will affect my ability to think on my feet in a courtroom.

Q: **What do you wish you had known before law school?**

A: I wish I'd known that there were resources out there that help you to improve your reading skills and efficiency. Once you are in the 'thick' of a semester—it's hard to find time to do any extra reading, even if that reading will help you become more efficient overall. I read a couple of books on how to do well, but none of them addressed law school from a conceptual, epistemological level—which for me is crucial.

Additionally, I wish I had really taken the idea of "stress management" seriously. There is so much to read, to learn, to study, to participate in, etc., ... that it gets overwhelming when you feel like everything you do is still not enough. I wish someone had just said on Day 1: "Relax, it's all going to be fine."

Q: What advice would you give to other law students who have (or may have) learning disabilities (or who simply think outside of the box)?

A: I would say that you need to find a good balance between school and the rest of your life. And, that balance is your own balance. Many people will tell you to make sure to get out and do something besides study. Sure, you can't study 24/7. But, what I would suggest is to think about how best to create a balance that is optimal for *you*. If you need to work on a Friday night so that you aren't up late on a Sunday night (so you are forced to start your week with only 4 hours sleep), then stay home on Friday, and don't be apologetic for doing so. You'll be happier on Monday that you spent some time on Friday preparing for the next week.

I would strongly recommend looking at course outlines before your classes begin if you are a "big picture" kind of person. This will really help to introduce you to key vocabulary terms in the course. And it will help you get more out of your class lectures. I know that there are workshops that introduce you to what you'll need to know for law school. I didn't take one, but I wish that I had at least looked into it.

Finally, just persevere and don't let one instance of poor performance psych you out. It was really interesting for me to see how the dynamic of my small (1L) section shifted after first semester midterm grades came out. People you think won't do well may end up acing the class that you just got a 'C' in—and you may end up getting an A in a class that you thought you'd have to retake. You can't let your report card and the dynamic between you and your classmates affect your self-image or confidence. In my first semester, I had a 4.0 and a 2.1. I couldn't tell if I was a total moron or a genius. The truth is, regardless what your grades come out to be, you are neither a moron nor a genius. Focus on learning the material, and not the grade. It sounds impossible, and I am still very grade- focused myself. But, the more I focus on learning the material and the less pressure I put on myself to get an A, the better I do generally.

Part II

Maximizing Your Academic Success While You're Deep *IN* the Trenches

While the first part of this book introduced you to various learning and study strategies that will benefit non-traditional learners in law school, the second part of this book looks more specifically at how to succeed in the law school classroom and in your exams. This part of the book also provides you with strategies for how to navigate successfully through your legal writing and legal research class. Further, Part II of this book discusses the topics of outlining, multiple choice exams and essay exams. While Part I of this book introduced you to learning more *generally* in the law school environment, Part II focuses on the specific writing and test-ing-taking strategies that will help you succeed in your classes and on your exams. Like the first part of this book, Part II approaches these learning and test-taking strategies from the perspective of those who learn differently (although these strategies are certainly applicable and appropriate for all learning styles.)

So let's begin the next part of our journey: how to maximize your success while you're in the trenches of law school!

Chapter 10

Writing in Law School: Legal Structure, IRAC (No, Not the Country ...) and TREAC

Every law school has an introductory class focused on teaching you how to research and communicate the law. The most typical form of this class is "Legal Writing" or "Lawyering Skills" or "Legal Rhetoric." Whatever the name of the course, this is one of the most important classes in law school and it focuses on teaching you the unique analytical structure of a legal argument. Legal Writing demands that you *do* the work of a lawyer: you research the law, communicate the law and predict a result on behalf of your client.

There is no doubt that learning how to write within the required structure of legal writing is challenging, but it is also one of the most important skills you will master in law school. Even if you struggle with writing generally, you should make this class a priority because it is foundational: it teaches you the essence of being a lawyer—how to find the law, how to conceptualize a legal issue, and how to communicate the result to your client.

Further, if you are a law student who learns differently, your legal writing class can be a class in which you excel. First, these classes tend to be smaller than other law school classes. Therefore, there will be more opportunities to contribute your ideas and experiences on a topic because more class time is spent in discussion versus in a lecture. Second, you will have opportunities to conference one-on-one with your writing professor. This is how you will truly learn the craft of legal writing. Accordingly, you will have opportunities to talk with your professor about different ways of approaching legal research and writing. You should take these opportunities whenever they are presented to you. Many professors who teach legal writing are very knowledgeable about diverse learning styles.[1] Make an appointment to talk to your writing professor. Perhaps

---

1. Law professors who specialize in this discipline spend a great deal of time researching and writing on teaching and learning issues. There are conferences several

the conversation will start out about your writing assignment but it may also cover learning strategies, study strategies, or any number of subjects. You have a rare opportunity in your legal writing classes to have a law school professor get to know you well! Email your professor and set up an appointment early on in the semester!

Finally, another distinctive aspect of your legal writing course is that you will have far *more* control over your work product than in your other classes. For example, you will get your writing problems several weeks before they are due. You will have time to perfect your work product *if* you use your time wisely. You may also have the opportunity to get feedback on your drafts before you turn them in. Again, ask your professor if he/she will review one of your drafts. If you can get feedback about your legal analysis before your assignments are due, you have the opportunity to excel in this class. Good writing is all about rewriting—you simply need to allow yourself the opportunity to rewrite!

There are many excellent books devoted specifically to the art of legal writing and analysis, and this chapter will not attempt to cover the material in those books. However, this chapter *will* approach legal writing and analysis very practically with a focus towards helping students who learn differently. Where do law students with learning differences get stuck in legal writing? Many law students get stuck because they fail to adopt the formula for good legal structure. What do I mean by legal structure? I mean the formula or paradigm for a legal argument—typically called IRAC or TREAC. These are simply acronyms to help students remember that a legal argument is made up of several important parts.

This chapter will begin by focusing on legal structure—specifically how to use IRAC and TREAC to outline your arguments. This chapter will show you examples of actual law student writing. What did these students do correctly? Where did they fall astray? My hope is that by critiquing *real* examples, you will start to become more comfortable with the structure of a legal argument—which forms the basis of all legal writing (and law school exam writing as well!).

A. The Process of Writing

Writing is hard work—particularly when you are learning a new structure within which to write. So if you've had trouble writing in the past, you may think that you're not good at it. But the reality is that it's a skill—like anything else. And with effort, guidance and practice, you can learn how to write effectively as a lawyer.

---

times a year that are devoted to educating professors about how law students learn most effectively, teaching methodologies, etc.

The key to success in Legal Writing is to approach it with deference. It will be difficult—probably more so if you learn or process information differently. It will take a lot of time (all writing does). But you *can* learn it. Ironically, those students that have the most writing experience often struggle more with legal writing than less-experienced students because legal writing focuses (initially) on a rigid structure. Many English majors cringe at the idea of incorporating their wonderful and creative ideas into what they feel is a confining and rigid structure. But the structure is just the beginning—and a necessary one at that. Up until law school, you may not have done analytical writing before. Writing to present an *argument* is a different type of writing altogether. You are *reasoning* within your writing—and in order to do this in a convincing manner, you need to become comfortable with the structure for legal analysis.

B. The Structure of Legal Writing = Lasagna

Legal writing is like lasagna.[2] (Stay with me—it really *is* like lasagna!) Consider the typical legal reader—a busy judge or another lawyer. The legal reader has certain expectations about the structure of legal writing.[3] The legal reader wants a familiar organization; she wants vocabulary that she recognizes and understands. If you meet the legal reader's expectations regarding structure, then the legal reader (the judge or lawyer) is comfortable and open to your arguments.

Consider that this situation is very much like making lasagna for your family. If you come home from work one night and tell your family that you're making lasagna, they have certain expectations about what lasagna should look and taste like. Your family would expect cooked noodles, red sauce and melted cheese in defined layers. What would happen if you changed the structure of your lasagna? Supposed you didn't cook the noodles and you simply put the sauce on the side of the uncooked noodles. Your family would be angry—"this is not the lasagna we expected at all!" And your family won't want to eat your lasagna. They would rather throw it away and eat leftovers for dinner.

This same situation occurs for the legal reader. If a judge or lawyer has specific expectations about what your legal memorandum should

---

2. This analogy is widely used in the legal writing curriculum but it was made famous by Professor Sheila Simon, Clinical Professor of Law, University of Southern Illinois Law School. Professor Sheila Simon and Professor Richard Neumann use this analogy (and have a video clip) in their book, Richard K. Neumann and Sheila Simon, *Legal Writing*, (1st ed., Aspen Publishers 2008) and on the publisher's website.

3. The most typical types of legal writing are a legal memorandum (a memorandum drafted to explain research results and how the cases apply to your factual situation) and a brief (a type of adversarial document written by lawyers and submitted to the court advocating that the court make a particular ruling).

look like and the type of language you should use, you want to meet those expectations. If you meet the legal reader's expectations, the judge will consider your arguments. But if you present the judge with a memorandum or brief that looks and sounds strange, the judge may not even bother with reading your document. Busy legal readers do not have the time to wade through sloppy poorly-written writing.

So although the structure I'm about to discuss will seem foreign to you (and likely bothersome as well), you will need to become comfortable with this new way of writing. If this is difficult for you (and it *is* for a lot of students), give yourself a bit more time than you *think* you need to complete your legal writing assignments. Start early and submit multiple drafts to your professor to receive feedback on your progress. In legal writing, the student who gets the first draft done early (to leave more time for revisions) typically is the student who is most successful in the class overall.

C. Structure = IRAC

In an earlier chapter, I introduced the basic legal formula or paradigm for a legal argument: IRAC. This acronym stands for the following: I = Issue; R = Rule; A = Application (or Analysis); and C = Conclusion.

This formula is a way to *begin* thinking about the structure of a legal argument. We will expand upon this formula when we discuss TREAC. However, let's begin by considering the meaning of each letter of the phrase IRAC.

I: Issue. The issue is the question that you're being asked to address—typically there may be a main issue and several sub-issues. When you brief a case, you seek out the legal issue which is typically the question being resolved by the court. When you write a legal memorandum, the attorney for whom you are writing may give you the legal issue that you need to address. The legal issue is comprised of the legal question combined with the client's unique facts. One of your first tasks in legal writing is to discern (1) the legal question; and (2) the relevant facts that apply to the question or issue.

R: Rule. The rule is most typically the law that applies to the particular legal issue. The rule can either come from a statute or a case—or a series of cases. You want to state the rule clearly and concisely, and there should always be a citation after the rule! (Lawyers love citations; law professors love legal citations, and judges love legal citations. And even though they are a pain to put into your writing, citations give your writing credibility and support.)

A: Application. The application section is the rule (that you've discerned from the law) as it is *applied* to the facts of your particular problem or case. This is the heart of your legal analysis. Your job is to take the rule and analyze how the rule applies to the facts of your case. You will develop possible arguments in favor of your client's position and against your client's position. You will support your arguments with cases and citations that support one position and then another. And you will come to some sort of conclusion or prediction as to the likely outcome of the legal issue. In other words, how would a court likely conclude and why?

C: Conclusion. Lastly, you will conclude ... again. Legal readers like conclusions (they like to be reminded of your prediction) and they like your conclusions to be clear and concise.

Here's a simple example of how IRAC works. The paragraph below uses the IRAC structure. Examine how the different sentences fall into the categories of IRAC. The appropriate label comes *before* each sentence.

> **ISSUE.** In *Smith v. Jones*, 123 F.2d 456 (1st Cir. 1993), the court examined the issue of complete diversity of the parties. **RULE.** In *Smith*, the court relied upon the rule which stated that for diversity to be complete, every plaintiff must hold citizenship in a state that is different, or diverse, from every defendant's citizenship. **APPLICATION.** In the present case, the plaintiff, Doe, and the defendant, Moe, are both citizens of the same state, California. The plaintiff and the defendant do not hold diverse citizenship for purposes of diversity jurisdiction. Complete diversity of citizenship is lacking and the federal court may not assert subject matter jurisdiction based on diversity of citizenship. **CONCLUSION.** A court will likely dismiss the claim for lack of subject matter jurisdiction.

D. A More Advanced Formula: TREAC

IRAC is a simple formula for ensuring that you have all the parts of a legal argument. When I teach legal writing to students, I like to expand on the IRAC structure. Whereas IRAC is good for exam answers or case briefs, it is not detailed enough for more complex legal writing. I like to think about legal writing in terms of an expanded version of the IRAC structure called: TREAC.

The TREAC formula is comprised of the following parts: T = Thesis sentence (or topic sentence); R = Rule Statement; E = Explanation of the Rule; A = Application of Rule to Facts; and C = Conclusion.

The purpose behind TREAC is very similar to the purpose behind IRAC (to ensure you have all the parts of a good legal argument) but it offers more detail in two important respects. First, TREAC begins with a "T" for a "thesis sentence" which reminds you to state your main point about the paragraph or section very clearly. A thesis sentence tells the reader what the paragraph is about—the legal reader appreciates and *expects* this type of guidance.

Second, in TREAC, the "R" of IRAC is subdivided into two separate concepts: "R" = Rule Statement; and "E" = Explanation of the Law. The rule statement is the same as in IRAC—it states the rule concisely and clearly. The "E" for Explanation is an important addition. The Explanation requires that you explain where the rule came from. Typically, in an Explanation section, you discuss the various cases that created the rule.

Finally, the "C" for Conclusion is the same in both IRAC and TREAC— it sums up your prediction clearly and concisely.

Let's consider TREAC specifically as it helps you think about how to formulate a strong argument within your legal writing assignment.

T = Thesis Sentence. Begin your paragraph with a strong, clear thesis statement of your main point or likely result.

> Example: *"Maddie Rice has a strong argument for showing that she and her step-mother have a 'close personal relationship.'"*

R = Rule Statement. The Rule Statement is a concise statement of the rule (or element) that applies to this part of the problem.

> Example: *"Under <u>Marchetti v. Parsons</u>, the plaintiff must be a 'close relative' of the victim in order to recover for Negligent Infliction of Emotional Distress."*

E = Explanation of the Rule. The Explanation of the Rule tells the reader where the rule comes from. Usually, this section describes the cases that describe the rule. When you discuss a case (or cases) that help explain a rule, you will explain the facts, issue, holding and reasoning of the case (like a mini-case brief). In this section, you will not delve into your *arguments* about the cases or about the facts of your client's case. This section is purely for the lawyer or judge to *see* the law—and only the law. If you're discussing your client's facts in this section, you are mixing explanation and application. Make sure to only discuss the law in this section.

> Example: *"In <u>Marchetti v. Parsons</u>, the Rhode Island Supreme Court clarified the requirements for a party to bring a claim for Bystander Negligent Infliction of Emotional Distress. In <u>Marchetti,</u> the parents of a child injured in accident brought action against driver who struck child. The court found… [The Explanation continues laying out the facts, issue, holding and reasoning of the court]."*

A = Application. The application section is where you do the work of a lawyer. In this section, you will take the law you have just discussed and apply it to the facts of your particular case. Sometimes I tell my students to *talk* this section out. If you were in front of the judge, what three points would you want to make about your case? Write those points down. Then find support for them. Is there a case that holds similarly? If so, state it and describe how it's similar. Are there opposing arguments? You'll want to have a paragraph dedicated to opposing arguments or counter-arguments. Typically you want to analyze all possibilities and discuss their strengths and their weaknesses in this section.

> Example: "*Maddie and Mary's relationship likely would meet the 'close relative' standard. Mary is the only mother-figure Mary has ever known and has been in her life for two years. They clearly have a parent-child relationship which has been consistently found to meet the first element of negligent infliction of emotional distress. The defense might argue that Mary is not Maddie's natural or adopted mother, but in all other ways Mary is Maddie's parent. Their involvement in each other's lives and Maddie's dependency on Mary will discount the technical aspects they are missing and allow Maddie to be defined as a close relative of her stepmother.*"

C= **Conclusion.** Your conclusion is a restatement of your prediction or conclusion on the issue. It is a nicely constructed sentence that restates your thesis sentence in a more concise form.

> Example: "*Maddie's physical symptoms will likely fulfill the second requirement easily.*"

The TREAC formula is the key to strong legal writing. In my opinion, TREAC works better for legal writing (than IRAC) because legal writing is more detailed and complex than writing an exam answer. Your professors may suggest that you use IRAC in an exam answer and this is good advice. You have limited time in an exam situation and you are writing quickly. Using IRAC for an exam ensures that you will address all the main components of a legal argument—in other words, it prevents you from skipping an important component of your analysis and losing points!

But Legal Writing tries to accomplish *far more* in terms of detail and depth of arguments and counterarguments than writing a one page exam answer. So a more detailed structure, like TREAC, is usually required. Think about TREAC as a building block to your legal writing. The next part of this chapter will walk you through the steps of how you would outline (and use TREAC) for a typical one-issue, legal memorandum assignment.

E. Beginning Your Legal Writing Assignment: Creating the Large-Scale Outline

Before you begin to implement TREAC, you should have worked through your legal writing problem in a detailed way, including reading and briefing the cases (that you've either researched yourself and chosen—or the ones given to you if this is a "closed universe" memorandum).[4] In addition, you should be able to articulate the major legal issues in your assignment. In other words, can you tell a friend what the legal issues are in the problem? Can you draft your Questions Presented?[5]

In creating your large-scale outline, your main or most significant legal issues will become the main headings in your legal memorandum (or brief). Your sub-issues will follow under these main headings. When you have completed a large scale outline of your issues, you *then* begin to form the structure of your argument by using TREAC.[6]

Below you will find an example of a first-year law student's large scale outline for a legal memorandum. The student was asked to write a predictive legal memorandum analyzing whether the client could recover for Negligent Infliction of Emotional Distress after witnessing her stepmother's car accident. The main issue in the case was whether or not the client, Maddie Rice, could meet the specific elements of this tort claim. The elements for this cause of action came from Rhode Island common law. In other words, the Rhode Island Supreme Court issued an opinion which set out the elements for recovery for Bystander Negligent Infliction of Emotional Distress.

The following example is a first year student's actual draft memorandum. Note in particular how the student uses the main legal issue and the elements of the Negligent Infliction of Emotional Distress claim to create the headings and subheadings/issues of the legal memorandum.[7] My comments are beside the memorandum and they describe in more detail the different elements of the large-scale outline.

---

4. A closed universe means that you are not allowed to do any of your own research.

5. The Question Presented is one initial component in a Legal Memorandum. A Question Presented is a statement of the legal issue in the case posed as a Question. It typically contains a statement of the rule, the legal question, and the legally significant facts. The Question Presented is followed by a Brief Answer.

6. Note that this method may not make sense for everyone, particularly if you happen to be a "free-flowing" writer. But if you're stuck with the structure of your legal writing, you might try this technique to at least begin to outline the major issues and sub-issues of your assignment.

7. Keep in mind that this is a student's *rough* outline—so there are sentence fragments, technically imperfect citations, etc. The purpose of this example, however, is to show you one way to beginning outlining the structure of a legal memorandum.

Large-Scale Outline of NIED Assignment

File: Maddie Rice

I. Whether Maddie Rice Can Recover for Negligent Infliction of Emotional Distress

This is the main legal issue students have been asked to address in the Legal Memorandum.

    A. Elements of Claim: Introduction/Thesis paragraph stating issues in case.

    "Relying upon the reasoning of our previous cases and our discussion today, we hold that in order to recover for a negligent infliction of emotional distress, a party must (1) be a close relative of the victim, (2) be present at the scene of the accident and be aware that the victim is being injured, and (3) as a result of experiencing the accident, suffer serious emotional injury that is accompanied by physical symptomatology." Marchetti v. Parsons, 638 A.2d 1052, 1053 (1994),

This is what is commonly called a Thesis paragraph or an Umbrella paragraph. It lays out the main issues of the memorandum. I recommend to students that this is where they should lay out the elements of the NIED claim.

    B. Main Discussion of NIED Issue:

Now we break down the elements of NIED and these elements become our sub-issues.

       1. Must be a Close Relative of the Victim.

       2. Must Be Present at the Scene of the Accident and Be Aware that the Victim is Being Injured.

       3. As a Result of Experiencing the Accident, Must suffer Serious Emotional Injury that is Accompanied by Physical Symptomatology.

    C. Conclusion

F. Filling in the TREAC

After creating a large-scale outline, fill in the details under each section and create sub-issues where necessary. This next example shows how the student filled in the large-scale outline with the TREAC components. In essence, the student created a mini-TREAC within each major element of the Negligent Infliction of Emotional Distress claim.[8] Again, using a TREAC for each element ensures that you have all the parts for a strong legal argument as it relates to that element.

---

8. Note that there is no right or wrong way to outline a legal issue. As long as you are using the right elements for the claim—you can format your outline in many different ways. The main point is to begin to organize *something!*

Outline of NIED Assignment

I. **Whether Maddie Rice Can Recover for Negligent Infliction of Emotional Distress**

   A. Introduction/Thesis paragraph stating issues in case.

     "Relying upon the reasoning of our previous cases and our discussion today, we hold that in order to recover for a negligent infliction of emotional distress, a party must (1) be a close relative of the victim, (2) be present at the scene of the accident and be aware that the victim is being injured, and (3) as a result of experiencing the accident, suffer serious emotional injury that is accompanied by physical symptomatology." <u>Marchetti v. Parsons</u>, 638 A. 2d 1052, 1053 (1994).

     1. **T: Thesis Statement**: Maddie Rice Can Likely Prove She Was a "Close Relative" of Her Step-Mother, Mary Rice.

     2. **R: Rule Statement**: The first element of NIED is that there must be a close relationship between plaintiff and the victim of negligence. (cite to *Marchetti).*

     3. **E: Rule Explanation:** Explain *Marchetti* (facts, issue, holding, reasoning). <u>Must be at Accident Scene and must be aware that the victim is being injured. (Witnessing the Accident is not a prerequisite):</u> Parents of a child injured in accident brought action against driver who struck child. Court held that parents could not recover for negligent infliction of emotional distress because parents were not present at the scene of the accident. Child was crossing the street and struck by a car driven by defendant. She was transported to hospital. Parents saw her on a stretcher in the hallway of the emergency room. She had not yet been treated; "appeared lifeless, was immobile and bloodied, and had a tube in her throat."

     The *Marchetti* rule came from *D'Ambra*: the court "identified a number of factors to be considered in determining the scope of a defendant's liability for negligent infliction of emotional distress to an accident bystander. These factors included "physical proximity [to the accident], the actual witnessing of the accident, and the personal relationship existing between the bystander-plaintiff and the victim." 338 A.2d at 531. "We went on to state, however, that there are "other factors which, given the right circumstances, may be of major importance in determining whether an adequate relation exits between the defendant's conduct and the plaintiff's injury." *Id.*

     The *Marchetti* court also discussed *D'Ambra*. The *D'Ambra* court stated: "We consider today whether witnessing an accident is a prerequisite to recovering for negligent infliction of emotional distress or, instead, whether it is a nonessential factor — one among many to be considered by a trial justice in determining if a defen-

Note how the student begins to put short summaries of the significant facts. The student also uses quotes from the most important part of the case. This technique allows the student to add the necessary legal support to the arguments.

It is a great idea to use actual quotes and citations in your detailed outline; it saves time because you don't have to search for the cites/quotes later as you write.

dant owes a duty to the emotionally injured plaintiff. We hold that in order to recover, a party must be present at the scene of the accident and be aware that the victim is being injured." 338 A.2d at 531.

Marchetti Holding: In order to recover for negligent infliction of emotional distress, a party must (1) be a close relative of the victim; (2) be present at the scene of the accident and be aware that the victim is being injured, and (3) as a result of experiencing the accident, suffer serious emotional injury that is accompanied by physical symptomatology. Absent these three elements, a plaintiff who seeks to recover for emotional distress arising out of an injury to a relative may not recover for negligent infliction of emotional distress.

4. **A: Application**. Applying the rule to the facts of this case:

In this case, a court would likely rule that Maddie and Mary Rice were "close relatives" under the *Marchetti* holding. They were step-daughter/step-parent. Mary would have adopted Maddie but for grandparents' concern. Mary was the only mother Maddie had known. Like parents in both *D'Ambra* and *Marchetti*, there is a similar-type relationship. (cite to facts of both *D'Ambra* and *Marchetti*).

> Here, the student begins to develop the arguments. The writer is applying the rule (related to the 'close relative' element) to the facts of the case.

Counterargument: The definition of "relative" implies a close familial relationship. Extending this definition to include step-parent/step-child relationship is too far. Likelihood for success: Not likely a successful counterargument because purpose of NIED is to compensate for loss of a close relationship. Maddie and her step-mother have that.

> Make sure not to forget counterarguments. Also provide an assessment of whether you think they are viable arguments.

5. **C= Conclusion:** Accordingly, Maddie will likely satisfy this first element of NIED.

B. Must Be Present at the Scene of the Accident and Be Aware that the Victim is Being Injured.

1. **T: Thesis Sentence:** Maddie can likely prove the second element of bystander NIED, that she was "present at the scene of the accident and aware the victim was being injured." [cite to case]. Although this may be a more difficult element to prove, Maddie can make a strong argument that she satisfies this element of NIED.

2. **R: Rule Statement:** The current rule is from *Marchetti* which states that a party must be "present at the scene of the accident and be aware that the victim is being injured." [cite].

3. **E: Rule Explanation:** Start with *D'Ambra* to show chronology: *D'Ambra* originally required that the victim actually witness the accident. However, the *Marchetti* court interpreted *D'Ambra* to require only an examination of several factors — not to require that the victim witness the accident. *Marchetti* required that "a party must be present at the scene of the accident and be aware that the

victim is being injured." However, the *Marchetti* court was not entirely clear on what this language means. Expand on possible in-
terpretations.

4. **A: Application**: Maddie certainly was present at the accident scene
and saw her mother in the ambulance, on the stretcher and covered
with a blanket. She saw her mother's car. She was aware her mother
had been badly hurt in the accident. However, the phrase "be aware
that the victim is being injured" seems to imply that the party view
the injury as it is occurring. However, given that *Marchetti* looks at
many factors, Maddie can make a convincing argument that she
was at the scene and saw her mother in an injured condition. If the
policy behind this requirement is to prevent fraudulent claims, this
interpretation would seem to keep that in place.

Counterargument: *Marchetti* is simply interpreting *D'Ambra*—but
not really changing the requirement of the court wanting the victim
to be at the scene and essentially witness the accident. Additionally,
the facts in *Marchetti* involved parents who weren't at the scene.
Court dismissed the claim based upon those facts. The court's discussion on what the *D'Ambra* court meant is simply dicta. Must go
back to the requirement in *D'Ambra* and *Caparco* that require witnessing the accident. And, the language "is aware victim is being injured" requires the literal interpretation of being at the scene and
witnessing part of the injury. This was not the case here.

At this stage of your outline, your writing does not have to be perfect. But having a detailed outline and using TREAC helps you strengthen
and maintain your organization as you begin to write.

Hopefully, this outline gives you a sense of how you can build your analysis in a legal memorandum by starting with a broad outline and then filling in the different parts with TREAC. And then—magically, you have
completed several pages of your outline and analysis, and you can begin
writing the narrative.

G. Filling in Your TREAC—Part II: Adding Arguments and Detail

The next step in your writing process is to fill in the parts of your outline (and TREAC) in more detail. Specifically, you will want to focus
on your Application section—the part of the outline where you address your client's strongest arguments and the possible counterarguments of the opposition. Have you used the facts of your case to support
your client's argument? Begin to flush out your client's strongest arguments. Have you analogized or distinguished the cases that you discussed in your Explanation section? Law professors like to see some

cites back to cases in your analysis section—combined with the facts of your case. This is a section that mixes fact and law—so make sure you have both.

And if you're really stuck on your memo, try to at least get working on one section—perhaps the Fact Statement. In a Legal Memorandum, the fact statement is comprised of the story of your client's case. Using the documents in your case file or your Assignment Memo, you can create a concise, well-written fact statement. The fact statement is often the easiest place to start when you experience writer's block.

I have found that the biggest hurdle in legal writing for law students who learn differently is to *get something on paper*. Your initial draft does not have to be brilliant or even passable. Good writing is all about re-writing! Your goal is to get a first draft done, i.e., put something down for each section in your outline. Then you can move onto the revising stage. The revising stage is typically the *longest* stage in the writing process.

H. Beginning to Write: Possible Challenges in Legal Writing for Law Students Who Learn Differently

In legal writing, you will develop and organize what you want to say and then put it down on paper (or on the computer). For law students who learn differently, having to organize a complicated assignment with many parts can be very challenging. A typical legal writing assignment will take several weeks to complete, and it often requires a series of stages including planning, writing, and revising. These steps are part of a recursive rather than a linear process, i.e., each step is revisited during the writing process and the steps do not always proceed in the same order. The following suggestions may help you avoid the common pitfalls of the non-traditional learner specifically as it applies to legal writing.

1. **Have a Plan of Action.** Have a well-developed plan of action for your writing. Make a calendar starting with the due date and work backwards to the present date. Plan out every specific stage of the writing process, including researching, outlining, writing, revising, citing, proofreading, etc., and write it on your calendar. Stick to the plan! Your plan will serve as a concrete step to allow you to *engage* in the writing process and it may help you move forward when you feel stuck. A plan also provides a permanent reminder about the content and structure of the writing task.

2. **Create a First Draft.** This is a very important step. Choose a specific date by which you will produce a first draft and stick to it! By giv-

ing yourself a firm deadline for a first draft, you can prevent procrastination problems. Many students with learning differences wait until the last minute. You cannot do this and succeed in law school. Legal writing simply takes too much time.

3. **Revising and Editing.** Revising and editing skills are critical to effective legal writing. You need to leave ample time (at least several days) so you can revise and edit your work. Plan to complete at least three complete drafts. You will need to revise each of those drafts. In addition, plan to leave one day for proofreading and citation. In my experience, some non-traditional learners begin the revising stage of their writing too late. As a result, these students turn in a paper that could have been great but was only average because of a lack of revising, editing and proofreading.

4. **Obtain Feedback.** If possible, try to obtain written feedback from your professor during the different stages of your writing process (and drafts). Many students are reluctant to ask for feedback—perhaps they don't want to bother their professor or they don't want to talk about their struggles with writing. But receiving feedback is *how you learn.* Frequent feedback can make a huge difference in the quality of your writing. Meet with your professor early on. (This will help you stay with the different stages of writing). Bring your drafts to a meeting and discuss your work to make sure you are not missing critical elements and/or cases. What are the assignment's strengths? What are its weaknesses? Ask your professor to give you feedback. Although this may be difficult at first, this can also open up an important dialogue between you and your professor. For students who learn differently, having this dialogue (and relationship) with your professor can significantly enhance your success.

I. Checking Your Structure

Now that you've completed a draft (and revised, and revised ...), it is time to check your legal writing structure. This occurs before your final 'proofing' stage. This section will end by simulating an important exercise I have my students complete prior to handing in their final memoranda. This exercise forces students to check their own legal structure within TREAC. Do they have a rule for every section? Have they addressed counterarguments in the application section?

---

9. This assignment is particularly helpful for visual learners and kinesthetic learners because you are seeing the elements and moving your highlighter over the words.

I direct my students to color-code the TREAC formula in their legal writing assignment.[9] In other words, I have them bring their colored highlighters to class. After they have completed a second or third draft of their writing assignment, I ask them to make sure they have all the components of good legal structure.

Using their highlighters, I ask them to highlight each component of the TREAC structure within the assignment.

The example that begins on the following page is the first section of a first year law student's motion brief (a brief submitted to a trial court).[10] This assignment involved a motion *in limine*[11]—a trial-level motion that asked the court to exclude a particular piece of evidence. This issue was governed by a state rule of evidence (Rhode Island Rule of Evidence 403) and several cases interpreting the rule.

In this example, see if you can identify the different components of TREAC within a fully written assignment. As you read through the comments (and the highlighted sections), evaluate the student's writing. Did the student explain the law well enough? Were you persuaded by the student's arguments in the Application section? Did the student address the counter-arguments thoroughly? These are the types of questions that you will use to evaluate your *own* writing as well.

---

10. Note that this is an example of persuasive writing—which is usually covered during the second part of your first year (or during your second year). During your first semester of legal writing, you will focus on predictive writing (which is more objective, with the purpose of evaluating a legal question and predicting a result). Persuasive writing advocates for a particular position. Therefore, it tends to be more one-sided in its exploration of the possible arguments, i.e., there may be less time devoted to articulating the counter-analysis.

11. *In limine* means "at the threshold." A motion *in limine* is a pre-trial evidentiary motion that litigants file in order to have the court rule on the admissibility of evidence before trial.

DISCUSSION

A. The Photograph of Ross Gellar Offers Relevant Evidence of Plaintiff's Emotional Distress Under Rule 402 and Proves Material Facts Essential to Ms. Green's Bystander Negligent Infliction of Emotional Distress and Wrongful Death Claims.

Good use of a heading to state the issue clearly and guide the reader.

T: The photograph of Plaintiff's husband, Ross Gellar, is necessary to demonstrate Ms. Green's experience to the jury. It is relevant to Ms. Green's bystander negligent infliction of emotional distress (henceforth NIED) claim and proves contested elements of material fact. Aside from some cleaning done by the Coroner to make the body less gruesome, the photograph shows Mr. Gellar's body as Rachel Green saw it on May 24, 2006. The injuries to Mr. Gellar's right shoulder and right torso are also apparent in the photograph.

Good thesis sentence/s. This clearly sets out the main point in this paragraph.

R: Under Rhode Island Rules of Evidence 402 and 403, all relevant evidence is admissible unless its probative value is outweighed by the danger of unfair prejudice ... or needless presentation of cumulative evidence. R.I. R. Evid. 402,403. The court has wide discretion in deciding whether photographs are relevant under Rule 402 and admissible under Rule 403. **E:** The Rhode Island Supreme Court has declared, "a photograph of a murder victim is admissible so long as it is competent evidence which reasonably tends to prove or disprove some material fact at issue, provided it is not offered for the sole purpose of arising the passions of the jury." *State v. Bowden*. 324 A.2d 631, 637 (R.I. 1974).

This quote is helpful as it tells the reader very specifically what the Rhode Island courts look at with regard to photographs.

The Rhode Island Supreme Court has generally allowed photographs as evidence under a test for admissibility developed in *State v. Belloli*: "If a photograph is of such a nature as to inflame the jurors and therefore prejudice them beyond the ordinary prejudice always sustained by the introduction of relevant evidence intended to prove guilt," then its probative value is outweighed by the danger of unfair prejudice under Rhode Island's Rule of Evidence 403. 776 A.2d 928, 930 (R.I. 2001). In *State v. Belloli*, the court allowed enlarged, gruesome autopsy photographs as evidence in order to illustrate the medical examiner's testimony and assist the state in establishing elements of torture and aggravated battery for first-degree murder. *Id*. at 931. The court held that the photographs provided "a proper understanding of the corpus delicti, the extent of the injury, the condition and identification of the body" and were relevant to the question of the degree of atrociousness of the crime." *Id*.

T: Thesis Sentence
R: Rule Statement
E: Explanation of the Rule
A: Analysis
C: Conclusion

Similarly, in *State v. Bowden*, the Rhode Island Supreme Court held that a photograph of a gruesome, water-distorted body was admissible in order to prove material facts of the State's claims. If the photograph proves a material fact in issue, "it is of no concern that a photograph may be unpleasant to view or that it may have influence beyond the strict limits or the purpose for which it was introduced." *Bowden*, 324 A.2d at 637. The court ruled that the photograph of a murder victim was admissible to assist in establishing that the corpse was that of the victim.

A: The photograph of Ross Gellar, though gruesome, invokes the ordinary prejudice necessary to establish Ms. Green's NIED claim. It is not offered for the sole purpose of arousing the passions of the jury. In order for the jury to determine whether Ms. Green can recover for NIED, they must understand what Ms. Green experienced at the time. Ms. Green fainted upon witnessing her husband's body. Other evidence indicates that she was in optimal health prior to witnessing the accident. While Atlantis Resorts admits breach of the duty of care in negligence, Ms. Green must prove that it was this breach of duty that caused her to experience emotional distress and, subsequently, go into acute hypertensive crisis that led to the loss of her child.

> Good, strong thesis sentence that begins the Application section. The reader clearly knows the writer's position.

Even though other forms of evidence are available, the jury could not fully understand the extent of the emotional trauma that Ms. Green experienced on May 24, 2006 without seeing a close representation of what Ms. Green witnessed before she fainted. The photograph is the only evidence available for this purpose. The photograph is a less-gruesome representation of what Ms. Green experienced at the accident. Ross Gellar's body has been partially cleaned up by the coroner, and thus gives a less-gruesome, less-prejudicial representation of what Ms. Green witnessed. Although less-gruesome, the image of Ross Gellar properly represents Mr. Gellar's injuries and is suitable evidence of what Ms. Green saw at the accident. Furthermore, in *State v. Belloli*, the photographs were enlargements of photographs already available as evidence and more gruesome than those presented in the present case. *Belloli*, 776 A.2d at 930. Yet, though cumulative, the court allowed the photographs as evidence to establish elements essential to the state's claims. *Id.* In the instant case, the photographs are equally essential to establish Ms. Green's bystander NIED claim.

> Good factual analysis, but still try to link the arguments <u>back to the cases</u> that were explained above. The writer does it below in the next paragraph, which is great. But, any time one can draw a comparison, the better. Be very specific with factual analogies. "Like *Belloli*, where the evidence was relevant because it proved an element in issue, the photo in the present case shows ..."

A P P L I C A T I O N

While this is not a prosecution for murder, and elements such as atrociousness of the crime and condition of the body are not generally necessary to NIED claims, the condition of the body and extent of the injury are essential to understand Ms. Green's negative reaction that led to her acute hypertensive crisis. The jury must decide that the accident could create similar reactions in reasonable people.

> By rearranging slightly, the student can make this first sentence SO much more persuasive. Start with the strong assertion, as this is the first thing the judge sees: "The condition of the body and extent of the injury are essential to understanding ...", and then end with "... despite the fact that it was a murder.... "

Finally, the photograph of Ross Gellar proves contested material facts in the case, including the location of the injuries, and is thus relevant to Ms. Green's wrongful death claim. The photograph shows the shark bites and is a faithful representation of the victim, Ross Gellar. Photographs that show faithful representations of victims are generally admissible to aid the jury in arriving at the proper understanding of the events in question, especially when some principle facts are in dispute. *Bowden*, 324 A.2d at 637. The court in Bowden highlights that evidence having a natural tendency to establish the facts in controversy should be admitted. *Id.*

C: The Plaintiff asks the to court admit the coroner's photograph of Ross Gellar to aid the jury in establishing whether Ms. Green can recover for Bystander NIED and wrongful death.

C O N C L U S I O N

> Good concluding sentence here. Link the conclusion on this issue with the rules again. Remember, you are always tying your arguments back with the law the court will apply.

The previous example represents a good start to the Discussion section (the argument section of the brief). The student followed the TREAC structure well.

As you read through examples of legal writing, train yourself to critically evaluate the writing. We learn the most about writing when we critique what we've read. Even the published opinions that you read each day for class could use further revisions. As you've probably gathered by this point in your law school career, judicial opinions are *not* always well-written!

J. When the TREAC Structure Is Missing

The prior example illustrated what a Discussion section looks like when a writer uses the TREAC structure. But what does it *look* like (and how does it *read*) when a student fails to conform to the ideal legal structure? Many law students' first or second (or even third) legal memoranda will lack a coherent legal structure. How does this adversely affect the clarity and credibility of the writing? Would you as a lawyer *trust* the writer's assessment?

In this next example, the student writer does not follow the TREAC structure. Read through this example. Can you identify the parts of TREAC formula? Although the writer certainly has some aspects of TREAC, consider how missing *some* elements (or changing their order) affects the overall writing. Evaluate the following example focusing on how the writer incorporated the TREAC formula.

DISCUSSION

I. EXHIBIT 24 IS A PROTECTED DOCUMENT PURSUANT TO THE LAWYER-CLIENT PRIVILEGE.

   A. The Lawyer-Client Privilege in Wisconsin Statute §905.03 applies to Exhibit 24.

Good to use the actual law here. Typically, the rule should be introduced with some text before jumping into a quote.

R: Section 905.03 (2) provides as follows:

(2) General rule of privilege. A client has a privilege to refuse to disclose and to prevent any other person from disclosing confidential communications made for the purpose of facilitating the rendition of professional legal services to the client.

RULE

T: Missing Thesis Sentence! The reader has to jump immediately to the law without a reference to the purpose of the law.

True, but what are the decisions and what's the cases' relevance to the client? This is an important thesis sentence and I think MORE can be done with it. It should say something about the interpretation of the case law.

This seems like the writer is talking about policy here, and she may want to introduce it as such. Use the cases to set out the policy behind the attorney-client privilege.

E: Wisconsin has decided cases regarding protected information. *Dudek v. Circuit Court for Milwaukee County,* 150 N.W.2d 387, 398. In *Dudek,* attorney Dudek was subpoenaed as a witness against his client. Dudek refused to reveal certain information he had because, "the questions inquire into matters that are privileged as attorney-client communications." *Id.* at 393-394. Although the court (insert how the court reacted to this) the Supreme Court went on to say of the issue of attorney-client privilege:

EXPLANATION OF RULE

T: Thesis Sentence
R: Rule Statement
E: Explanation of the Rule
A: Analysis
C: Conclusion

"The administration of justice is thought best promoted by a rule which encourages clients to reveal the facts fully to their attorneys. By encouraging revelation of the facts to the attorney, the privilege is also calculated to serve the basic objective of the jurisprudential system. Without the rule, parties would not reveal all of the facts because of fear of detriment or embarrassment. It is better to have otherwise concealed facts within the knowledge of the person charged with the direction of the lawsuit, even though he must not reveal the communication, than to have those facts or opinions buried within the knowledge of the client."

I'm not sure what this means. Transparency? Does the writer mean "communication" or "relationship"? Try to be very precise with the use of words.

Id. at 398. The purpose behind Wisconsin Statute §905.03(2) is to protect transparency between attorney and client. This transparency is necessary for an attorney to advocate on behalf of their client's interests.

A: Missing Application of the law. This section simply ends without an actual application of the law/rule just discussed to the facts of the case. The Application section is perhaps the most important section of the brief.
C: Missing Conclusion.

B. Exhibit 24 Is a "Confidential Communication" Made For the Purpose of Facilitating Professional Legal Services in accordance with Wisconsin Statute § 905.03(d).

T: Missing Thesis. Usually, a writer wants to have a thesis sentence that states the main point before jumping into the rule/statute. It lets the reader know the overall framework of the section and why the statute is relevant.

Section 905.03(1)(d) provides as follows:

**R
U
L
E**

(d) A communication is "confidential" if not intended to be disclosed to 3rd persons other than those to whom disclosure is in furtherance of the rendition of professional legal services to the client or those reasonably necessary for the transmission of the communication.

E: Missing Explanation of Rule and/or Discussion of Cases. Once again, this is a substantive omission. What cases have discussed and/or interpreted this rule? The judge needs to see how the law has been applied in this jurisdiction.

Typically, introduce the reader to your application/ analysis by starting with a strong thesis sentence to organize the paragraph. Further, address the first element of this analysis more explicitly: make the point here or earlier that Exhibit 24 *IS* a confidential communication. State the law first, facts/analysis second.

Substantive concern: Note that the Explanation of the rule, i.e., the case discussion, is missing above.

**A
P
P
L
I
C
A
T
I
O
N**

A: In his affidavit, Jon Peters specified to attorney Block that "These, [the statements] are for your eyes only." (Affidavit 2). Mr. Peters further commented, "I left [attorney Block's office] believing that I had handed over my communications to Sam Block and that they were confidential communications." (Affidavit 2). Sam Block corroborates Mr. Peters' statement in his affidavit noting that he heard Mr. Peters say something to him to the effect of, "Here you go … these are for your eyes only … " (Affidavit 1) once Mr. Peters handed him the document.

Additionally, Exhibit 24 was produced 'in furtherance of the rendition of professional legal services to the client.' Section 905.03(1)(d). In his affidavit, Jon Peters stated, "I wrote the documents for the sole purpose of communicating this information to my attorney in preparation for the deposition." (Affidavit 2). This deposition was being taken in light of a divorce action which was under way between Jon Peters and his wife Macy Peters.

Good use of the facts of the case. Weave in the law/cases as well. The judge is interested in the facts, but the writer's job is to persuade the judge by illustrating how the law supports the case as well as the facts. Compare (analogize) the facts of the case to like cases in the jurisdiction. This is the heart of persuasion. Is the case similar or different from the *Dudek* case discussed above? How?

Without proof to the contrary, Exhibit 24 is a "confidential communication" within the spirit of Section 905.03(1)(d) because Jon Peters had not intended the document to be disclosed to 3rd persons.

**C
O
N
C
L
U
S
I
O
N**

C: Additionally, Jon Peters made Exhibit 24 exclusively for the purpose of rendering professional legal service in the spirit of Wisconsin Statute 905.03(1)(d) and Exhibit 24 should therefore be barred from the case at hand.

What did you think of this argument section? Did it persuade you that the writer's position was supported by the law? This paper was missing some very important substantive discussion, including the explanation of the cases that discuss the attorney-client privilege and the application of the law to the facts of the present case. With some additional effort, this student's paper could certainly be revised to minimally include all the elements of the TREAC formula. However, if this was the student's final draft, the student would receive a low grade because so much of the substance is missing from the assignment.

Note also that whenever an essential element of the TREAC structure is missing in a legal argument, the argument is far less complete and persuasive. Even if you are writing an objective (or predictive) legal memorandum, your writing lacks support and credibility without each element of the TREAC formula.

As you begin to write your first legal writing assignment, try to become comfortable with this type of legal structure. It is difficult at first, but it is also something that will help you in every aspect of law school. As you progress as a legal writer, you will be able to stray from this structure when appropriate. However, as a new legal writer, the structure of TREAC helps make sure that your legal argument on an issue contains all the relevant parts. Remember that your legal reader expects a certain structure! Try your best to incorporate that structure as you write your assignments in law school.

Chapter 11

Tips for Organizing Your Legal Research

This chapter will offer several tips for how to begin your legal research projects in an organized and efficient manner. Legal research is most typically a component of your Legal Writing course in law school although some law schools teach legal research as a separate course. Legal research is another topic (like legal writing) that warrants an entire book (and there are several excellent legal research textbooks out there already).

Therefore, the purpose of this chapter is offer a few suggestions that will help law students who learn differently organize and complete their legal research assignments more efficiently. Over the years, I've seen that students who struggle with legal research seem to get stuck in similar places. For example, many students with learning differences love to research and they are very good at it—their natural creativity allows them to see the legal issues differently than other students, and therefore, they consider arguments and legal sources that other students overlook. However, sometimes these non-traditional learners *love* to research *so much* that they cannot *stop* researching! In other words, these students get stuck in the process of legal research—they continue looking for cases believing that there must be a perfect case out there. Accordingly, these students spend too much time on the research phase of an assignment and too little time on the writing and revising stages of an assignment.

This chapter will provide you with a plan of action (and research outline) to help you make your legal research more manageable and efficient.

A. Organizing Your Legal Research: Using a Research Log

If you tend to think "outside of the box," legal research may be initially overwhelming. With the advent of electronic research, i.e., specific research databases such as Westlaw, Lexis or LoisLaw, legal research is faster than ever before. But legal research is also exponentially more abundant—meaning that you have access to thousands of cases and sources. If you have problems processing and organizing information, you may find yourself getting *too much* information too quickly. Further, many students begin their legal research too quickly—in other words, they jump onto the computer immediately and input searches without truly identifying the specific questions or research terms that apply to their client's case. Using imprecise or haphazard search terms can lead to imprecise and inefficient search results. In the end, this wastes time because you have to sort through all those irrelevant search results before you begin to narrow down the correct legal issue.

When you begin working on your first legal research assignment, you need a game plan—just like the process for legal writing. For the first several research assignments in my class, I have my students complete a Research Log. The purpose of the Research Log is to organize the legal issues and to systemize the way you search for legal sources. The Research Log gives you a concrete plan of action. Filling out a Research Log may seem tedious at first. Eventually, however, you will become familiar with the steps of legal research and you will perform these steps automatically. Until this happens, however, you want to approach legal research with the following plan.

The example that begins on the next page shows an initial research project in a first-year Legal Writing Class. The first part of the assignment presents the Research Log. My students are instructed to fill out the different parts of the Research Log as they complete their legal research for this assignment. I also require my students to use both electronic resources and print resources from the library. You should do this as well. Verifying your research results with both types of research allows you to 'check' your research!

In addition, I ask the students to create a statement of the legal issue by answering important questions in the Preliminary Steps portion of the Research Log. Students then identify the Primary Sources of Law and move to the Secondary Sources of Law. Although you may research the law in any order, i.e., go to secondary sources first, the Research Log ensures that you check both types of sources.

Research Log 1 : Assignment and Template

Bystander NIED in California

Prof. Christensen
Legal Writing I

We will be representing Rachel Gellar, a young woman who was on a boat while her fiancé, Ross Gellar, received fatal injuries as a result of a shark bite (during a shark dive hosted by the Atlantis Resort). Among other claims, Rachel would like to bring suit against Atlantis Resorts for Bystander Negligent Infliction of Emotional Distress for the distress she suffered as a result of viewing a portion of the accident which caused the death of her fiancé. Rachel lives in Los Angeles and we will bring suit in California state court (Atlantis Resorts is incorporated in California). Therefore, please research what is required in California for our client to recover for Bystander Negligent Infliction of Emotional Distress. I will provide additional facts after receiving your initial research log.

Requirements: This research journal should be the product of your own effort. Although you may talk with others in the class about the process of research, what you've found, etc., all written work (and decisions about how and why the authority is relevant) the actual writing MUST be your own work.

Please also note that I am requesting you provide two *sources from the library*, i.e., proof that you have gone to the library and copied directly from the reporters and/or other sources from the library. Please attach the copies of the sources to the Research Log when you hand it in. For your other research, you may use either electronic resources or book research, or a combination of both (i.e., find a case from the digests in the library and print them off from the electronic resources).

I. **Preliminary Steps:**

 A. Before you start to research, **record** your preliminary steps. This section will describe the preliminary steps you've taken for this assignment before you've begun researching. Make sure you understand the research question and the issues that are presented by the problem.

 Please respond specifically to the questions listed below.

 Is this problem an issue of state or federal law?

 What authority will be mandatory?

 What authority will be persuasive?

 What jurisdiction am I in?

 What are potential research/search terms?

 Where do I think I'm going to look first?

 Where should I start, the library or the computer?

 B. **Prepare a preliminary statement of what you believe the issue/s to be at this point.**

II. **Primary Authority Research:**

This is an issue governed by common-law, so there are no applicable statutes. Therefore, you can proceed to identify the relevant cases.

A. **Five Most Relevant Cases and Your Analysis of Them**:

Select and describe the five best cases you have found (not the first five cases you have found). Provide a *full and correct* citation to the case and briefly describe how each case may be useful to our situation (and specifically what issue to which it may apply). Your descriptions should include a brief statement of the facts, issue and holding of the case, and you should explain how the case is helpful or harmful to the issues in your case, etc. Note also whether the cases are mandatory or persuasive authority.

1.

2.

3.

4.

5.

B. **Other cases**.

Provide a list of other cases that you located that may not be the five best cases. Explain how you found them (but you do not have to go into detail about the case's relevance). Please also provide a full and correct citation for each of these cases (limit of 10 cases).

IV. **Secondary Sources:**

A. **Explain the steps** that you took to locate secondary sources and authority. **List at least three secondary sources** that you would use to analyze the issues raised in the problem. Briefly explain how you located each authority and why it may be useful to this particular issue for our client.

V. **Am I Done Yet?**

A. Did the authorities that you have located refer back to each other? Did the new authorities that you located fail to reveal any significant new information, i.e., this is one way to check that you've found all the relevant information.

VI. **What was the most surprising thing about the research for this problem?**

The Research Log allows you to begin your research in an organized fashion. Remember that research is a recursive process—it is not linear but cyclical. You may begin pursuing one avenue only to find out that it was a dead end. Begin again and take a different path. But try to record your different paths so you know where you've been and where you're heading.

B. Final Tips for Legal Research

The following section offers four final tips to improve your efficiency with legal research: (1) know when to stop researching; (2) limit the number of cases you ultimately choose to write about; (3) organize your research; and (4) begin to write.

1. The Biggest Challenge: Knowing When to Stop!

One of the most important skills to develop as a law student is to learn when to *STOP* researching your problem. As you become more practiced at the skill of legal research, you will gain an intuitive sense of when to stop researching, and when to begin outlining and writing. Until then, give yourself a firm deadline as to when you will stop your research. Choose a date on the calendar, e.g., one week after the date you receive your assignment, and do as much research as you can until that point, and then stop![1]

The biggest mistake I see *all* law students make is the tendency to believe that there is one 'right' case out there if only you can find it. The reality is that there is no 'perfect' case that answers the issue completely. As with most legal problems in real life, your job as a lawyer is to take the cases you *do* find and synthesize the cases (see how they fit together) into a rule that a lawyer can use. You then apply that rule to the facts of the case to predict a result. This is the *work* of lawyers.

2. You Cannot Write About 50 Cases!

Another issue that may appear for non-traditional learners is that they want to write about too many cases. When you begin to research your legal issue, you will likely find that there are hundreds of cases that may apply. Interestingly, however, when you actually begin to narrow down your

---

1. This doesn't mean that you won't go back and perform more research after you begin to write your assignment. In fact, it is likely that you will need to search for another case. My point here is that you need to begin writing so that you can learn where you have holes in your analysis such that you can fill those holes with more research.

list to the most relevant cases, you will actually rely upon only four or five cases in your writing assignment. Part of the *process* of legal research is to refine your issues as you go along. In other words, once you have that initial pile (or list) of cases, you will need to sift through them to determine which ones truly help you resolve your problem—and which ones do not. If you are not going to use a particular case, write it on the top of the case: "Not Helpful." Put it into a different pile.

For the cases you think you will use, write on the front of the case why it's relevant: "Good Case for NIED Issue." This helps you stay organized. Ideally, you want to end up with around 3-6 cases about which to write for each separate legal issue in your problem. You cannot write about many more than that number of cases and write about them *well*. Hopefully, your professor will guide you about the number of cases she expects you to use in your particular problem. If not, *trust* yourself that you can pick out the most relevant cases. You *will* be overwhelmed if you try to incorporate too many cases into your legal memorandum or brief.

3. Organization Is Key

Keeping organized can be particularly challenging for law students who learn differently. Some students believe they are conducting effective legal research when they sit down at the Westlaw or Lexis printers— and print off hundreds of cases. Perhaps these students are thinking that if they print off everything of potential relevance—then they will *have* everything. Yes, you may *have* the case—but the question is: will you be able to find it?

Organization is the key to effective legal research. If keeping organized is a particular challenge for you, make sure to address this right away. Get yourself a three-ring binder or a set of file folders. Divide your cases up as they relate to your different legal issues. If your first three cases support the negligence issue, then clip those cases together and write "Negligence Issue" on the top of the case. Divide the cases up based upon the issues they support. Write the main issues/holdings of the cases on the first page of the case as well. This will help you sort through and organize your research. Instead of paging through cases to re-orient yourself to the case, you can locate the most relevant cases more efficiently.

Consider placing your actual writing assignment and your notes about the assignments into a binder or separate computer file as well. If you have all your information in one place (and not scattered about in your apartment), you'll feel much more in control of your assignment. And, BACK UP your computer files. Send yourself your work product in emails—keep multiple electronic copies. Having your computer crash (and losing your work) is not typically a reason for which professors give you extensions!

4. Begin to Write — Soon!

Finally, begin the writing process sooner than you want to! Legal research and writing is a cyclical process. In other words, you tend to go from one to the other, and then back again. You will research for awhile, then you will write your outline. You may realize that you need another case or two. So you'll go back to researching for awhile, but it will be more directed at this point. Then you'll work on writing the draft of the memorandum. This recursive cycle is a *good* thing. It ensures that you are actively involved in thinking throughout the problem — analyzing the issues critically — and realizing the need for further support.

Another reason to begin writing soon is to prevent yourself from getting stuck in the researching phase. For non-traditional learners, they tend to enjoy researching a great deal. For a kinesthetic learner, research is *doing* something versus sitting in the classroom. For the visual learner, research involves reading and examining cases and books. Some students want to stay in this phase forever! However, you need to give yourself enough to time complete the writing phase as well. If you have three weeks total for your entire legal writing assignment — give yourself at least two-thirds of that time for the writing process. In other words, limit your initial research phase to approximately one week. Don't worry — you can always do a bit more research later!

Chapter 12

Outlining: It's So Much *More* Than Simply Creating a *Really* Long Document on Your Computer

In law school, outlining seems to be something mysterious that all law students *do* in order to prepare for law school exams. Yet there is typically no explanation of how best to go about outlining or even what the purpose of outlining is on a basic level. Further if you learn differently, you may need to outline differently as well. Therefore, this Chapter is devoted to discussing the purpose of outlining in law school and providing you with several approaches to law school outlining to help you maximize your exam preparation.

A. What Is the Purpose of Outlining in Law School?

Outlining in law school is a way to organize all the information you've accumulated throughout the semester in your classes. Outlining helps you prepare for law school exams in three specific ways: (1) you will be able to see the big picture and how the individual cases or rules fit into the big picture; (2) you will force yourself to practice your deductive reasoning, i.e., applying the general rules to a new factual hypotheticals; and (3) you will organize all the information from your casebooks, class notes, case briefs and commercial outlines.

Keep in mind that most of your classroom experiences in law school involve *inductive* reasoning. Inductive reasoning is a type of reasoning which involves moving from a set of specific facts (the cases you read) to a general conclusion or application. In class, you begin with a case that sets out a rule. Your job is to read and understand the case, and then to pull the rule *out* of the case so you can apply the rule to future cases.

But when you take law school exams, you will actually use *deductive* reasoning. In other words, you do somewhat the opposite of what you do in class. In class, you read specific cases and extracted general rules.

When you take a law school exam, you will use deductive reasoning: you will reason from a general rule to a specific conclusion. Most law school exams require you to identify issues, state the general legal rules that apply, and then analyze a set of facts in light of the general rule to formulate a conclusion. Applying this general rule to a set of specific facts (that your professor gives you in the form of an exam hypothetical) uses *deductive* reasoning.

Therefore, one key to outlining successfully in law school is to recognize that you must prepare for your exams differently than you prepare for your law school classes.

B. Should You Make Your Own Outline or Use a Commercial Outline—or Both?

Law students often question whether or not they should make their own law school outlines, buy commercial outlines or borrow others' outlines. Realistically, you will likely use some content from all of these sources. Although some law professors will tell you that you must create your own outline, I have always felt that students benefit from seeing different perspectives, i.e., those perspectives from other students' outlines and commercial outlines. Sometimes seeing a concept explained differently is very helpful—particularly if you process information in a different way.

However, your outline should be very course specific. When you begin outlining, use your course syllabus, your case book (the table of contents, in particular), your class notes, *and* your favorite commercial outline.

C. How Do You Begin?

Begin by focusing on the larger picture. Start by looking at how your course syllabus divides the different segments of the course. Compare the course syllabus to the table of contents of your casebook. Look to see how your professor and the author of the casebook divide the concepts into larger categories.

For example, perhaps you studied Intentional Infliction of Emotional Distress in the first two weeks of the semester. A larger concept like this will become one of the main headings in your outline. Then proceed to add different levels of detail. After the main heading, your next level should be the specific rules or elements of Intentional Infliction of Emotional Distress. What is the majority rule? What is the definition of the rule? What are the elements? The next sub-level of your outline will include case examples that you've either read or discussed in class. Add material as you review your notes and put in as many examples or hypotheticals as you can find.

After you have the larger framework of your outline (including the rules and cases), the most important layer of your outline may be examples of the *application* of these rules. In law school, we test your application of the general rules to new factual situations. You need to train yourself to recognize these types of fact patterns. Commercial outlines are particularly helpful for this aspect of outlining because they often have examples of how to apply the rule.

When I review students' outlines, I often find that they fail to take this critical step in outlining: they fail to add in factual hypotheticals for every concept so they can *see* the application of the rule next to the rule itself.

When you find a commercial outline (or another student's outline) that you like, find specific examples or factual hypotheticals for each of the main concepts for that part of the course. For example, if the concept involves "proximate causation" from your Torts outline, find specific examples of factual hypotheticals that implicate this issue. For many students with learning differences, they can teach themselves the legal concept through these examples.

In addition, adding in hypotheticals for each legal concept teaches you to see the issues as they relate to the legal concept. In other words, you are more likely to recognize or spot the proper issue in an exam because you have considered the most common factual hypotheticals that tend to "trigger" those issues. In addition to using outside sources such as outlines, you should also review your class notes. Insert into your outline any examples that your professor gave you to illustrate a particular concept.

The following example illustrates a section of a course outline in a first-year Property course. What do you notice about the outline? Is it simple to read? Does it incorporate examples? Evaluate the outline to see if it helps you understand the general rules and various specific examples to which the rule might apply. We will talk more specifically about how to make your outline an effective learning tool. Initially, however, I encourage you to spend a few minutes looking at this example and then progress to the general tips on outlining. We will then look specifically at how to create outlines and how to make them work *for* you!

Property Outline[1]

Obtaining and retaining ownership
Methods of acquiring title

Adverse possession is a method of acquiring title by using or possessing property. An action for adverse possession is by statute, incorporating common law elements – essentially, the statute of limitations for an action in ejectment.

If you bring a successful adverse possession claim you get title to the property in question that can be recorded.

> Trigger facts:
> Boundary disputes
> Use of property without record of title
> Title is unclear or in dispute
> Long time squatters/trespassers
> Misplaced fences or encroachments

Adverse possession:
Statute + 4 common law elements
1. Actual entry and exclusive possession
2. Open and notorious
3. Adverse, hostile and under claim of right
4. Continuous for the statutory period

Elements:
1. Actual entry and exclusive possession
Type of entry/use that true owner would make of that property such that neighbors and other observers would regard the occupant as exercising exclusive dominion (Ewing)

Sufficient acts depend on nature, character and location of land and potential uses
Camper, outhouse, fish rack, reindeer pen on northern portion (Nome 2000)
Cattle grazing OK (Quarles)
Gravel pit OK (Ewing)

> Notes from review session:
> Likely on the multiple-choice section.
> Know case names.

Can be demonstrated by residence or with fences and cultivation

Have to have entry with intent to **own.**

Before we analyze the strategies for creating the most effective outlines, here are a few general tips.

1. Include appropriate defenses and remedies in your outline as well as principal claims;
2. Cover the application of the legal principles from every side (from both a pro side and a con side).

---

1. This example outline was created by Alison M. Nissen, Director of Academic Success, Visiting Clinical Associate Professor, Rutgers School of Law—Camden. These materials were developed by Professor Nissen for the 2009 AALS Annual Meeting, San Diego, California, Academic Support and Teaching Methods Workshop: "Show Us Your Stuff" and they are used in this book with the author's permission.

3. Consider the bigger picture or larger context of a principle or rule of law. Commercial outlines can be very helpful.[2]

4. Try *not* to simply type in all of your class notes into your outline or your document will become too detailed to be helpful.

5. Think about larger concepts and try not to get lost in the minute details of the cases—*specific holdings in most cases are not nearly as important as the larger legal concepts or claims.* Law school exams rarely ask you to discuss specific cases. It is far more important to ask yourself the following: for what *proposition* does each case stand? In class, you often discuss the details of the cases. This is because professors want you to grasp the basics of the case so you can extract the rule, i.e., inductive reasoning. However, on a law school exam, the details of a case are far less important than the application of the rule to a new factual hypothetical, i.e., deductive reasoning. Therefore, you want to prepare your outline with that reality in mind.

D. How Early Should I Start Creating My Outline?

As with everything else in law school, time management is very important. Like studying and attending class, you want to set aside specific blocks of time each week to work on your course outlines.

Begin outlining early in the semester. Consider your learning style. Consider your tendencies (or lack thereof) for procrastination. Make a specific plan of attack for changing your prior habits—*if* they need changing. Set a schedule. Determine what class you want to tackle first. Should you tackle your most difficult class? Probably yes. And just do a little bit each week. You will feel much better knowing that you've already started working toward your exams.

E. Specific Outlining Strategies for Law Students Who Learn Differently

Research has shown that they way in which we present information on a page or on a computer screen, i.e., the way information is presented *visually*, can have a large impact on how our brain processes and retains information. Many first year law students will obtain course outlines

---

2. You need to know how to apply the law in an exam, but you also need to consider social, political, economic, moral or policy arguments, too. These are secondary to the rules of law but they can be important in an exam answer.

from upper-level students. Having someone else's outline is often a good way to *begin* the outlining process. You can gain some valuable insights by examining how another student has organized the class material. However, the prior outline is only the beginning and you will want to add to this outline to create something that specifically enhances your own learning. If you learn differently, the process of making an outline *yours* is particularly important. Further, if you process information in a particular way, tailor your outline to match your information processing style. Do you like to work with flow charts? Do you need lots of examples to see how a principle works? Allow your learning style to guide the way in which you outline.

The example below is another section of a first-year Property outline dealing with the subject of Adverse Possession.[3] Even if you have not yet studied Adverse Possession, examine the outline. Do you find its organization logical? Do you like the way it looks? Examine the font and the use of highlighting. Does anything stand out? Is it easy to read? Does the outline incorporate examples of *how* the legal concepts apply to different factual scenarios?

PROPERTY OUTLINE[4]

FALL 2009

ADVERSE POSSESSION

1. ACTUAL ENTRY AND EXCLUSIVE POSSESSION

* type of entry/use that true owner would make of that property such that neighbors and other observers would regard the occupant as exercising exclusive dominion (Ewing)

* sufficient acts depend on nature, character and location of land and potential uses camper, outhouse, fish rack, reindeer pen on northern portion (Nome 2000)
cattle grazing OK (Quarles)
gravel pit OK (Ewing)

* can be demonstrated by residence or with fences and cultivation

* have to have entry with intent to OWN

* may have to occupy "whole" parcel; only to get title to what is actually used; if reside in a house then may get possession (b/c this is how ordinary owner would use a house) but if trying to possess multi-acre farm would have to cultivate just like ordinary owner would do

* possession must be exclusive – not shared with either true owner or public
does not have to be absolute, occasional, isolated visits by third parties (think hunters; hikers) will not impact exclusivity

---

3. Once again, my appreciation to Professor Alison Nissen for her permission in allowing me to use her examples. *See* Nissen, *supra* n.1.
   4. *Id.*

2. <u>OPEN AND NOTORIOUS</u>

* possession must be sufficiently visible and obvious to put reasonable owner on notice to true owner that someone is using the property with intent to claim possessory rights (<u>Smith v. Hayden</u> – garage on neighboring property)

* acts sufficient to satisfy open and notorious = residing; building fences; other improvements; cultivation
wall enclosing property OK (<u>Tippet</u>)

* concealed use (like cave) does not equal open use

* how "open" the use needs to be is in keeping with the character of the property, however rural property that is extensive and wooded may require more than minimal activity to put owner on notice (<u>Nome 2000</u>)

3. <u>ADVERSE, HOSTILE AND UNDER CLAIM OF RIGHT</u>

→ THREE DIFFERENT APPROACHES:

OBJECTIVE STANDARD – WHAT THE ADVERSE POSSESSOR THINKS ABOUT TITLE IS IRRELEVANT, HOSTILITY WILL BE IMPLIED BY ADVERSE POSSESSOR'S ACTIONS IN USING/OCCUPYING THE PROPERTY

GOOD FAITH – ADVERSE POSSESSOR NEEDS TO BELIEVE THAT HE/SHE HAS TITLE TO THE PROPERTY, THAT ADVERSE POSSESSOR HAS MADE AN HONEST MISTAKE ABOUT OWNERSHIP

HOSTILE TRESPASSER – ADVERSE POSSESSOR KNOWS PROPERTY BELONGS TO ANOTHER, BUT INTENDS TO TAKE TITLE AWAY

Also, the possession must be continuous for the statutory period – number of years required varies from state to state.

Although the substance of this outline is accurate, the *way* in which the information is presented could be improved.

For a law student who learns differently, consider adjusting your outlining strategy in three specific ways: (1) use summaries and roadmaps; (2) adopt visual strategies (font and contrast); and (3) use trigger facts.[5]

The next section of this chapter will discuss these three strategies and illustrate how to apply them to the example outline above.

---

5. Again, my appreciation to Professor Nissen as I adopted these terms from her presentation.

1. Use Summaries and Roadmaps

As you examine the 'before' and 'after' excerpts from the Property Outline below, what do you notice? What are the differences between them? Is the second outline easier to understand? Why? Is the second outline easier to read? The 'after' outline incorporates summaries and roadmaps. Can you pick out where these elements are?

Before	After
PROPERTY OUTLINE	Property Outline
ADVERSE POSSESSION	**Adverse Possession**
1. ACTUAL ENTRY AND EXCLUSIVE POSSESSION	Adverse possession is a method of acquiring title [6] by using or possessing property. An action for adverse possession is by statute, incorporating common law elements – essentially, the statute of limitations for an action in ejectment.
• type of entry/use that true owner would make of that property such that neighbors and other observers would regard the occupant as exercising exclusive dominion (Ewing)	If you bring a successful adverse possession claim you get title to the property in question which can be recorded.
• sufficient acts depend on nature, character and location of land and potential uses camper, outhouse, fish rack, reindeer pen on northern portion (Nome 2000) cattle grazing OK (Quarles) gravel pit OK (Ewing)	**Adverse possession:** **Statute + 4 common law elements** [7] 1. Actual entry and exclusive possession 2. Open and notorious 3. Adverse, hostile and under claim of right 4. Continuous for the statutory period
* * *	**1. Actual entry and exclusive possession** Type of entry/use that true owner would make of that property such that neighbors and other observers would regard the occupant as exercising exclusive dominion (Ewing)

Summaries are simply short paragraphs of information that give you the larger picture of a legal concept before getting into the individual elements. In legal writing, we often call these types of summaries "roadmaps" because they give the reader a short synopsis or "roadmap" of where the text is heading. Summaries can help you learn the bigger picture of the concept as well as the individual elements.

The 'after' outline incorporates short summaries and roadmaps. In this outline, the summaries provide a brief snapshot of the concept of Adverse Possession. The 'before' outline does not contain summaries.

---

6. Advance Organizer: Using a Summary Defining Adverse Possession.
7. Advance Organizer: Using a Roadmap Laying out the Elements Clearly.

In addition, using summaries to define concepts in your outline will allow you to self-monitor your learning. In other words, because the concepts are clearly articulated, you will get a better sense of whether you truly understand the concept or not.

2. Visual Strategies: Changing Fonts and Contrast (Bold/Regular Text)

Research has found that our eyes focus better and read faster when we use some fonts over others.[8] For example, it is very time consuming for your eyes to read a sentence in ALLCAPS. In outlining, you may think initially that using ALLCAPS will emphasize a certain point or principle. In reality, it will take your brain longer to process that material. Consider the example outlines below. What are the differences between the 'before' outline and the 'after' outline? Which font is easier to read—the bolded text or the ALLCAPS? Does it take longer to read in ALLCAPS?

Before	After
PROPERTY OUTLINE	**Property Outline**
ADVERSE POSSESSION	* * *
1. ACTUAL ENTRY AND EXCLUSIVE POSSESSION	Elements:
* * *	**1. Actual entry and exclusive possession**[9]
	* * *
2. ADVERSE, HOSTILE AND UNDER CLAIM OF RIGHT	**2. Adverse, hostile and under claim of right**
→ THREE DIFFERENT APPROACHES:	3 different approaches:
OBJECTIVE STANDARD – WHAT THE ADVERSE POSSESSOR THINKS ABOUT TITLE IS IRRELEVANT, HOSTILITY WILL BE IMPLIED BY ADVERSE POSSESSOR'S ACTIONS IN USING/OCCUPYING THE PROPERTY	**A. Objective standard:** What the adverse possessor thinks about title is irrelevant, hostility will be implied by adverse possessor's actions in using/occupying the property
GOOD FAITH – ADVERSE POSSESSOR NEEDS TO BELIEVE THAT HE/SHE HAS TITLE TO THE PROPERTY, THAT ADVERSE POSSESSOR HAS MADE AN HONEST MISTAKE ABOUT OWNERSHIP	**B. Good faith standard:** Adverse possessor needs to believe that he/she has title to the property, that adverse possessor has made an honest mistake about ownership
	* * *

---

8. Ruth Anne Robbins, *Painting with Print: Incorporating Concepts of Typographic and Layout Design Into the Text of Legal Writing Documents*, 2 J. Ass'n Legal Writing Directors 108, 114 (2004) (*citing* Miles A. Tinker, Bases for Effective Reading 15 (U. of Minn. Press 1965) (summarizing his scientific studies on reading and legibility of text)).

9. *Id.* at 119 (describing how using bolded text increases comprehension).

The 'before' outline uses ALLCAPS. Does it slow down your reading? The research illustrates that using ALLCAPS increases your reading time by 9%–19%.[10] This means that your eyes are working harder (and getting tired more easily) when you format your outline to look like the 'before' outline. In the 'after' outline, the headings use font with a light/dark contrast. The use of contrasting (**bolded** versus non-bolded text) maximizes readability and comprehension. Further, the 'after' outline uses lower case letters instead of ALLCAPS. Studies have shown that 90% of readers prefer lower case typeface over ALLCAPS.[11]

These small adjustments in the look of your outline may actually enhance the way your brain processes this information. This may be particularly helpful if you learn differently—if you are a visual learner—or if you simply take longer to process information overall.

3. Add "Trigger Facts" and Examples into Your Outline

Finally, a third technique for good outlining is to add "trigger facts" or examples into your outline. "Trigger facts" are nothing more than typical hypotheticals used to illustrate a particular legal concept.

As you know, law school classes tend to focus on extracting rules *out* of the case law (inductive reasoning). On an exam, you will need to recognize the issue and apply the general rule of law to the factual hypothetical (deductive reasoning). As part of your exam preparation, you will need to practice 'spotting' legal issues. In other words, you will need to be able to recognize the more typical fact patterns that fall within a particular rule or legal concept. These types of factual scenarios are rarely in your casebooks. Unfortunately, many law students fail to incorporate these types of factual hypotheticals or "trigger facts" into their outlines.

Yet it is precisely your ability to recognize the typical fact patterns that will determine your success on a law school exam. Therefore, you need to incorporate "trigger facts" or examples into your outline.

"Trigger facts" are those facts that will alert you to the application of a particular rule or cause of action. In the example outline below, one "trigger fact" is a boundary dispute. Boundary disputes often involve issues of Adverse Possession. Therefore, if you see an exam question that deals with a boundary dispute, it is likely that you will need to discuss some aspect of Adverse Possession. Having "trigger facts" in your outline will allow you to remember and spot these issues more easily.

The following example contains "Trigger Facts." The example also uses lower case letters and contrast (bold) in the headings. Does this outline provide additional information in a format that is more readable?

---

10. *Id.* at 115.
11. *Id.*

Property Outline

Obtaining and retaining ownership
Methods of acquiring title

Adverse possession is a method of acquiring title by using or possessing property. An action for adverse possession is by statute, incorporating common law elements – essentially, the statute of limitations for an action in ejectment.

If you bring a successful adverse possession claim you get title to the property in question that can be recorded.

Adverse possession:
Statute + 4 common law elements
1. Actual entry and exclusive possession
2. Open and notorious
3. Adverse, hostile and under claim of right
4. Continuous for the statutory period

Elements:

Trigger facts:
Boundary disputes
Use of property without record of title
Title is unclear or in dispute
Long time squatters/trespassers
Misplaced fences or encroachments

1. **Actual entry and exclusive possession**

   Type of entry/use that true owner would make of that property such that neighbors and other observers would regard the occupant as exercising exclusive dominion (Ewing)

   Sufficient acts depend on nature, character and location
   of land and potential uses
   Camper, outhouse, fish rack, reindeer pen on northern
   portion (Nome 2000)
   Cattle grazing OK (Quarles)
   Gravel pit OK (Ewing)

   Notes from Review Session:
   Likely on exam. Know the different cases here.

   Can be demonstrated by residence or with fences and cultivation

   Have to have entry with intent to **own**

   May have to occupy "whole" parcel; only to get title to what is actually used; if reside in a house then may get possession (b/c this is how ordinary owner would use a house) but if trying to possess multi-acre farm would have to cultivate just like ordinary owner would do

   Possession must be exclusive – not shared with either true owner or public
   Does not have to be absolute
   Occasional, isolated visits by third parties (think hunters; hikers) will not impact exclusivity

2. **Open and notorious**

   Possession must be sufficiently visible and obvious to put reasonable owner on notice to true owner that someone is using the property with intent to claim possessory rights (Smith v. Hayden – garage on neighboring property)

   Acts sufficient to satisfy open and notorious = residing; building fences; other improvements; cultivation

   Wall enclosing property OK (Smith v. Tippet)

   Concealed use (like cave) does not equal open use

How "open" the use needs to be is in keeping with the character of the property, however rural property that is extensive and wooded may require more than minimal activity to put owner on notice (Nome 2000)

3. Adverse, hostile and under claim of right

3 different approaches:

A. Objective standard:

What the adverse possessor thinks about title is irrelevant, hostility will be implied by adverse possessor's actions in using/occupying the property

> **Hypotheticals from Class:**
> Example of neighbor who placed fence over property line believing that it was on his property.

B. Good faith standard:

Adverse possessor needs to believe that he/she has title to the property, that adverse possessor has made an honest mistake about ownership

C. Hostile trespasser approach:

Adverse possessor knows property belongs to another, but intends to take title away

4. Continuous for the statutory period

Number of years – required varies from state to state
Exception: tacking
Successive periods of adverse possession by different persons may sometimes be combined together to satisfy the statutory duration requirement

---

Final Tip: As you create your outlines during the course of the semester, make sure to add in any examples that your professor has given you in class. Write these examples into your outline—it is likely that these examples will clue you into what your professor sees as important. In addition, commercial outlines often provide good examples of hypotheticals associated with particular rules or concepts. Add in these examples as well!

Chapter 13

The Law School Essay Exam

There is no doubt that the law school essay exam is mysterious to most law students. You've likely heard the joke that law professors grade essay exams by simply throwing the pile of exams down the stairs and the paper that lands closest to the bottom gets the A. But the real difficulty in conquering the law school essay exam lies in understanding the format of the exam. There are two main differences between law school essay exams and other types of exams. First, the law school essay exam is a timed test; you have only a limited amount of time to put down all the information you've learned during the semester. For most students, if they had a full day to complete the essay exam, they would likely do well. However, law students typically are given between three and four hours to complete a final exam in a course. Answering all the questions in that limited amount of time is very challenging.

Second, law school essay exams ask you to *apply* the information you've learned in class to a new factual situation and come to a conclusion based upon that analysis. In other types of exams, you are frequently asked to *give back* all the information you've learned during the course. However, in a law school exam, we assume you can write down what you've learned in class. After all, you are very smart—you wouldn't be in law school otherwise! But law professors are asking you to go one step further. We want to see if you can *identify* a legal issue within a factual hypothetical, *apply* the rules you've learned in class to this factual situation, and *predict* a likely outcome based upon both the facts and the law.

In other words, the method by which we test you in law school is different than the way in which we teach you. In class, you talk about different cases and extract the rules out of the cases you read. You prepare for class by focusing on case reading and analysis (i.e., the Case Method). But the typical law school essay exam requires you to *apply* the rules you've learned to a new problem. Another way to think about this is that the exam assumes (in most cases) that you are an attorney *applying* the law to a new set of facts as if you're talking to a client that has come to your office (i.e., the Problem Method). Therefore, if you approach studying for your law school essay exam by simply reviewing the cases and their rules, you may not do as well as you would like. Instead, you need to go one step further and *practice* how to *identify* the legal issues in a fact pattern and *apply* the rules. This is what you will be asked to do on your essay exams.

The key to essay exam preparation is to prepare for your exams by concentrating on what your professors will *test* on the exams, i.e., you need to *practice* how to read through a fact pattern quickly, *identify* the key issues, *analyze* the law as applied to the facts, and *conclude*. Further, you need to *practice* how to quickly outline your answer before beginning to write.

Outside materials, including commercial outlines, can be a big help with exam preparation. Once you have chosen some helpful study aids (that match your learning style),[1] your job is to replicate the essay exam experience *before* you take exam. Quite simply, you need to teach yourself how to *take* the exam almost as much as you need to study the substance of the course material.

Generally speaking, law professors are testing two main skills in essay exams: first, whether or not you can *spot the legal issue* in the problem; and second, whether you can *analyze* the issue, i.e., apply the law to the facts of the hypothetical. In order to properly prepare yourself for your essay exams, you need to have a game plan in place early on in the semester. In addition, you will need to consider how your individual learning style or learning differences will affect your exam preparation. The way in which you learn will factor into the materials and methods you will choose to prepare for exams. This section will provide you with various strategies for understanding and mastering the law school essay exam.

A. The First Step: Issue Spotting

Most of your essay exam questions will begin with a lengthy factual situation commonly called a 'hypothetical.' In an exam, your job is to read through the hypothetical carefully and efficiently. Some facts will be very relevant to your analysis of the problem and other facts will not be relevant to your analysis of the problem. The purpose of these long (and sometimes silly) factual hypotheticals is to test your ability to spot the relevant issues.

Issue spotting requires you to identify the facts in a hypothetical that relate to a legal concept or claim that you've covered in class. A law professor packs a number of issues into any given essay question. Your job is to read the facts in order to determine whether the facts give rise to a particular legal issue. This is difficult to do—under pressure—and in a time-limited situation.

First, begin your exam preparation by understanding that there is no *perfect or right* answer to any given question on an essay exam. Your job

---

1. See Chapter 7 for a comparison of the different study aids, commercial outlines, etc.

is not to give the professor the *perfect* answer but to think creatively about the problem and give the professor all the potential *possibilities* that come from the hypothetical. In order to see all the possible issues that flow from an essay fact pattern, you need to train yourself in the skill of 'issue spotting.'

In longer essay questions, there will be as many as ten to twelve different legal issues in a factual hypothetical. You are awarded points for each issue you spot and analyze; if you fail to spot and discuss the issue then you will not receive points for that issue. Therefore, it is essential that you become adept at issue spotting.

Consider the following issue spotting exercise.[2] The author of this exercise based the problem on a California Bar exam question. The purpose of this exercise is to sensitize you to the words that convey fact patterns and to discipline yourself to read the facts of questions carefully.

Step 1: Assume you have just completed your study of the crime of burglary. You are about to take your Criminal Law midterm and you receive the following factual hypothetical on the essay exam. Read the following factual hypothetical and circle all the facts that you think might be important as you analyze the problem for the elements of burglary.[3]

> One evening Albert was told that his estranged wife Zola was having overnight male guests in their residence. He immediately stormed out of the Sleezy Saloon, where he had been all evening, and drove his car wildly to the residence.

Step 2: Pull out (and rewrite) the key facts that may lead to legal issues. You should end up with a list of key words.

Key Words
evening
Albert
told
estranged wife
Zola having overnight male guests
their residence
he immediately
stormed out

---

2. This example was adapted from an Issue Spotting exercise from http://www.law schoolsecretstosuccess.com/Issue_Spotting.html (last visited 2/24/09).

3. Assume that you studied common law burglary, which is typically defined as the breaking and entering of the house of another in the nighttime, with intent to commit a felony therein, whether the felony be actually committed or not.

Sleezy Saloon
been all evening
drove car wildly
to residence

Step 3: Each of these key words could become a separate issue in your exam answer. At this point, you may not even need to look at the exam hypothetical again! You can simply refer to your list of key words. Now you will begin **issue-spotting**. Your job is to recognize the legal issues presented by the key words. Remember that each key word or phrase *may* be a possible issue in the problem. But you cannot write about every word—so you must decide which terms are *relevant* to the crime of burglary and which are not. For example, you might analyze the first three key words from the list as follows.

> "Evening" represents the common law crime of burglary. The associated facts to burglary are "their residence" and "been there all evening," which suggest that it may still evening or it may be sunrise and also the issue of burglarizing one's own residence.

> "Sleezy Saloon" suggests intoxication, a defense, and is supported by the fact that he had "been there all evening" and "drove his car wildly". The latter indicates a charge of drunk driving and a possible mitigation to the provocation suggested by the fact that his "estranged wife" had "overnight guests". The fact that it took time to drive to the residence and that he might have had a chance to cool off or maybe a reasonable person would have done so would also mitigate the provocation.

> "Estranged wife" suggests the issue of provocation and is supported by the facts that he "immediately stormed out" and that she has "overnight guests," which on further analysis could also suggest a possible charge of adultery.

All of the individual facts relate to one another in various combinations. If you find that you're not using all of the facts presented, you may not be spotting all the issues.

Being able to spot the legal issues in an exam hypothetical is a necessary skill and it is also a skill that requires practice.

Pay attention to 'key words' in any factual hypothetical that can highlight issues for you. For example, in the above hypothetical, there are some basic words that suggest an issue such as 'evening' for burglary and the use of 'the Saloon' for intoxication. Other words are used more subtly but also highlight potential issues such as the description of "storming" out of the Saloon, the "wild driving," and the "estranged wife."

Each of these phrases relates to the legal issues of burglary, provocation, drunk driving, intoxication, and adultery. Of course, there may be other crimes that come into play in this hypothetical as well—such as drunk driving, speeding, and adultery. Although these secondary issues may be of less significance when compared to the primary issue of burglary and murder, being able to spot sub-issues will show your professor that you have an in-depth understanding of the law.

Remember: all issues are derived from the facts in the problem. *Read the factual hypothetical very carefully.*

Once you feel like you've gotten a handle on the basic substance of the course, spend some time teaching yourself *how* to spot the legal issues in an exam situation. In other words, *practice* issue spotting explicitly.

Go through different hypotheticals related to the subject of the course. You can find hypotheticals in commercial outlines, study aids, prior exams, etc. The main point is that issue spotting is a skill—and you will need to set aside some specific time to acquire this skill in order to be successful on your exams.

And this is particularly true for law students who learn differently. Based upon your unique way of learning, you may have more trouble reading quickly through the fact patterns under pressure or you may become overwhelmed by the number of facts in the hypothetical. Practice as much as you can so you begin to develop a consistent plan for how you will approach issue-spotting on an essay exam.

B. The All-Important Analysis in the Essay Exam: A Mini-IRAC for Each and Every Issue

After you spot the issues in the factual hypothetical, you will analyze the issues and come to a conclusion. On an exam, you *will* receive some points for simply spotting the issue. However, the bulk of your points on an essay exam will come from a well-written analysis for each legal issue.

In law school, when we say that we want an *analysis* of a legal issue, we want you to apply the rule of law to the set of facts, and come to a conclusion. Does this sound familiar? This is the same type of analysis that you have done in your legal writing class. The main difference between a Legal Writing IRAC and an essay exam IRAC is that the essay exam IRAC is what I call a Mini-IRAC, i.e., it's shorter and more focused than the legal structure used in more formal legal writing. Law professors often complain that law students forget to do a proper 'analysis' in their essay exam answers. What they really mean is that students forget to include *all* the necessary elements of a Mini-IRAC for a legal issue. Using an IRAC structure for your exam answers is helpful for two main reasons. First, IRAC helps you organize your writing so that your professor can more easily *see* the legal reasoning in your answer. Second, IRAC ensures that you won't forget to address important elements for any legal issue.

When your professors are reading your essay exams, they are evaluating whether you can (1) spot the legal issue; (2) understand and identify the applicable rule; and (3) analyze different possible arguments for the application of law to the facts; and (4) come to a conclusion. Again, you should not worry about an *absolute* right or wrong answer; instead, law professors are looking for your *analysis*.

Law school essay exams are typically made up of two types of questions: the short answer essay question and the long answer question. In a short answer essay question, the professor will ask you to review a shorter and more focused factual hypothetical (likely containing two or three legal issues). A long-form essay question contains a lengthy factual hypothetical. Typically, this type of essay question contains ten to twelve legal issues. Your strategy in answering either type of essay questions should be very similar.

1. Short Answer Questions

Typically, a short essay question will have a one paragraph factual hypothetical that is focused on one to three legal issues. If you spot the issue/s quickly in this type of question, you can write an efficient and concise answer and gain time to use on other questions. Here's an example of an actual short answer question from one of my Evidence exams.

Question A: Short Answer Example

Donald ran a red light and collided with Ellie. Donald died in the crash, and Ellie was severely injured. In the wreckage of Donald's car, police found a dozen boxes of Peppie's Take-Out. Ellie sued Peppie's, claiming that Donald was delivering the food and that Peppie's was responsible for Donald's negligence. Peppie's claimed that it had no connection with Donald and that he must have stolen the food boxes. In response, Ellie offers evidence that Donald was insured under Peppie's group health insurance plan. <u>Is this evidence admissible?</u>

The 'call of the question' is underlined here. Pay special attention to this part of the question. Many students read the 'call' of the question first to frame the way in which they read the facts.

How would you go about writing an answer to this type of question? The best exam answers are written with a coherent structure. Here is the IRAC structure which is often used in exam writing.

I = Issue   (State the legal issue.)
R = Rule   (State the main rule that applies to the legal issue)
A = Analysis   (Apply the rule to the facts of your case. Examine the issue from both sides of a possible argument, discussing the strongest argument and possible counterarguments.)
C = Conclusion   (Prediction of a likely result.)

The IRAC structure makes answering essay questions more efficient because you don't have to think about how to organize your exam answer. You know *ahead* of time how you will approach each exam question.

In addition, using the IRAC structure ensures you will discuss each essential part of a legal argument, i.e., you won't forget to state the *rule* or to *analyze* the issue as you are writing quickly in an exam setting.

The most important element in IRAC is the A (Analysis). Students sometimes forget to properly *analyze* the legal issue and provide reasons for their conclusion. Your reasoning is precisely what your law professors *want* to see!

Further, don't spend *too much time* answering short answer essay questions. You need to know when to *stop writing*—so you don't waste valuable time that takes away from other questions. Just because there *could be* a potential legal issue related to a factual hypothetical does not mean that you *must* take the time to write about it. You will not likely receive much (if any) credit for bringing up extra issues. Therefore, part of becoming an efficient test-taker is knowing when to *stop writing* and move on. This is particularly important for short answer essay questions.

Let's look at a student's answer to the above-referenced question from my Evidence exam. This student received full credit for her answer to this essay question. Below I indicate each component of the IRAC structure to illustrate how using IRAC helps organize an exam answer.

Question A: Student Example Answer 1

I: The issue in this case is whether Federal Rule of Evidence 411 will bar Ellie from using the fact that Peppie's insured Donald under its group health insurance. **R:** The rule is that FRE 411 bars evidence of liability insurance to prove negligence. **A:** In this case, we are dealing with group health insurance which is medical insurance and not liability insurance. Because these facts deal with medical insurance, it is quite possible our facts will fall outside the protection of FRE 411 and be admissible as evidence. However, some courts have construed FRE 411 to include medical insurance. If a court does consider medical insurance to fall within FRE 411, then we must apply FRE 411 to determine whether 411 will preclude admissibility on these facts. FRE 411 excludes evidence of insurance for liability, but not for other purposes, such as ownership or control. On these facts, Ellie offers the insurance to show agency or control. **C:** Therefore, this evidence will be allowed because it is offered for some purpose other than liability.

Issue

Rule

Analysis

Conclusion

I: Issue
R: Rule
A: Analysis
C: Conclusion

This was a concise, well-written answer and the student received 15 out of 15 points. Notice how the student was very economical with her words but still discussed each element within the IRAC structure.

Note also that there was a sub-issue involved in the answer to this question, i.e., whether Rule 411 applied to health insurance. This student picked up on the sub-issue and chose to address the sub-issue within her main issue analysis of Rule 411. Many students who answered this question failed to see this sub-issue.

Consider a different student's answer to this same question in Student Example 2. Does this second answer use the IRAC form? As a law professor, I had a more difficult time locating each IRAC element in this student's answer. In addition, this student added some *additional information* to her answer regarding the topic of relevance. I had not expected relevance to be an issue in drafting this exam question. Typically, law professors simply read over "extra" material that students add to an exam answer and move on to the issues that directly address the question. In other words, adding extra information will not likely help you but it will rarely hurt you either. The danger is wasting time that you could use for other questions.

Note that in the following IRAC example, I've added a new category for "extra information" in the key below. I have also inserted several comments that I had as I reviewed this exam answer.

Question A: Student Example Answer 2

X: First, we want to determine whether this evidence is relevant under rules 401 and 402. The fact that the pizza place had insurance may have some relevance, i.e., may help make more probable the fact that the company was able to pay for the claim and was potentially liable. Once relevance is established we can examine **I:** whether the evidence should be admissible. **C:** I don't think this evidence will be admissible because it is insurance. **R:** The federal rules do not allow another party to mention health insurance except in specific circumstances. **A:** Ellie probably wants to use the insurance to show that Donald was liable which is a restricted use. However, insurance can be used for other purposes such as ownership or control. **C:** Evidence will probably be excluded.

I: Issue
R: Rule
A: Analysis
C: Conclusion
X: Extra Information

Extra Information. The student addressed the relevance issue which was not an incorrect analysis, but it was also not exactly what I was looking for in this short answer. I simply read over the relevance issue until I got to the Rule 411 issue.

Rule. This is an accurate statement of the rule generally. But the student fails to identify which Federal Rule of Evidence governs the issue, i.e., Rule 411. Also, this rule statement needed more specificity with regard to what the rule states.

Analysis. This is the beginning of the student's analysis but it is not complete. True, Ellie may use the evidence of insurance for this purpose, but more likely it will be for another purpose, i.e., to establish that Donald worked for Peppie's Pizza. Partial credit. More analysis needed.

Issue. This is the larger issue, i.e., admissibility, but the issue is not specific enough. It should involve the particular rule at issue: FRE 411.

Conclusion. This is the writer's conclusion. It's fine to begin with a conclusion, and to end with one. However, this conclusion doesn't give me the reason why the evidence should be excluded. Is it because of Rule 411? This conclusion is too vague.

Conclusion. It's probably not a correct outcome given the facts of this case but I'm not as concerned with that as I am with the fact that the conclusion doesn't state any reasons for the result. In other words, there is no analysis here—just a result.

This student was able to identify some of the important issues in this question but didn't follow through with enough detail about the rule itself or the analysis as to why the general rule would not apply in this case, i.e., that the policy was really health insurance versus liability insurance. This was an average to below-average answer to this question. This student received 8 out of 15 points.

Consider another example of a short-answer essay question.

Question B: Short Answer Example

Susan sued Mark for stealing a pair of running shoes from her athletic supply shop. Mark took the stand at trial and denied that he took anything from Susan's shop. "I don't even shop there," Mark said. "She has shoddy, out-of-date merchandise." On cross-examination, Susan's attorney offered evidence that Mark had been convicted three years earlier for illegally downloading music from the internet. Mark's conviction was for a misdemeanor defined as "making unauthorized copies of audio recordings for commercial advantage or private financial gain." Is evidence of the conviction admissible?

A good student answer is reprinted below. I have also pointed out the different components of IRAC.

Question B: Student Example Answer 1

Conclusion — **C:** Possibly admissible. **I:** The main issue is whether or not the conviction is admissible under Rule 609. **A:** Here, it is a misdemeanor. Misdemeanors do not fall under Rule 609. **R:** Rule 609 addresses a felony that results in a year or more in prison. **A:** So it would be admissible under 609 ONLY if it was a crime of dishonesty. The question then becomes whether illegally downloading music could be considered a crime of dishonesty. Although courts come to different conclusions, there's a good argument that it IS such a crime. Congress recently tightened that definition; did not want theft to constitute "dishonesty." **C:** If this court agrees that it is a crime of dishonesty, then evidence is admissible without any balancing—not even under Rule 403.

—— Issue
—— Analysis
—— Rule

I: Issue
R: Rule
A: Analysis
C: Conclusion

— Analysis

— Conclusion

Note that this answer contained mostly Analysis in the answer. Although there could have been a more specific and thorough rule statement, the analysis in this answer was quite good. The student was very concise in his answer but he hit all of the essential issues. The student received 23/25 points.

Consider a different student's answer to this question. This student also received 23/25 points. This answer contained more overall explanation of the rule and also addressed a few additional issues that were not necessarily required to receive full points—but the answer demonstrated an in-depth understanding of the legal issues.

Question B: Student Example 2

Question 4: Is evidence of the conviction admissible?

Headings. Using Headings helps your professor follow your answer.

Extra Information. The student did a nice job discussing the relevance of the evidence and a possible FRE 403 argument. I had not expected students to go into this aspect of the question but I chose to recognize it as an issue when grading the exam.

Issue Missing: The student actually failed to clearly state the issue although I could tell that the student was discussing FRE 609 here. The student lost two points for failing to state the issue.

I: Issue
R: Rule
A: Analysis
C: Conclusion
X: Extra Information

Extra Information. Here, the student was discussing this evidence as possible character evidence. Once again, the student identified a different issue, i.e., one that I wasn't testing in this problem. This discussion certainly didn't hurt the student in her answer but it wasn't necessary either.

X: First, evidence of the conviction may be admissible only if it is relevant. Relevant evidence (401) is any evidence that has any tendency to make a fact of consequence more or less probable. The governmental interest in allowing evidence in is evidenced by the words "any tendency" so evidence regarding a prior bad act that has something to do with the D's nature regarding truthful conduct is relevant. The evidence may be unfairly prejudicial to the D. The conviction does suggest an inference to the jury that if he stole music, he may steal shoes. Under 403, a defense attorney may be able to bar this evidence because its unfair prejudice outweighs the probative value.

Second, **R:** convictions are admissible against a witness under 609 if the conviction was one that resulted in more than 1 year in prison. **A:** I believe, as a misdemeanor, this crime would not result in a year or more in prison and therefore the evidence is likely to be overly prejudicial and therefore barred. Also, 609 applies to witnesses other than the accused (unless he is on the stand perhaps) and therefore the evidence may also not come in during under 609.

X: Third, because this is cross exam discussion, I assume that Mark is on the stand and therefore his character comes into play regarding his reputation and opinion. (404). Assuming that a person represents themselves to the best of their abilities, it is likely that his character is in play and the prosecutor could attack his character under 404(a)(1) with specifics. The prosecution may also attempt to avoid a character issue by admitting the evidence under 404(b) but there is little evidence to provide a MOPPIIK reason. The specific instance of conduct may be admissible under 405 to prove that his statement that he didn't steal the shoes and sporting gear should be treated with caution as to its truthfulness may come in under 405(b).

Note that the answer I was looking for with this question is located in the middle of the student's answer (the A: Analysis portion). Most of the other issues discussed in the answer were extra issues that the student was not required to discuss.

When it doubt, it may not hurt to address extra issues *as long as* you've fully discussed the main issue in the question (and you've given yourself enough time to complete all the other exam questions). *Sometimes students delve too deeply into a single question which takes far too much time away from answering the other questions on the exam.* Don't fall into this trap. Set yourself a time limit for short answer questions and move on once you have used up your time for that question!

In order to prepare for short answer essay questions, *practice* writing in an IRAC formula as much as possible prior to your exams. Find out how many short answer questions will be on your exam. Calculate the time you will spend for each. And practice, practice, practice! Use examples or hypotheticals from commercial outlines. Develop different questions with your study group. You can also write short answers to multiple-choice hypotheticals. Use the fact pattern and write out an answer before you look at the answer choices.[4]

2. Long Essay Exam Questions

Long essay exam questions can be more difficult for several reasons. First, longer essay questions have multiple issues within the lengthy factual hypothetical and it is challenging for anyone to spot all the issues in a timed situation. Second, you need to manage your time very carefully on long essays. In other words, you don't want to write several paragraphs about a few issues and fail to write anything about several other issues. By not addressing issues, you are guaranteed to lose points on the exam! And writing extensively about only a few issues will not earn you any extra points. In an essay exam, you need to ascertain exactly how much time you can spend on each separate question and stick to it! If you have three long essays in a one hour exam (or section), then you should budget 20 minutes per section. Once you hit 20 minutes on a question, wrap it up and move on. This is a hard technique to master so you need to begin *practicing* taking timed exams as soon as possible.

Here is a game plan to tackle longer essay exam questions.

Step 1: Page through the exam (or section). Note how many questions are on the exam. (Students often forget to answer *all* the questions!) Allocate your time carefully. Know exactly how much time you can afford to spend on each question in the exam.

Step 2: Skim the call of the question first so you know what the question is asking for specifically. You may be able to direct your reading of the factual hypothetical more efficiently if you know the issue beforehand.

Step 3: Skim the facts.

Step 4: Re-read the facts again and begin to pull out the different issues. Circle key facts that may lead to legal issues. Write a list of key facts on the margin of your paper.

Step 5: Draft Mini-IRAC's for each separate key fact and/or issue that stems from the factual hypothetical. Note your different issues specifically so your professor can identify the separate analysis.

---

4. This will also help you reason through answer choices for the multiple-choice questions.

Let's see how this works with another example.[5] The purpose of this example is to show you how to begin to outline multiple-issues in a longer essay question. Or in other words, after you have identified each issue, you will draft an individual IRAC for each issue.

Example C: Longer Essay Question

Jane represents Roger, an unknown songwriter, in a copyright infringement action against the star singer Beyonda. Roger claims that Beyonda based one of her best-selling hits on an obscure song that he composed. Roger sends a fax to Jane's office that reads "I realize my infringement claim is far-fetched, but I'm relying on you to get me something in settlement. Beyonda has plenty of dough to spare. We can allege anything and get some money!" Hector, another one of Jane's clients, is standing near the fax machine when Roger's fax arrives. Hector has no connection with Roger or Beyonda, but he has always admired Beyonda's work so he calls her to tell her what Roger wrote. Beyonda moves to dismiss Roger's claim as frivolous, attaching an affidavit from Hector that relates the contents of Roger's fax. Does admission of the affidavit violate the attorney-client privilege under current federal law?

Example C: Answer Example 1

Here is *my* sample answer to this question.[6] As in the other examples, I have coded the answer to reflect the different parts of IRAC.

There are four overall issues in this question. **I:** The first issue is whether and how the attorney-client privilege applies in this case. **I:** Second, whether there was a "confidential communication" from the client (Roger) to the attorney (Jane) such that the attorney-client privilege attaches to the communication. **I:** And the third issue is whether there was an Inadvertent Disclosure of the document under Federal Rules of Evidence 502(b) of the Rules. **I:** Lastly, there may be a final issue involving the fraud exception to the attorney client privilege.

An introductory paragraph laying out the four main issues is helpful for the professor. Therefore, even if you don't have time to get to all the details, you've at least outlined the main issues and you'll likely get partial credit.

Issue — **I:** The first issue is whether the attorney-client privilege applies in this
Rule — case. **R:** In order for the privilege to attach, the common law requires that there was a "confidential communication" from the client (Roger)
Analysis — to attorney (Jane). **A:** In this case, Roger was sending a fax to his attorney's office, so he did reasonably have an expectation that this was a confidential communication. Roger intended the communication to go

---

5. Note that this question is likely a bit shorter than most long-answer essays but the process you use to read and pick apart the issues is the same.
6. I hand out sample answers to my students after exams. Note that this is more organized than most of the actual student answers to this question.

to Jane, his attorney. It was not unreasonable to assume that since it was being faxed to Jane at her office that she or a representative from her office would pick up the document. **C:** This was a confidential communication protected by the attorney client privilege.   —— Conclusion

Issue 2: **I:** The second issue is whether there was an inadvertent disclo-   —— Issue
sure to Hector and whether that disclosure waived the attorney-client
privilege. **R:** Under new Federal Rule of Evidence 502, Inadvertent Dis-   —— Rule
closure, the fax was inadvertently disclosed. **A:** Roger had every belief   —— Analysis
that he was faxing it to his attorney **C:** and therefore, the disclosure was —— Conclusion
inadvertent.

Issue 3: **I:** The next issue is whether the inadvertent disclosure waived   —— Issue
Roger's attorney-client privilege because of such disclosure. **R:** Under   —— Rule
FRE 502, if the communication was inadvertently disclosed, the disclosure does not operate as a waiver in Federal proceedings if: (1) the disclosure is inadvertent; (2) the holder of the privilege took reasonable
steps to prevent the disclosure; and (3) the holder promptly took reasonable steps to rectify the error. **A:** Here, there was likely an inadver-   —— Analysis
tent disclosure, and Roger took reasonable steps to prevent disclosure
(faxing to his attorney's office was reasonable).

C: There is a question here as to whether Roger or Jane took steps to rec- —— Conclusion
tify the error, but they did not know that Hector saw the fax. We would
need additional facts as to what exactly Jane did upon receiving notice
that the information had been disclosed. However, assuming that Jane
took steps to rectify the error, it is likely a court would find that there
was an inadvertent disclosure and would uphold the privilege.

Issue 4: **I:** There is one additional issue that may arise on the facts of   —— Issue
this case. If the claim is completely groundless (as suggested by Roger's
statement), Roger is arguably asking Jane to aid in illegal conduct; this
might defeat privilege. **R:** The attorney-client privilege can be waived if   —— Rule
the client asks the lawyer to engage in illegal behavior. **A:** In this case, —— Analysis
however, it's fairly arguable that the claim Roger is asking his attorney
to bring isn't illegal—**C:** so this alone would not waive the privilege.   —— Conclusion

Note that the rule statement for each issue is actually a very small part of the overall answer. I've seen many student answers that focus too heavily on explaining the rules and they spend too little time explaining their analysis, i.e., applying the rule to the facts of the case—addressing the arguments and counterarguments. The majority of your discussion in most exam answers should be devoted to the *analysis* of the issue.

Certainly, however, the number of sentences you use to analyze the issue will depend upon the complexity of the issue (and the arguments surrounding it). If it's a straightforward resolution of an issue, less space is required. If it's a complicated issue that has authority to support both sides of an issue, then you need to spend more time developing the arguments and counter-arguments. Note that the sample above provides *at least* one sentence for each element of IRAC. Minimally, you want to write one sentence per IRAC element and often you want to provide *more* than one sentence per IRAC element (particularly in the analysis section) for more complex issues.

Under exam conditions, you probably won't write as coherently about every issue as I did in the example above. That's okay! Professors realize that you are under pressure and we do not expect perfection in your answers. The idea is to practice writing an exam answer like the sample answer and to try and identify and explain as many issues as you can in the time amount given. If you get confused and scratch out portions of your answer—don't worry. You can still get credit for your answer.

Here's an example of an *actual* student answer to Example C that received 19 out of 24 total points on this question. Although the student got the main issue correct, i.e., whether an attorney-client relationship existed, the student missed two of sub-issues, i.e., the inadvertent disclosure issue and the fraud issue.

But because the student identified the main issue, the student did fairly well on this exam question with regard to the total number of points received.

As you read through the student's answer, evaluate it as if you were the professor reading the answer. Did the student follow the IRAC formula? Can you identify the individual parts of IRAC? Did the student actually *see* an additional issue within the problem?

Example C: Student Example Answer 2

Question C: Does the affidavit violate A-C privilege?

Extra Issue. The student addressed a "relevance" issue. Although "relevance" was beyond the scope of what was originally intended with the question, I gave the student some credit for this addition. This offset slightly the points the student lost on the missing issues of inadvertent disclosure and fraud.

I: Issue
R: Rule
A: Analysis
C: Conclusion
X: Extra Information

X: First, evidence of the plan to squeeze Beyonda may be admissible only if it is relevant. Relevant evidence (401) is any evidence that has a tendency to make a fact of consequence more or less probable. The governmental interest in allowing evidence in is evidenced by the words "any tendency" so evidence regarding a conspiracy to extort money and the fact that there is a bogus case is likely relevant to a judge when considering the validity of a case in a Motion to Dismiss.

Issue ——
Rule ——
Analysis ——

I: Whether it violates A-C privilege depends on **R:** whether (1) the privilege existed and (2) whether it was violated. First, the privilege may have existed. **A:** Jane was an attorney, Roger was her client, he contacted her for legal advice regarding a (supposed) copyright infringement action, the fax was presumably meant to be confidential as a statement such as this if it were not would be very damaging to the person who communicated it to their attorney. The privilege only "may" exist rather than "certainly" exists because the communication seems to be sent to Jane in hopes that he can make a fraudulent claim (and likely an illegal act) with the help of his attorney. **C:** This action taken by Roger fits the crime fraud exception to A-C privilege voiding the privi-

Conclusion ——

lege. **I:** The fact may also not be found to be privileged for the fact that — Issue
the statement was readily observed by another client. **R:** The presence — Rule
of a third party waives the privilege and although the privilege exists
for individuals under the attorney's employ, the presence of a client ob-
serving the communication destroys the privilege. **C:** The admission of
this likely does not violate A-C privilege.

Missing Analysis. The student jumps from the Issue to the Rule with no Analysis.

— Conclusion

X: Additionally, the statement by Hector would avoid hearsay and be
admitted under 801(d)(2)(1) as an admission by a party (Roger); or it
could be admitted as it is not meant to prove TMA under 801(c) but
rather that R had knowledge that he does not have a viable claim
against Beyonda.

— Extra Information

Note that the student's answer was not perfect but it did discuss the
main issue of whether the attorney-client privilege had attached. Further, even though the student missed two sub-issues (inadvertent disclosure and fraud), the student added two issues (relevance and
admissions) which provided the student with a couple extra points. Note
also that the student's answer wasn't in perfect IRAC form. For the most
part, however, the elements were distinct enough that I could find the different elements as I read through the answer. And the student did a nice
job on the overall analysis, which is what law professors look for to assess your overall understanding of the legal issue.

In addition to using the IRAC formula in constructing organized
exam answers, you may also want to practice the ability to quickly
outline difficult long-essay questions before you begin writing. This is
particularly important if you learn differently or become easily overwhelmed with long fact patterns. Long-form law school essays tend to
have *very* detailed and complex hypotheticals that are full of legal issues. Law professors are testing your ability to recognize the legal issues but also your ability to organize the issues and rules into a coherent
discussion, and to note relevance information and discard irrelevant
information.

For many students, if they fail to outline their answers before they
begin to write, their essay answers are jumbled and difficult to follow,
and they typically miss issues. The key to the outlining step in exam writing is to become so familiar (and practiced) with your *process* for outlining that you can know exactly what you will do when you get to this
type of question.

Therefore, when you take your practice exams, work on outlining the
longer and more difficult questions. Practice in a timed situation, i.e.,
limit the time in which you allow yourself to outline. Replicate this *process*
as many times as you can before your actual exam.

Consider the following long essay question from an Evidence exam. This
was a difficult question that addressed several hearsay exceptions in both
a criminal and civil context. Very few students got all the issues involved

in this essay question. However, the students who did get most of the issues spent some time outlining the issues on their test booklet before writing. Consider the outline that follows this essay question.[7]

Example D: Long Form Essay Question
You will have one hour to answer this essay question.

Tricia Adams broke into John Vicker's house to steal his bobblehead collection. While Adams was in the house, Vicker came home with a man Adams recognized as Paul Brown. Adams hid behind a curtain; Vicker and Brown could not see her, but she could see them. Adams watched from behind the curtain as Brown killed Vicker with a knife. Brown then ran from the house.

Adams forgot about the bobbleheads and used her cell phone to call a friend named Fred White. Adams told White that she "desperately needed a place to hide out for a few days and chill from some major stress." According to White, Adams was "sobbing and hysterical on the phone."

White allowed Adams to stay at his apartment for four days. At the end of that time, Adams confided to White that she had broken into Vicker's house, intending to steal his bobblehead collection. While in the house, she told White, she had seen Brown stab Vicker to death. "I'll never forget the sight of his bleeding body," Adams said, starting to cry again. She composed herself and returned to her own home.

White was horrified by Adams' revelation. After thinking about the matter for a week, he called Adams and told her that he could not keep silent about the crimes. White then went to the police and reported everything Adams had said about breaking into Vicker's house and witnessing his murder. The police drove to Adams's house to interview her, but found that she had committed suicide shortly after receiving White's call about notifying the police.

In addition to White's report, the police gathered some circumstantial evidence linking Brown to Vicker's murder. A grand jury indicted Brown for homicide. Vicker's widow also sued Brown for the wrongful death of her husband.

   (A) In the civil suit against Brown, will Vicker's widow be able to call White as a witness to testify about Adams' statements (1) during the

---

7. This example was created by Deborah Jones Merritt, John Deaver Drinko-Baker and Hostetler Chair in Law; Courtesy Professor of Sociology; Courtesy Professor of Public Policy and management, and Associate Faculty Member in Women's Studies, The Ohio State University, Moritz College of Law. Professor Merritt is a wonderful teacher and mentor. This example and the following outline are used with her permission.

phone call to White, and (2) after she had stayed at his apartment? Explore all plausible bases for admitting these hearsay statements.

(B) Can White testify for the prosecutor about Adams' statements during the homicide trial? In answering this subpart, build upon your previous answer. Focus, in other words, on how admissibility of the statements in the homicide trial differs from that in the wrongful death suit.

Here is an example outline of an answer listing the various issues in this essay. What do you notice? The outline is very detailed, and you may not have enough time to fill in all of the details. But having something to help you organize the many issues in any long form essay will be very helpful. In the end, you will write a better answer to your long essay questions.

(A) The Civil Suit

1. Statements made during the phone call. Hearsay: Does any exception apply?

    Exception for excited utterance
    - Witnessing murder is a startling event
    - Adams' statements related to this event
    - Was Adams speaking under stress of excitement?
      Subjective standard
      As a criminal, would illegal activity bother her less?
    ○ But sobbing and hysterical
    ○ Words suggest she was under stress
    ○ How much time passed before she called?
    ○ Cases suggest statement made within 30-40 minutes of major stress ok

    Exception for state of mind
    - Admits statements of emotion or feeling
    ○ "Desperate need" could be an emotion
    ○ "Stress" could be a feeling or a reason for feeling; latter inadmissible under this exception
      - Feelings must be contemporaneous with statement: Within confines described above, these statements fit

    Adams is not a party, so can't use party-opponent exception
    Others possibilities that people discussed were present sense impression.

2. Statements made after staying with White. Also hearsay: Applicable exception?

    Not excited utterance: four days is too long to sustain stress
    State of mind might admit "I'll never forget the sight of his bleeding body" as statement of contemporaneous feeling. But other statements are memory/explanation; inadmissible under this exception.

Statement against interest

- Adams is unavailable (dead)
- Against interest

○ Subjected her to criminal liability (breaking and entering)

○ Reasonable person wouldn't have made unless true

○ Against interest at time made

○ She was open to prosecution

○ No evidence that she then intended suicide

- Not offered to exculpate criminal defendant; don't need corroboration
- Judge might redact, limiting references to Adams' own crime

○ Her attempted burglary was entirely separate from murder

○ But Adams had no legal reason to be in the house; very fact she could see murder was against her interest

○ Statement seems reliable, particularly valuable, and it's offered in civil case: all reasons supporting admission

Other points

No Sixth Amendment issues in civil case

Statements during phone call may not help plaintiff unless later statements are also admissible. Former statements alone could suggest that Adams, rather than Brown, committed murder.

(B) Criminal prosecution

1. Sixth Amendment's Confrontation Clause[8] applies.

   a. If the statement was testimonial, admissible only if Adams is unavailable and Brown had a previous opportunity to cross-exam. First condition is met, but not second.

   b. To admit statement, therefore, prosecutor must persuade judge it was non-testimonial. Prosecutor seems to have a strong case:

   - Both statements were made to a friend, not a government official
   - Circumstances surrounding statements were not formal
   - First statement was made under stress, possible emergency
   - Second statement was more factual
   - No evidence that Adams intended either statement to be used for prosecution. In first, she asked friend for place to stay. In second, she sought comfort from friend
   - Fact that Adams committed suicide when White went to police supports conclusion that she did <u>not</u> intend statements to be used prosecutorially

---

8. Note this example does not take into account recent case law involving the Confrontation Clause and the Sixth Amendment.

Whether or not you outline (and how much time you spend on an exam outline) depends in large part on how you learn. Some students hate outlining—either for papers or for exams. Obviously, you will *not* want to outline your exam answer before you begin to write if you find that it does *not* help you. But even if you are not inclined to write a detailed outline, it *is* beneficial to write at least a list of issues that you intend to cover as you write. Minimally, having a list of the main issues in a problem will prevent you from *missing* issues as you write your exam.

3. How Do We Grade?

It's worth considering how law professors grade before you begin taking your exams. Law professors typically come up with a point system for grading. Your professor will develop a checklist for each issue and assign a certain number of points per issue. Although style, grammar and readability do matter, these factors do not carry as much weight as substance. In other words, you don't usually accumulate additional points for writing well. However, you may lose points for not writing well. Consider that writing an organized, grammatically-correct exam answer will make sure that your professor *sees* all of your issues and analysis, and this will maximize your points on the exam.

Law professors read through exam answers quickly but we often read them two to three times each. The first time we read an answer is more of a 'skim' to get a gut feeling as to whether the student got the main issue/s or not. The second time, we may go through and actually check off the major issues you've identified and analyzed. The third pass is to ensure that we haven't missed any of your issues! A third read through is often necessary in a poorly organized exam answer. If at all possible, you want write clearly and concisely so your answer can be easily read— so it doesn't require that your professor read it again to search for issues.

So, for example, in a long essay, there may be 100 total points for the entire essay question. But the essay is likely divided into 10 different issues—each with a different Mini-IRAC. So each issue will be worth 10 points each. Again, under this system—time management is an important key to success. If you write beautifully on only six issues, you will still get points for only those six issues (and miss almost 40 points on the exam!). Make sure you leave enough time to address all of the issues in the essay question. Write down the time allotted for each overall question and try to stick to it.

Over the course of law school, you will develop your own method for taking essay exams (and all of your exams). The key is to develop your game plan early on in the semester of your first year. Many students wait until after their first semester midterms or exams (or even into their second year) before they consider *how* to take exams. This is particularly true for students who learn differently. You may score below average on your midterms and feel like there's no way to improve. Or you may think that you received the grade you did on an exam simply because you didn't understand the substance of the course well enough—or that your professor was less than fair on the exam, etc. Any or all of these things may be true. However, you should also consider that you might need to spend some of your time preparing for the *taking* of the exam itself. The key to success in taking law school exams it to develop a specific strategy for the exam and to practice your strategy or plan *before* the exam. You don't have to write a perfect answer—you simply need to catch the major issues and write an IRAC analysis for most of the issues. If you can accomplish this, you will perform well on your law school essay exams.

Chapter 14

Taking the Multiple-Choice Law School Exam

Law school multiple-choice exams are very different than any multiple-choice exams you have taken before law school. In your prior multiple-choice exams, the questions most likely tested your ability to *recall* information. However, the law school multiple-choice exam (and the multi-state bar exam as well) tests your ability to *analyze* a fact pattern and come to the correct conclusion. Like the law school essay exam, law professors are asking you to perform the same type of skills in a multiple-choice exam: read a factual hypothetical, identify the legal issue, and apply an IRAC analysis to come to the correct conclusion. Although you have a closed universe in a multiple-choice exam, the questions themselves are quite complex and time-consuming.

Law professors often justify their use of multiple-choice exams by claiming that they want to simulate bar exam questions. This may be partly true. We do want to prepare you for the bar exam after you graduate from law school. But law professors also like multiple choice exams because they are objective and they are easy to grade! That being said, however, drafting a good multiple-choice question is very difficult. So, as with any other type of exam, I would suggest trying to obtain copies of your professors' prior multiple-choice exams early on in the semester.[1] You will need to practice taking multiple-choice exams as a separate skill set in law school. The types of multiple-choice questions used in a law school exam are unique. So even if you do not have access to a particular professor's prior multiple-choice exam, consider asking your professor if there is a particular study aid that the professor recommends.[2] Minimally, you need to simulate the types of questions you might find on multiple-choice exam in that particular course.

---

1. This may be somewhat difficult, however, because many law professors have policies that prevent them from giving students copies of the multiple-choice questions so that we can reuse multiple-choice questions on different exams.

2. For example, I often suggest the Q & A series which has hundreds of multiple-choice questions for any subject. You can practice writing Mini-IRACs with the questions, or use them for multiple choice practice as well. This series is a good supplement to your own outline. It's not a bad idea to have many different study sources. They each give you a different but helpful perspective.

Law school multiple choice questions are very difficult for several reasons.[3] First, the factual scenarios or hypotheticals that precede the answer choices are complex and detailed. Second, several of the answer choices seem equally correct. Third, the answer choices often contain distracting information designed to lure you away from the real focus of the question.[4] Therefore, to do well on these exams, you must not only understand the rules applicable to a given issue in the question, you must also understand the formula a law professor uses to create multiple-choice questions. You are less likely to feel ambushed by your first series of multiple-choice exams if you become familiar with the types of questions used in a law school multiple-choice exam.[5] This chapter will explain these different types of multiple-choice questions and provide you with important strategies for mastering this type of exam.

A. The Terminology of Multiple-Choice Questions

First, let's begin with some basic terminology of the different components of a multiple-choice question. There are three parts to any multiple-choice question: the 'root' or factual hypothetical; the 'call' of the question (sometimes called the question or 'stem'); and the 'options' (or answer choices).[6] First, the 'root' is the fact pattern that precedes the actual task being demanded of the law student. The root likely contains all of the facts needed for a knowledgeable examinee to answer that question. A well-written root uses concise language and minimizes extra characters, names or information. However, many law professors may not give you a "well-written" factual hypothetical. Sometimes, we will use silly names or put in extra information in the fact patterns (which is not helpful to you but fairly typical). So you should be prepared to distill the *relevant* facts from the 'root' as quickly as possible. Like the factual hypothetical in an essay exam, you want to begin reading the root by circling any key phrases or words that signal issues.

---

3. Rogelio Lasso, *Taking Multiple Choice Exams,* (*citing* Michael Josephson, *Evaluation and Grading in Law School*, (1984)) (updates to Professor Josephson's work on multiple choice exams provided by Rogelio Lasso, John Marshall Law School, Chicago and Professor Vernellia Randall, University of Dayton Law School. Professor Lasso's handout is at Appendix D at the end of the book.

4. *Id.*

5. *Id.*

6. Michael Josephson, *Learning and Evaluation in Law School*, *Volume 2: Test Construction, Scoring, Grading, and Ranking Institutional Policies* (1984), Submitted to the: Association of American Law Schools Annual Meeting; January 4, 1984 Teaching Methods Sections.

Second, the 'call' of the question is a short, focused question that asks you to perform a particular task. Sometimes the call of the question will add facts to the initial hypothetical. Other times, the call of the question will require you to make certain assumptions before answering the question. Or the call may specify what cause of action or theory to advance. Whatever the particular call, make sure to read the call very *carefully* so that you know precisely what you are being asked to do!

Third, the answer choices or 'options' are the lettered choices given to you as potential answers to the call of the question. One of the answer choices, called the 'key,' should be clearly better than the other options (called 'distractors.'). A well-written series of answer choices or options should be parallel in language and structure; should be as concise as possible; should not contain new facts; and should not contain additional conditions. Once again, however, since not all law professors are trained to write *good* multiple-choice questions, you may see questions on your exams that do not always follow these rules.

In the following example,[7] I have labeled each of these parts in a typical law school multiple-choice question:

Root or Factual Hypo
1. Pam sues for injuries after her car is struck by a truck driven by Reginald. On direct examination, Pam's lawyer asks her: "Isn't it a fact that you were driving well within the speed limit prior to the collision and keeping a careful lookout for other cars?"

Call or Stem — The defense attorney objects. The judge should:

Options A–C are distractors.

A. Sustain the objection because leading questions are never allowed on direct examination.
B. Overrule the objection because leading questions are permissible in some introductory situations on direct examination.
C. Sustain the objection because the witness should testify in a narrative form.
D. Sustain the objection because leading questions are generally not allowed on direct and the attorney is not asking simply introductory material.

Key (correct answer). Although leading questions are sometimes allowed for introductory material, in this situation, the lawyer is planting the information and the leading question goes too far under Rule 611.

Why do law professors use multiple choice questions? The multiple choice exam is a very flexible form of objective testing that is similar to the essay exam in terms of analytical requirements and substantive knowledge. Essay questions can be converted into multiple choice questions and professors can alter multiple choice questions easily to make them more or less sophisticated by adjusting the complexity of the facts or by changing the manner in which the call of the question is worded. In addition,

---

7. *Id.* at 349–378.

a law professor can make a question more challenging by posing options which are both complex and close to each other in terms of similarity between answer choices. It is then up to the student to read carefully and closely in order to determine the subtle differences between the listed options.

B. What Are the Different Forms of Multiple-Choice Questions?

There are several different forms of multiple-choice questions but the most common form types are as follows: (1) the simple fact pattern; (2) the complex fact pattern; (3) the two-tiered option; (4) overlapping options; and (5) the question series.[8] Having a sense of the different types of multiple-choice forms (and becoming comfortable with them) will help you reduce test-anxiety. In addition, you may want to develop a strategy where you can spot easier multiple-choice questions versus more difficult forms of questions. Keep in mind that the typical law school multiple-choice exam will have some of each of the five types of questions. In my experience, approximately 25% of the multiple-choice questions are of low to moderate difficulty; 50% of the questions are of moderate difficulty; and approximately 25% of the questions are of high difficulty. The remainder of this sub-section will describe the different forms of law school multiple-choice questions and provide you with an example of what they look like.

1. The Simple Fact Pattern

The simple fact pattern is comprised of a straightforward factual hypothetical that focuses on a single legal issue. Your strategy for this type of question is to read the question carefully in order to make sure you get it right! This question form is likely a lower difficulty question type so you want to maximize your opportunities for getting these types of questions correct. Here is an example of a 'simple fact pattern' type of multiple-choice question.

> John was fired from his job. Too proud to apply for unemployment benefits, he used his savings to feed his family. When one of his children became ill, he did not seek medical attention for the child at a state clinic because he did not

8. These remaining examples in this chapter are based upon prior bar exam questions; *see* Josephson, *supra* n.6 at 352 (noting that the illustrations used in the book are taken from "Multistate Bar Examination Questions VI" (1981) by the National Conference of Bar Examiners)).

want to accept what he regarded as charity. Eventually,
weakened by malnutrition, the child died as a result of the
illness. John has committed:

(A) murder
(B) involuntary manslaughter
(C) voluntary manslaughter
(D) no form of criminal homicide

In this example, the answer choices are fairly straightforward as well.
Therefore, if you know the answer fairly quickly, fill in the answer and
move on to a more complex question. Sometimes you can efficiently answer these types of questions which will leave you more time for higher
difficulty questions.

2. The Complex Fact Pattern

This type of multiple-choice question involves a more complex factual hypothetical that may take you a bit longer to read and digest. Some
students can be overwhelmed by the details of these longer factual scenarios. Take your time reading the question and don't panic. The challenge of this type of question is to sort through the facts carefully and
methodically to pick out the relevant facts from the less relevant facts.
Here is an example of a complex fact pattern type of multiple-choice
question.

Homer and Purcell entered into a valid, enforceable written
contract by which Homer agreed to sell and Purcell agreed
to purchase Blackacre, which was Homer's residence. One of
the contract provisions was that after the closing Homer had
the right to remain in residence at Blackacre for up to 30
days before delivering possession to Purcell. The closing
took place as scheduled. Title passed to Purcell and Homer
remained in possession. Within a few days after the closing,
the new house next door which was being constructed for
Homer was burned to the ground, and at the end of the 30-
day period Homer refused to move out of Blackacre; instead,
Homer tendered to Purcell a monthly rental payment in ex-
cess of the fair rental value of Blackacre. Purcell rejected the
proposal and that day brought an appropriate action to gain
immediate possession of Blackacre. The contract was silent
as to the consequences of Homer's failure to give up possession within the 30-day period, and the jurisdiction in which
Blackacre is located has no statute dealing directly with this
situation, although the landlord-tenant law of the jurisdiction requires a landlord to give a tenant 30 days notice before a tenant may be evicted. Purcell did not give Homer any

such 30-day statutory notice. Purcell's best legal argument
in support of his action to gain immediate possession is that
Homer is a:

(A) trespasser ab initio
(B) licensee
(C) tenant at sufferance
(D) tenant from month to month

Note that the answer choices are fairly straightforward; the difficulty
lies completely with the factual hypothetical itself. Some law students
handle these types of multiple choice questions using the following
strategy.

First, skim the facts to get a general idea for the subject matter; second, read the call of the question first to get the focus on the question;
third, re-read the facts more carefully, actively marking key words and
phrases that relate to the legal issues; and fourth, begin going through answer choices to eliminate wrong answers and narrow in on the correct answer. Note that these types of multiple-choice questions may require a bit
more time to work through the factual hypothetical so keep that in mind
as you work through your exam.

3. The Two-Tiered Option

In this type of multiple-choice question, there is an initial factual hypothetical that is fairly straightforward. Following the hypothetical, you
will see a two-tiered option section which provides *two possibilities* that
might reasonably flow from the factual hypothetical.

Your task is to assess whether the options in either I. or II. are correct
based upon the information given in the factual hypothetical. And there
is one additional step to this type of question. After reviewing the options, you then need to go to the answer choices to evaluate the different choices. The answer choices will ask you to determine if none, either
or both options are correct.

This type of question is challenging because is adds an additional
step in your reasoning process. Therefore, although the factual hypothetical is not overly complex, the additional requirement of reasoning
through the two options (I. and II.) and *then* moving to the answer
choices can make this type of multiple-choice question challenging.
Here is an example:

On March 1, Zeller orally agreed to sell his land, Homestead,
to Byer for $46,000 to be paid on March 31. Byer orally
agreed to pay $25,000 of the purchase price to Quincy in sat-
isfaction of a debt which Zeller said he had promised to pay
Quincy. On March 10, Byer dictated the agreement to his secretary but omitted all reference to the payment of the

$25,000 to Quincy. In typing the agreement, the secretary mistakenly typed in $45,000 rather than $46,000 as the purchase price. Neither Buyer nor Zeller carefully read the writing before signing it on March 15. Neither noticed the error in price and neither raised any question concerning omission of the payment to Quincy. In an action by Quincy against Byer for $25,000, which of the following is (are) correct?

I. Byer could successfully raise the Statute of Frauds as a defense because the Byer-Zeller agreement was to answer for the debt of another.

II. Byer could successfully raise the Statute of Frauds as a defense because the Byer-Zeller agreement was for the sale of an interest in land.

(A) I only
(B) II only
(C) Both I and II
(D) Neither I nor II

Strategically, if you can determine that one of the options is definitely *wrong*, you can narrow down your answer choices immediately to eliminate any reference to that option. For example, if you determine that option I. is incorrect in the above-example, then you can eliminate answer choices (A) and (C) immediately. The challenge is to focus on the options first and then move onto evaluating the answer choices. These types of questions are very typical on law school multiple-choice exams so it is important to recognize this type of question.

4. Overlapping Answer Choices

The fourth type of multiple-choice question is the "overlapping answer choices" type of question. In this multiple-choice question type, you are presented with a simple fact pattern and you are given a series of answer choices that overlap. Therefore, the challenge inherent in these types of questions is to reason through the overlapping answer choices. Typically, the answer choices will ask you to decide between two different possibilities, one possibility or neither option. Here is an example:

Defendant was tried for robbery. Victim and Worth were the only witnesses called to testify. Victim testified that Defendant threatened her with a knife, grabbed her purse, and ran off with it. Worth testified that he saw Defendant grab Victim's purse and run way with it but that he neither saw a knife nor heard any threats. On this evidence the jury could properly return a verdict of guilty of:

(A) robbery only
(B) larceny only
(C) neither robbery or larceny
(D) both robbery and larceny

One good thing about this type of multiple-choice question is that you are being asked to assess *only* two options. Therefore, you will focus your analytical process on whether the answer is both options, one option, or possibly neither option. Typically, you can eliminate at least two of the answer choices very quickly which will allow you to focus on the answer choices if you must choose quickly.

5. The Question Series

Finally, there is a fifth type of multiple-choice question called the question series. Like its name implies, the question series multiple choice question begins with an initial factual hypothetical that will apply to more than one multiple-choice question. In one sense, this is an economical type of question; you can read through the initial hypothetical and apply the factual scenario to more than one question. One key to answering this type of multiple-choice question is to read the initial hypothetical very carefully and write out notes in the margin so you can refer back to key issues quickly without re-reading the facts. Here is an example of a question series.

Questions 53-55 are based on the following fact situation.

Harry met Bill, who was known to him to be a burglar, in a bar. Harry told Bill that he needed money. He promised to pay Bill $500 if Bill would go to Harry's house the following night and take some silverware. Harry explained to Bill that, although the silverware was legally his, his wife would object to his selling it.

Harry pointed out his home, one of a group of similar tract houses. He drew a floor plan of the house that showed the location of the silverware. Harry said that his wife usually took several sleeping pills before retiring, and that he would make sure that she took them the next night. He promised to leave a window unlocked. Everything went according to the plan except that Bill, deceived by the similarity of the tract houses, went to the wrong house. He found a window unlocked, climbed in and found silver where Harry had indicated. He took the silver to the cocktail lounge where the payoff was to take place. At that point the police arrested the two men.

53. If Harry were charged with burglary, his best argument for acquittal would be that:

(A) there was no breaking
(B) he consented to the entry
(C) no overt act was committed by him
(D) there was no intent to commit a felony

54. Bill's best argument for acquittal of burglary is that he:

(A) acted under a mistake of law
(B) had the consent of the owner
(C) reasonably thought he was in Harry's house
(D) found the window unlocked

The question series is a fairly common type of multiple-choice question on a law school exam. Keep in mind, however, that the question that follows the initial factual hypothetical may add *additional* facts for you to consider. Therefore, you will need to apply the facts from the initial hypothetical to any additional facts given to you in the separate question. Finally, if you find yourself running out of time on your exam, you may want to look for this type of question. It may be possible for you to move through a question series more quickly.

C. What Are the Different "Calls" to a Law School Multiple-Choice Question?

In the last section, we examined the different types or *forms* of multiple-choice questions. In this subsection, we will consider the most typical question stems or calls of the question. In other words, there are four typical tasks that a law school multiple-choice question will ask you to complete. Becoming familiar with each of these tasks may help you move faster through your multiple-choice exam.

A multiple-choice question will typically ask you for one of the following: (1) the "one correct answer;" (2) the "one incorrect answer;" (3) the "best answer" (relative to the choices given); and (4) the "best reasoning" (among the choices given). This subsection will give a short explanation of each type of question call or task.[9]

1. One Correct Answer

In this type of question, only one of the answer choices is correct and it is *absolutely correct*. The remaining options are incorrect. Your job is either to locate the correct answer immediately (because you know that

---

9. Adapted from Josephson, *supra* n.6, at 355–366.

it is clearly the correct answer) or to eliminate the answers you know are incorrect. The exact language used in the call of the question may vary somewhat, e.g., see the two examples below, but these types of multiple-choice questions always ask you to find the one correct answer. Consider using the following strategy with this type of question. As you read each answer choice, think of the answer choice as a true/false question. Thus, you can derive the correct answer either by knowing it when you see it or by the process of elimination (i.e., eliminating answers you know are incorrect). In the following examples, I have highlighted the call of each question as it represents the one correct answer variety.

Example 1:

Which of the following statements is most accurate?

(A) Payment of Daniel of the $100 was a condition precedent to Paul's duty of performance.
(B) The performances of Paul and Daniel under the contract were concurrently conditional.
(C) Payment by Daniel of the $100 was a condition subsequent to Paul's duty of performance.
(D) Performance by Paul under the contract was a condition precedent to Daniel's duty of payment of the $100.

Example 2:

In a collision case, Plaintiff offers in evidence a photograph showing the scene of the accident while the cars were still in place. **A proper foundation must include, as a minimum, testimony by which of the following?**

(A) The photographer
(B) A person who was present at the time the photograph was taken.
(C) A person who observed the cars while they were still in place.
(D) A person in whose custody the photograph has been since it was developed.

2. One Incorrect Answer

The second type of question stem or call of the question involves a variation of the single correct answer but it is the negative form of the question. The one incorrect answer stem asks you to pick out the one incorrect answer from a set of options. The remaining options, the distractors, are all correct statements. Like the strategy described above for the one correct answer question type, you can use a process of elimination to narrow down your answer choices. The only difference: eliminate the *true* statements and select the *false* statement. In the following two examples, I have highlighted the call of the question that illustrates the one incorrect answer format.

Example 1:

Which of the following crimes is **LEAST likely** to result in a felony murder conviction if the victim dies during the perpetration of the crime?

(A) rape
(B) robbery
(C) larceny
(D) kidnapping

Example 2:

Which of the following statements regarding the legal effect of Daniel's illness is **LEAST accurate**?

(A) Daniel's illness and the related development excused Paul from his obligation to deliver the cards on or before December 15.
(B) Prompt notice by Daniel to Paul of Daniel's recovery from illness was an implied condition of Paul's duty under the circumstances.
(C) Paul was under a duty of immediate performance of his promise to deliver the cards, as of December 15, by reason of the express language of the contract and despite the illness of Daniel and the related developments.
(D) Daniel's conduct after his illness constituted a waiver of the necessity of Paul's performing on or before December 15.

3. One Best Answer

The third variety is the one best answer question stem, which is also the most common multiple-choice question because it provides law professors with the most flexibility in creating subtle differences between answer choices. In other words, law professors can make the answer choices sound very similar and it's up to the student to determine which answer choice is the best answer.

Thus, this question stem or call tests a student's relative judgments and does not require the law professor to draft answer choices that are absolutely true/correct or false/incorrect. Instead, this form allows for a wide variety of question types which can test students' understanding in several different ways. Consider the following list of possible question stems within this category of one best answer.

a. Which is the **best, more likely or most probable** result?

b. What is the **best reasoning** supporting a stated result?

c. What is the **best argument** supporting a particular position or party?

d. What is the **best defense** under these circumstances?

e. What is the **best cause of action** that applies to the fact pattern?

f. Which facts will **most help** a particular party advocate for a particular argument/position?

Consider the following two examples of this variety of question stem.

Example 1:

Roofer entered into a written contract with Orissa to repair the roof of Orissa's home, the repairs to be done "in a workmanlike manner." Roofer completed the repairs and took all of his equipment away, with the exception of a 20-foot extension ladder, which was left against the side of the house. He intended to come back and get the ladder the next morning. At that time, Orissa and her family were away on a trip. During the night, a thief, using the ladder to gain access to an upstairs window, entered the house and stole some valuable jewels. Orissa has asserted a claim against Roofer for damages for the loss of the jewels. **In her claim against Roofer, Orissa will**

(A) prevail, because by leaving the ladder Roofer became a trespasser on Orissa's property.
(B) prevail, because by leaving the ladder Roofer created the risk that a person might unlawfully enter the house.
(C) not prevail, because the act of the thief was a superseding cause.
(D) not prevail, because Orissa's claim is limited to damages for breach of contract.

Example 2:

The State of Rio Grande entered into a contract with roads, Inc., for construction of a four-lane turn-pike. Prior to commencement of construction, the legislature, in order to provide funds for parks, repealed the statute authorizing the turnpike and cancelled the agreement with Roads, Inc. Roads, Inc., sued the state to enforce its original agreement. **In ruling on this case, a court should hold that the state statute canceling the agreement is:**

(A) Valid, because constitutionally the sovereign is not liable except with its own consent.
(B) Valid, because the legislature is vested with constitutional authority to repeal laws it has enacted.
(C) Invalid, because a state is equitably estopped to disclaim a bid once accepted by it.
(D) Invalid, because of the constitutional prohibition against impairment of contracts.

These types of questions tend to be fairly challenging on a law school exam because students are required to read through each answer choice to evaluate both the stated *conclusion* in the first part of the answer and the *reasoning* which lead to that conclusion in the second part of the answer choice. So, in the above example, a student must first determine whether the court's decision is either valid or invalid; and second, the student must analyze the reasons justifying the end result. These types of questions tend to take more time because students need to read the answer choices very carefully.

4. Best Reasoning Supporting a Stated Position

The fourth and final type of question stem asks the student to analyze the best reasoning for a particular position or conclusion. Once again, like the one best answer variety described in (3) above, the best reasoning question can be equally time-consuming because it requires you to evaluate the reasoning of each answer choice. Consider the following two examples of the best reasoning variety:

Example 1:

> Tess occupied an apartment in a building owned by Len. She paid rent of $125 in advance each month. During the second month of occupancy, Tess organized the tenants in the building as a tenants' association and the association made demands of Len concerning certain repairs and improvements the tenants wanted. When Tess tendered rent for the third month, Len notified her that rent for the fourth and subsequent months would be $200 per month. Tess protested and pointed out that all other tenants paid rent of $125 per month. Thereupon, Len gave the required statutory notice that the tenancy was being terminated at the end of the third month. By an appropriate proceeding, Tess contests Len's right to terminate. **If Tess succeeds, it will be because:**

(A) a periodic tenancy was created by implication.
(B) the doctrine prohibiting retaliatory eviction is part of the law of the jurisdiction.
(C) the $200 rent demanded violates the agreement implied by the rate charged to other tenants.
(D) the law implies a term of one year in the absence of any express agreement.

Example 2:

The State of Missoula has enacted a new election code designed to increase voter responsibility in the exercise of the franchise and to enlarge citizen participation in the electoral process. None of its provisions conflicts with federal statutes.

Which of the following is the strongest reason for finding unconstitutional a requirement in the Missoula election code that each other must be literate in English?

(A) The requirement violates Article I Section 2 of the Constitution, which provides that representatives to Congress be chosen "by the People of the several States."
(B) The requirement violates Article I, Section 4 of the Constitution, which gives Congress the Power to "make or later" state regulations providing for the "Times" and "Manner" of holding elections for senators and representatives.
(C) The requirement violates the due process clause of the Fourteenth Amendment.
(D) The requirement violates the equal protection of the laws clause of the Fourteenth Amendment.

For this type of question, try to eliminate wrong conclusions quickly. This will eliminate at least two answer choices. Then work to analyze the reasoning and determine which answer choice contains the most thorough and accurate reasons for the stated result.

C. Pay Attention to the Role That the Question Asks You to Play

In addition to the different forms of multiple-choice question types (and the different varieties of question stems), you should also pay attention to the role that the question asks you to play.[10] You may be asked to assume a certain role in the call of the question. Typically, you will be asked to assume one of three roles: a judge; a lawyer (or advocate); or a scholar (or policy-maker). You may answer the question differently depending

---

10. *See* Professor Lasso, *supra* n.3, at 4.

on the role to which you've been assigned. If you learn to recognize these different roles, you can use your role to eliminate wrong answer choices quickly.

1. The Judge[11]

One common role that a multiple-choice question will ask you to assume is that of a judge. Many multiple-choice questions use this type of format. For example, consider the following question stem: "If John sues Mary for battery, **the court should** find in favor of ..." Once you recognize this type of question, you want to make sure to begin your analysis with no particular result or conclusion in mind. A judge will be open to both sides of any argument. Second, try not to decide questions of fact (in the answer choice) because judges focus on questions of law. In addition, be alert for misstatements about facts in lawyers' arguments. As a judge, you want to wait to resolve any issue until you have considered all the arguments presented in the answer choices. Examine each option in turn. Ask yourself whether the facts and law are accurately stated. Is the conclusion offered consistent with the argument advanced? The correct option is the one where the argument advanced is based on *accurate* statements of fact and law, and is consistent with the conclusion offered. Select such an answer choice even though you may not personally agree with the result.

2. The Lawyer[12]

You may be asked to assume the role of a lawyer or advocate. The following example illustrates this type of multiple-choice question: "Which of the following is the most effective argument in favor of Mary's position?" For these types of questions, make sure to examine each answer choice in turn. Is the law accurately stated? Are the inferences on which the answer choice is based supported by the facts given? Could the argument result in victory for the client? The correct option is the one where the argument advanced is based on accurate statements of fact and law and is consistent with the conclusion offered. Once again, select that answer even if you don't really believe that your client can win.

3. The Scholar[13]

You may also be asked to assume the role of a scholar or academic, i.e., someone who considers the policy of the law more than its applica-

---

11. *Id.*
12. *Id.*
13. *Id.*

tion. Here is an example: "The interest in Blackacre which John had on the day after Testatrix's death is best described as a …"

In answering these types of multiple-choice question, try to refrain from determining or trying to determine the actual outcome of the factual hypothetical. Use your knowledge of the law to recognize the legal significance of a particular fact or to select the most applicable rule. Try to focus on the specific and limited issue that you're being asked to consider. Resolve the issue in your own mind first, and then examine each of the options carefully and select the one which comes closest to the selection you have already formulated. And once again, select the answer even if you don't really believe it's the best or just result.

D. Answer Choices: Recognizing Distractors[14]

One key skill in taking multiple-choice exams is to eliminate wrong answer choices or distractors. Consider that three out of the four answer choices in *every* multiple-choice question will be a wrong answer. A wrong answer or distractor is an answer that initially may seem correct but either ends up having faulty reasoning or the answer choice is incorrect but it uses the correct *reasoning*. Law professors want to test your knowledge and analytical abilities with multiple-choice questions but they do not want to be too obvious with the correct answer. Therefore, several of the answer choices will look correct on a superficial level. Your goal is to read each answer choice carefully so you can eliminate distractors as you move through the answer choices. All of the answer choices are designed to give a look of plausibility. Therefore, you must read them carefully!

Here are some potential pitfalls as they relate specifically to *distractors* in a multiple-choice context and some suggested approaches to deal with them.[15]

1. Watch Out For Incomplete Definitions and Arguments[16]

Sometimes an answer choice or a definition will seem correct superficially but it actually contains an incomplete definition. Don't accidentally add in the remaining definitional components or arguments to the answer choice. Focus on the text given. Here's an example. Assume that the answer choice states: "Murder is the unjustified killing of a human being." Although there doesn't seem to be anything wrong with this definition, it is likely an incorrect answer choice. The full definition of murder is as

---

14. *See* Lasso, *supra* n.3 at 2–4; *see also*, Josephson, *supra* n.6 at 350.
15. *Id.* at 3.
16. *Id.*

follows: "Murder is the unjustified killing of a human being _with malice aforethought_."

Try not to complete the definition or argument in your mind and conclude mistakenly that an incomplete answer choice is correct.

2. Deal Only with the Facts Given: Don't Add Facts and Don't Ignore Facts![17]

In examining answer choices, you want to assume _nothing_ in addition to what has been established or given in the answer choice. For example, if the question states: "The Prosecutor proves that John shot Mary and that Mary died an hour later. Is John guilty of murder?" The answer is likely, "No." You must also prove that John's bullet _caused_ Mary's death. The facts, as given, may not demonstrate murder.

In addition, don't _ignore_ facts either. Typically, you will find facts in an answer choice for a particular reason. For example, you may have been taught in criminal law that an intoxicated person cannot usually drive a car in a reasonable manner. Assume that the factual hypothetical states that "although Mary drank two quarts of whiskey, she was driving her car in a reasonable manner when she collided with Paul." The call of the question asks: "Was Mary negligent?" Mary is not negligent. Negligence is _unreasonable_ conduct. Since the facts tell you that Mary was driving her car in a _reasonable_ manner, you must conclude that she was not negligent.

3. Don't Overlook the Obvious[18]

Sometimes the answer choice is so obviously correct that there is no rational excuse for missing it. Don't ignore an obviously correct answer. Remember that some of the questions on the exam will be easier than others.

4. Watch Out For Unfamiliar Phrases[19]

As you've no doubt learned in law school, there are many legal phrases to learn. But be careful of an answer choice that seems to suggest a familiar but slightly 'off' legal theory. For example, on a property exam, the following characterization is incorrect despite the fact that it uses a legal phrase: "A plaintiff could not be the holder of a certain easement because "an incorporeal hereditament lies only in grant." If you've never heard of a doctrine or a rule then the answer is probably incorrect. Note also

---

17. _Id._
18. _Id._
19. _Id._ at 4.

that you might encounter answer choices that describe familiar concepts in non-traditional words. For example, instead of saying: "John owed Mary a duty of reasonable care only if he created a foreseeable risk to her," a correct option would say: "John had no obligation to Mary unless it appeared that John's conduct would injure her." Remember that *substance is more important than form.*

In summary, as you skim through answer choices on your multiple-choice exam, make sure to keep in mind the following rules: (1) watch out for incomplete definitions or reasoning; (2) deal with only the facts given; (3) don't overlook the obvious answer; and (4) be wary of unfamiliar language or phrases.

E. Final Strategies to Enhance Your Performance on the Law School Multiple-Choice Exams

This final sub-section will address some specific strategies for taking multiple-choice exams. Although you will know the material in your course well, you may experience other issues that affect your exam performance. Perhaps you have test-anxiety or time management issues that prevent you from illustrating your true understanding of a subject. Or perhaps you are a slower reader and struggle to make it through the factual hypotheticals. I've had many students over the years that have scored perfectly on the essay portion of my exam but did poorly on the multiple-choice section of the exam. I know these students worked very hard in the course and that they knew the material. But something about the multiple-choice questions tripped them up. When I talk with students about their exam performance, they often state: "I'm just bad at multiple-choice exams!" I respond: "You may feel that way, but you need to figure out how to get better at them because you will see these type of exams throughout law school and on the bar exam."

For students who have trouble with multiple-choice questions, I try to encourage them to go on a 'multiple-choice' diet. I recommend that they work on multiple-choice questions at least one hour per week (beginning the second or third week of the semester) per course. The reality of the situation is this: if you have difficulty with multiple-choice questions, you may need to spend some additional time teaching yourself *how* to take these types of exams. Although you may struggle *more* with multiple-choice exams than essay exams, you *can* get better at taking them.

For law students who learn differently, one of the biggest roadblocks with regard to multiple-choice exams is time management. On the bar exam, you will have only about 2 minutes per multiple choice question. In this type of 'timed' test, you need to become *so* comfortable with the types and format of the questions that you can read through the questions and answer choices efficiently. So—decide to put yourself on a 'multiple-choice diet' and commit yourself to improving your comfort level the types of questions in a law school multiple-choice exam.

The remainder of this section offers ten strategies for practicing and taking multiple-choice exams. Try to integrate these strategies into your practice sessions as much as possible and then you will internalize the strategies before the exam.

1. Control Your Test-Anxiety (As Much as Possible)

We all get nervous when taking exams. For any law student, the pressure of doing well on an exam that counts for 50% to 100% of your entire course grade is enormous. But for those law students who learn differently, you may have different or additional pressures with regard to taking exams. It is particularly important for you to control your test-anxiety as much as possible. Panicking will inhibit your memory and make it impossible to read and comprehend the questions.[20] One way to control your test anxiety is by being as prepared as possible. Another way to control your test anxiety is by simulating the exam experience as much as possible before the exam. This means you need to begin 'practicing' taking the exam early and often during the semester. Try to obtain some past bar exams questions, commercially-prepared multiple-choice questions, and/or prior multiple-choice questions from the professor teaching your class. It's not enough that you know the rules or the law. You must train yourself to analyze the fact patterns and answer choices of multiple-choice questions carefully and efficiently. The more comfortable you are with the different types and forms of multiple-choice questions (in addition to knowing the substance of your course), the less anxious you will be on your exam.

2. Spaced Practice Is Better Than All-at-Once Practice

Research has shown that spaced practice is generally superior to 'massed' practice, i.e., practicing for fewer but longer sessions. For example, if you have only one remaining day to study for your Torts exam, you'll get more mileage out of several 2-hour blocks of time than studying for 12 hours

---

20. Test anxiety can have a significant effect on one's performance. *See* Keith A. Kaufman, V. Holland LaSalle-Ricci, Carol R. Glass, Diane B. Arnkoff, *Passing the Bar Exam: Psychological, Educational, and Demographic Predictors of Success*, 57 J. LEGAL EDUC. 205, 207 (2007). In studying how test anxiety affects performance on the bar exam, Kaufman states, "Test anxiety, for example, is characterized by the disposition to react with intrusive thoughts, mental disorganization, tension, and physiological arousal when exposed to evaluative situations." *Id.*

straight. Cramming is a recipe for poor retention, mental and physical fatigue, and test anxiety. Try your best to schedule how and when you will study for your multiple-choice exams. Plan to spend one to two hours per week simply working on multiple-choice questions in each of your courses. Doing a little bit each week will relieve some of your stress about multiple-choice exams because you are *doing* something early on in the semester to become *better* at taking this type of exam. The reality is that you the more you practice any skill—the better you become at it. And this holds true for taking multiple-choice exams as well!

3. Budget Your Time For Each Test Question and Stick to It!

You will often know ahead of time how many multiple-choice questions will be on your exam. For example, I will often give students 25 multiple-choice questions in a one hour period. Therefore, students know that they have between two and three minutes per multiple-choice question for that section of the exam. On easier questions, try to stick to the two minute mark. On more difficult questions, you may need three minutes or more to answer the question. As much as you can, try to stay within that average of two to three minutes per question. Remind yourself to check your progress every five questions or so (no more than 15 minutes should have passed). If you run across a question where you have no idea how to answer it, try not to waste valuable time. You could be using that time answering questions in which you *do* know the answers. If you're stuck, choose your best guess and move on.

4. Develop a Plan for Attacking the Factual Hypothetical of Each Question

As you practice, you will get a sense about the way that you like to approach multiple choice questions. For example, some students like to skim the facts of the hypothetical first. Next, they read the 'call' of the question. Then they go back and read the factual hypothetical again in detail—circling the key phrases and issues. Or perhaps you are a visual learner. You may want to draw a diagram or picture of the facts on the margin of your exam. When you develop an approach that you can use throughout the exam, you will feel more comfortable with taking the exams. Another tip for dealing with factual hypotheticals includes focusing *only* on the facts given. For example, in a breach of contract case, if someone was talking on the telephone— this may be an important fact. Circle it. In addition, try to use the simple interpretation of the facts—do not make them more complex than they are. Pay attention to your instincts. And pay special attention to seemingly meaningless details—it's possible they are in the fact pattern for a reason.

5. Reword the Call of the Question

Sometimes rewording the call of the question can be very helpful. This allows you to rewrite the task of the question so you understand more clearly what the question is asking you to do. This may be particularly helpful as you work through your practice exams. Consider the following examples:

Actual Question Call	Revised Call
What is the most likely outcome?	What is the result and why?
Which claim is most likely to succeed?	Which is the only claim that can succeed on these facts and why?
What is the defendant's best defense?	Why won't the defendant be guilty on these facts?
If party X loses, the most likely basis	Party X lost because …

You probably won't have time to re-write all the question calls but you may choose to use this strategy if you run across a call that is particularly confusing to you.

6. IRAC Your Answer Before Looking at the Choices

After reading through the factual hypothetical, consider doing a quick IRAC of the factual hypothetical before you go through the answer choices. This is the same process that you'd use in an essay exam. The idea behind this suggestion is that doing an IRAC *before* looking at the answers will help you solidify your reasoning. In addition, it may prevent you from being seduced by a distractor because you have already thought through a possible answer. It's good to get a gut sense of the correct answer before you look at the different options.

7. Eliminate Incorrect Responses

In a perfect world, the correct answer to the multiple-choice question would simply jump out at you. However, law school is *not* a perfect world! Therefore, the best (and sometimes only) way to arrive at the correct answer to some multiple-choice questions is to use a process of elimination. Go through the answer choices of the three questions you believe are wrong and determine specifically *why* the answers are wrong. Hopefully, you can eliminate incorrect answers. Read very carefully. Check the *reasoning* of each option. If the reasoning is not correct then the answer cannot be correct. How are options likely wrong? An answer choice is likely wrong if it mischaracterizes the facts; misstates the law; or ignores a central issue. If an answer choice does *any* one of these three things, you can eliminate the answer choice and move on.

8. Choosing Between Two Possible Answers

Many students tell me that when answering a multiple-choice question, they can usually narrow down the answer choices to two likely possibilities. How do you choose? Sometimes answers can both be *technically* correct but one answer is a *better* answer choice. Note that an answer ultimately can be the wrong choice even though it's factually and legally correct; but it may not be as precise or effective as another option. For example, an option that is easier to prove is more likely to be correct than an option that is difficult to prove. A more precise answer is better than a less precise answer. Also double-check the reasoning of the choices: does one overstate the requirements of the law or cite rules that do not apply? Does another option assume a particular fact is true when it is actually in dispute?

9. Okay, Sometimes You Gotta Guess!

Let's face it. Between time constraints and anxiety, you may have to guess at some questions. Try to eliminate wrong answers. Then go through your remaining choices. Be wary of answer choices that have language of certainty, i.e., "always," "never," "cannot," "must." Be wary of answer choices that focus on the results. Be wary of answer choices of theories or doctrines that seem unfamiliar to you. If two answers are opposites, one is probably true. Remember that some questions test your knowledge of rules; but others test your knowledge of exceptions. Don't waste too much time. If you don't know, guess. Then come back ONLY if you have time. If you waste too much time guessing, you may be missing points on questions where you DO know the answer.

10. Final Tips:

Don't skip questions without filling in an answer choice. You might forget to come back. Write on your exam — note facts, issues, rules. Make the fact patterns visual; create flow charts to match your learning style. Do not let one question influence your answer on the next question. And remember to breathe. You have studied hard and you can reason through the questions to get to the correct result.

Multiple-choice questions are indeed difficult in law school. However, with diligence and practice, you can become more proficient at taking these types of exams. Get as many example exams and/or questions as you can and begin practicing now. You can succeed in law school!

Conclusion

Law school will be one of the most challenging experiences of your life—regardless of how you learn! But if you learn differently, law school may be particularly challenging—at least initially. The key to success, however, is to believe in yourself and to maximize your potential. Everyone has unique gifts—the key is to use your gifts to your advantage and to limit your weaknesses to the extent possible. I hope that this book has given you some helpful advice about how to approach law school learning, studying and test-taking. Now the rest is up to you—but you *can* do it! Good luck!

Appendix A

In the Matter of Thonert

This is the full text of the opinion used in the reading studies described in Chapters 5 and 6.

In the Matter of Richard J. THONERT
No. 02S00-9902-DI-151.
Supreme Court of Indiana, Aug. 22, 2000.

Richard J. Thonert, Respondent pro se.

Donald R. Lundberg, Executive Secretary, Dennis K. McKinney, Staff Attorney, Indianapolis, IN, for the Indiana Supreme Court Disciplinary Commission.

PER CURIAM.

The respondent in this attorney disciplinary matter is charged with failing to disclose to an appellate tribunal controlling authority known to him, not disclosed by opposing counsel, that was directly adverse to his client's position. He also failed to advise his client of the adverse authority when his client was contemplating his legal options.

This matter is presented to this Court upon the Disciplinary Commission's and the respondent's *Statement of Circumstances and Conditional Agreement for Discipline,* entered pursuant to Ind.Admission and Discipline Rule 23(11)(c), in resolution of this matter. That agreement is before us now for approval. We note that our jurisdiction of this matter derives from the respondent's admission to the practice of law in this state in 1974.

The parties agree that the respondent represented a client charged with operating a motor vehicle while intoxicated. Prior to the client's initial hearing and before the client met with or hired the respondent, the client was advised by videotape of his rights. He pleaded guilty to the charge, and the matter was set for sentencing hearing. Prior to that hearing, the client met with the respondent to discuss the possibility of withdrawing his guilty plea. During their meeting, the respondent told the client of another criminal case, *Snowe v. State,* 533 N.E.2d 613 (Ind.Ct.App.1989), in which the respondent had prevailed on appeal for the defendant. He provided a copy of the Indiana Court of Appeals decision to his new client. The respondent agreed to represent the client for $5,000, which the client paid.

Snowe also involved a prerecorded videotaped televised advisement of rights, but the record in that case failed to indicate whether the defendant had ever viewed the tape advising him of his rights. Further, the opinion held that a trial court judge cannot rely solely on displaying a videotape advisement of rights, but instead must also determine whether the defendant knows of and understands his rights, the nature of the charge or charges against him, the full import of the rights waiver in his guilty plea, and the sentencing possibilities for the charges against him. *Snowe*, 533 N.E.2d at 617.

At the client's initial hearing, it was established that he had viewed the videotape, that the videotape advised him of his rights and the sentencing possibilities under the charges filed against him, that he understood the charge against him and his rights as explained in the videotape, and that he voluntarily waived those rights and pleaded guilty.

On May 30, 1996, the respondent entered an appearance on behalf of the client and filed a motion to withdraw the guilty plea. The trial court denied the motion without hearing. The respondent appealed that ruling, alleging that his client had a right to withdraw the plea because, due to the absence of counsel at the time he entered it and the fact that the record did not reflect that the trial court properly examined the client as to waiver of his rights, the client had not made it knowingly, intelligently, or voluntarily. The respondent further argued that the client had a right to a hearing on his motion to withdraw the plea.

The respondent represented the defendant in *Fletcher v. State*, 649 N.E.2d 1022 (Ind.1995). In that case, this Court addressed the questions that the respondent raised in his client's case. The ruling in *Fletcher* was adverse to the arguments that the respondent offered on appeal of his client's case.[1] The respondent had served as counsel of record for defendant Fletcher in the appeal before this Court. This Court's ruling in *Fletcher* was issued on May 1, 1995, over one year before the respondent filed his appeal on behalf of the client. In his appellate brief filed on behalf of the client, the respondent failed to cite to *Fletcher* or argue that its holding was not controlling authority in the client's case. The respondent also failed to argue that the holding in *Fletcher* should be changed or extended. Although he advised his client of the *Snowe* case, he failed to advise him of *Fletcher* or explain any impact *Fletcher* might have on his case. Opposing counsel had not previously disclosed *Fletcher* to the Court of Appeals.

Indiana Professional Conduct Rule 3.3(a)(3) provides that a lawyer shall not knowingly fail to disclose to a tribunal legal authority in the

---

1. In *Fletcher*, we noted, "The defendant's admission during the initial hearing that he had seen and understood his rights contradicts his subsequent claim that his plea was unknowing and involuntary...." *Id.* at 1023. As to the right to a hearing on a motion to withdraw a plea, the opinion provides that, "[c]onvening a hearing is merely a discretionary option of the trial court." *Id.*

controlling jurisdiction known to the lawyer to be directly adverse to the position of the client and not disclosed by opposing counsel. The concept underlying this requirement of disclosure is that legal argument is a discussion seeking to determine the legal premises properly applicable to the case. *Comment* to Ind.Professional Conduct Rule 3.3. The respondent's intimate familiarity with *Fletcher* is established by his having served as counsel to the defendant. Accordingly, we find that the respondent violated the rule by failing to disclose *Fletcher* to the Court of Appeals in his legal arguments on behalf of the client.

Professional Conduct Rule 1.4(b) provides that a lawyer shall explain a matter to the extent reasonably necessary to permit a client to make informed decisions regarding a representation. A client should have sufficient information to participate intelligently in decisions concerning the objectives of the representation. *Comment* to Prof.Cond.R. 1.4. By failing to advise his client of a ruling in the controlling jurisdiction that was adverse to the legal arguments contemplated for his client's case on appeal, and instead choosing only to advise the client of an earlier appellate decision favorable to his position, the respondent effectively divested his client of the opportunity to assess intelligently the legal environment in which his case would be argued and to make informed decisions regarding whether to go forward with it. Accordingly, we find that the respondent violated Prof.Cond.R. 1.4(b).

The parties agree that the respondent should be publicly reprimanded for his misconduct. We agree that a public admonishment is appropriate in this case, given the negative impact on the efficient resolution of the client's appeal occasioned by the respondent's lack of disclosure and its attendant deception of the client as to the viability of any efforts to withdraw the guilty plea. Accordingly, we accept the parties' agreement and the discipline called for therein.

It is, therefore, ordered that the respondent, Richard J. Thonert, is hereby reprimanded and admonished for his violations of Prof.Cond.R. 3.3(a)(3) and 1.4(b).

The Clerk of this Court is directed to provide notice of this order in accordance with Admis.Disc.R. 23(3)(d) and to provide the clerk of the United States Court of Appeals for the Seventh Circuit, the clerk of each of the United States District Courts in this state, and the clerks of the United States Bankruptcy Courts in this state with the last known address of respondent as reflected in the records of the Clerk.

Costs are assessed against respondent.

Appendix B

Advocacy Template

This is an example of another way to case brief, called the Advocacy Template.[1] By considering the story that came *before* the legal confrontation, you have the opportunity to examine the roles the attorneys play as the dispute evolves. In addition to the structural elements of a traditional case brief, the Advocacy Case Brief takes you to a new level: it allows you to explore the human drama of a case while applying "the law" at the same time. Consider the Advocacy Template for a possible way to enhance your case briefing in law school.

ADVOCACY TEMPLATE ONE		
For Holographic Examination of _____ (case caption).		Casebook page _____.
Citation (optional) _____ Decided _____ (date) By _____ (student).		
Context Boxes	Each box of questions give you a reason for finding succinct answers in the relevant segment of the judicial opinion. By having a reason for your reading of this complex material, your answers will provide an understanding for examining how the actors in the human story morphed this into the legal story.	**Notes & Questions**
HUMAN INTEREST FACTS: **Operational** **5 Ws & an H**	In trial court, which label from this doctrine fits π/Δ at the time of the contract, transaction or event? (e.g. Landlord/tenant) Who did What to Whom, Where, When and Why? How did this conflict ripen into litigation? [diagram or chart events; or write as a very brief narrative]	

Template continues on next page

---

1. J.J. Brown, supra note __ at ____.

Resurrect the WHOLE STORY when assigned to role play as a simulation.	There is a many dimensioned human drama (a story of conflict) behind this appellate decision. It precipitated the client's seeking help or desiring to go to court. What facts do you think are missing that would fill out details about the dispute? Make and write your best estimate from the printed facts in the majority and dissenting opinions. Re-create that drama as you envision it. Write a hypothetical scenario starting with each layperson's statements or actions to each other or to their attorneys (i.e., fictional dialogue that highlights the incident or transaction on which there was disagreement and/or dispute). If you are called upon to role-play as one of the parties, you may use incidents and personalities from your own life experiences to fill out details of your story. Consider using events from the Supplemental Context.	
Supplemental Context	What was occurring around the same time these facts were developing? Cite to extra-legal facts: biographical (e.g. parties, family of significance, the Judge) geographical (what city, state, or part of country; any map as to location, what about the neighborhood?) historical, political (local or nat'l), social, economic, financial.	
Core of Conflict	What thing-fact-condition-attitude is keeping the parties at odds? Strip away the fine details of this story; write 1–2 sentences which describe the essential tension in this dispute. If it's a quarrel, was it caused by a personal insult, an undermined ego, or an injustice? If a business dispute, was it about a financial loss, a contract term/price, or an act or omission?	
Cause of Action & Remedy	What is π's legal action and remedy? Injunction, Replevin, Specific Performance, Trespass, Declaratory Judgment, Damages, Rescission, Reformation, Partition, Quiet Title, or _____?	
Judicial	Trial court was located at ____ and π/Δ (circle one) prevailed? π/Δ appealed to _____ (court jurisd. & name) where π/Δ prevailed? π/Δ appealed to the _____ (jurisd. & name) where π/Δ prevailed? Who authored this last appellate decision? How long do you estimate the parties spent on these court phases?	

Note how the template is divided into a series of context boxes which contain different questions for you to consider. The boxes will help you make sense out of the complexity of any opinion. Working through this process gets easier and faster the more it is applied.

For example, the **Human Interest** story asks you to think about the human element that is often hidden within the appellate decision. You are also asked to consider the basic information, the **Operational Facts**. This section simply asks you to answer the Who, What, Why, When and Where questions typically used by good journalists.

The next box asks you to consider the **Supplemental Context** of the case. You are no doubt already proficient at online research, so this will allow you to find information about the parties and dispute in the case. This helps you place the case into a context that makes sense for you. What was occurring around the same time these facts were coalescing into the story?

The **Cause of Action** and the **Judicial** stages boxes are straightforward. The **Doctrine** content box asks you to look for and place the case's ruling into the body of doctrine within that section of the casebook that you are studying. It forces you to consider how this case fits into the larger legal doctrine that you are studying. Further, this box helps you realize that that substantive doctrines and principles cannot be understood from one or two judicial opinions.

Next, before you can truly analyze precedent, they should identify the **Benchmark** traditional rule that would solve the typical conflict of this type. You must understand the underlying rule before you can fully appreciate how it is altered by the final decision you are reading. This knowledge then allows you to consider the next two parts of the brief: Common Law Precedent and New Rule Emerging.

Appendix C

Sample Psychoeducational Evaluation

Brenda M. Peterson, Ph.D.

Name: Sam Sample
Date of Birth: 5-23-83
Age: 24
Testing Dates: 7-15, 7-17 and 7-25, 2009
Date of Report: 8-1-09

PRIMARY REFERRAL CONCERNS

Sam is a 24 year old male who has just completed his first year of law school at Baxter Law. He reported that his first year of law school did not go well and that he is in the bottom third of his class. According to Sam, his grades do not reflect his ability and understanding. He reported that there is a significant difference between what he knows and how he tests. Sam explained that he has trouble organizing his thoughts on timed tests. In addition, he miswrites words and misspells words frequently. He believes that his work on timed tests is disorganized. In comparison, Sam seems to do well in writing classes where he had more time to edit his work and improve his structure and organization. Sam also reports that it takes him a very long time to read the material as he must reread the material several times to retain it. In order to learn the material effectively, Sam takes notes as he reads and uses index cards. Sam has never been tested for learning disabilities or attention deficit disorder in the past and has never received accommodations in school. This summer, Sam is working as a law clerk in a civil litigation firm.

Before entering law school, Sam worked as a paralegal in the legal department of a law firm.

BACKGROUND INFORMATION

Developmental/Family: Sam was the product of a full-term pregnancy with no significant complications during the pregnancy or the delivery. Sam's development proceeded normally, and there are no developmental delays reported that would impair Sam's academic progress. There is a family history for the presence of learning disorders and ADHD on the maternal side, with Sam's uncle and grandfather both displaying symptoms of short attention span and learning difficulties in the area of reading. Sam's uncle has self-medicated with drug use and dropped out of college due to these difficulties. Both of Sam's parents were good students. Sam's mother completed college and his father runs a successful family business. Sam resides with his parents and his younger sister who is a high achiever academically. **Health/Medical:** When Sam was 4-years-old, his tonsils and adenoids were removed to alleviate chronic problems with breathing, allergies, colds, and infections. This surgery helped, but Sam continued to suffer from allergies and has taken medication throughout his life for this condition. He has been receiving allergy shots for over two years, and currently receives one shot each month to manage his symptoms.

Social/Emotional: Sam has enjoyed positive social relationships and has established and maintained many friendships. Sam's girlfriend described him as "mellow and easy-going." There are no social/emotional conditions reported that would impair Sam's academic progress.

Educational: Sam has attended both public and private schools throughout his school years. He Attended Hometown Elementary School for grades kindergarten through six. His third grade teacher expressed concerns about his slow progress in reading and a referral was made to receive Reading Specialist services. Sam continued with these specialized services at school twice a week for three years. Sam has attended Hunter Academy, a private school, since the 7th grade, and has maintained a "B to C" average, with the help of intensive private tutoring on a regular basis. Progress reports were reviewed and Sam's teachers describe him as a positive, upbeat student who "seeks advice, responds well to criticism, and strives to improve his skills". There were, however, concerns expressed about his inconsistency. There seemed to be a pattern of poor test performance but of maintaining his grades by doing homework and re-doing assignments when allowed by the teacher. Teachers recommended tutoring sessions and offered to meet with him weekly, noting that he "responds well to one-on-one instruction".

In describing his learning process, Sam indicated that he has always had trouble maintaining his attention and that he has always taken longer than others to learn material and to complete his homework. He has always been a slow reader, and needs to read at a slow pace to acquire full comprehension. Even though he uses his finger to mark his place while reading, he still loses his place, which results in skipping words and whole lines in the text. He indicated that he needs a lot of help from his tutor to write essays and reports.

Sam recently graduated from Cal State University in June of 2007 with a major in political science. He stated that he received an overall G.P.A. of 2.5, but that his G.P.A. in his major classes was closer to a 3.5. Sam has always found math classes to be the most difficult for him and often he had to retake these classes to receive acceptable grades. Sam also struggled with the LSAT exam. He had to continue taking LSAT practice exams with the Kaplan Program for six months before he was able to achieve a score that was greater than 149. While in college, Sam worked as an intern in a law firm and a legal aid office.

Sam continues to have trouble focusing and reported that he is very distractible lately. Sam feels very disorganized although he wants to have things organized. He recalled that he used to lose credit cards frequently, but has trained himself to take better care of them. He has difficulty organizing his thoughts in writing. He is not able to work normally or think clearly unless he works in a very quiet environment. Sam often cannot finish a task that he has started and he jumps from one thing to another.

MENTAL STATUS and BEHAVIORAL OBSERVATIONS

Sam is a 24 -year-old Caucasian young man who used his right hand for all written work. He was Well-groomed and casually but appropriately dressed at each testing session. Sam cooperated fully with all assessment procedures and appeared to exert full effort on all tasks. I did have to repeat directions frequently so Sam could understand and respond appropriately. He was fully oriented to his surroundings and demonstrated appropriate interpersonal skills. His eye contact was normal, and his speech was regulated in its speed, rhythm, and tone. There was no evidence of disturbance in his emotions or his thoughts. Based upon the testing environment and Sam's level of motivation, the test results appear to be valid and interpretively useful.

ASSESSMENT RESULTS AND IMPRESSIONS

Cognitive Functioning: Based on the results of the WAIS-III, Sam's general cognitive ability is estimated to fall within the above average range and to be greater than 82% of the individuals his age. Sam has better developed verbal than nonverbal ability. Sam's verbal IQ score was 121 (92nd percentile; superior range), while his performance scale IQ score was 106 (66th percentile; average range).

In reviewing the WAIS-III Index scores, Sam's average verbal comprehension (VCI, 53rd percentile) is significantly more developed than his low average processing speed (PSI, 18th percentile), with the difference between these scores seen in 32.4% of the standardization sample. Additionally, there is a significant difference between Sam's average Working Memory (WMI, 66th percentile) and his low average Processing Speed, with this difference seen in only 17.2% of the standardization sample. This weakness in processing speed was also seen on supplemental subtests administered from the WJ-III (Processing Speed, 15th percentile).

Verbal Comprehension is the ability to use language for thinking and for problem solving. Sam's verbal comprehension abilities are well-developed at the above-average level (VCI, 87th percentile), and he demonstrated adequate skill in providing oral definitions to vocabulary words (Vocabulary, 73rd percentile).

He scored at the average to low average level in his ability to formulate abstract verbal concepts, answering in an unusual pattern of missing easier items while getting more difficult items correct (Similarities, 25th percentile). His knowledge of general information fell within the high average range (Information, 85th percentile). Sam's knowledge of socially appropriate behavior is within the average range (Comprehension, 63th percentile).

Auditory Processing/Phonemic Awareness: Sam's performance varied significantly on two measures of auditory processing, with his overall score falling within the average range (WJ-III, Phonemic Awareness, 43th percentile). In listening to words presented one sound at a time and then blending the sounds together to create a word, Sam scored at the low average level (WJ-III, Sound Blending, 17th percentile). However, when required to identify words that were pronounced with missing sounds/syllables, Sam scored at the high average level (WJ-III, Incomplete Words, 88th percentile).

It is unusual to see this degree of variability in these auditory skills, but it appears that Sam's test behavior interfered with his performance on the Sound Blending subtest. Both of these subtests are administered via a standardized tape recording, and Sound Blending was the first of these two subtests administered. On this subtest, Sam repeatedly answered before listening to the entire item, despite directions to wait until he heard the beep on the tape, which signaled the end of the item. On this subtest, there is the pattern of missing easier items while answering more difficult items correctly. By answering difficult items correctly, it appears that Sam possesses this auditory processing skill and that his low score is due to an impulsive response style.

Attention: Functioning in this domain was assessed through case history, school records, observation, self-report, and a variety of subtests, some of which also provide information about memory and processing speed. The results of those subtests are presented in those specific sections of the report and a later discussion will provide an integrated interpretation. Sam's responses on the Conners-Wells' Adolescent Self-Report Scale: Long Version (CASS: L) revealed significant difficulties in the areas of inattention and hyperactivity/impulsivity. Based upon Sam's self-report, his scores were significant on scales measuring Cognitive Problems/Inattention (T-Score = 65) and on the scales aligned with the current diagnostic criteria for ADHD: DSM-IV: Inattentive (T-Score = 74), DSM-IV Hyperactive/Impulsive (T-Score = 65) and DSM-IV: Total (T-Score = 73).

He endorsed items reflecting the following:

"I forget things that I have learned." – VERY OFTEN

"I tend to learn more slowly than I would like to." – VERY OFTEN

"I make careless mistakes or have trouble paying close attention to details." – VERY OFTEN

"I don't like schoolwork where I have to think a lot" – VERY OFTEN

"I have trouble finishing my schoolwork or chores." – VERY OFTEN

"I tend to squirm and fidget." – VERY OFTEN

"I have trouble concentrating on one thing at a time." – VERY OFTEN

"I like to be on the go rather than being in one place." – VERY OFTEN

"I am distracted when things are going on around me." – VERY OFTEN

Working Memory is a complex memory skill that requires holding information mentally while performing some active manipulation or calculation with it. Memory skills were assessed in auditory and visual domains.

Auditory Memory: All of the subtests on the WAIS-III Working Memory Index present numerical data orally, and Sam scored securely within the average level (WMI, 66th percentile), with even performance across tasks. He demonstrated average to high average strength in his ability to remember and re-organize letters and numbers (Letter-Number Sequencing, 75th percentile). His immediate recall of digits forwards and backwards was adequately developed (Digit Span, 50th percentile), as was his ability to perform mental math calculations (Arithmetic, 53th percentile). His auditory memory for language, specifically a series of unrelated words, was also within the average range (Memory for Words, 71th percentile).

Visual Memory: Sam scored at the average level when processing purely visual information (WJ-III, Picture Recognition, 38th percentile). On this subtest, Sam was required to recognize a subset of previously presented pictures within a field of distracting pictures. *Visual-Auditory Memory*: When required to learn and recall new information that was presented to him simultaneously with visual and auditory stimuli, Sam's performance suffered, and he scored at the low average level (WJ-III, Visual-Auditory Learning, 14th percentile).

Visual-Perceptual Organization is the ability to organize visual information and to reason and problem solve with visual data. This WAIS-III index score fell within the average level (POI, 42th percentile), with some variability performance across tasks. *Visual-Spatial*: Sam exhibited average ability on the Block Design subtest, which required him to use two-color cubes to construct replicas of two-dimensional, geometric patterns. This subtest assesses ability to mentally organize visual information. More specifically, this subtest assesses his ability to analyze part-whole relationships when information is presented spatially. Visual- spatial perception and visual perception-fine motor coordination also may influence performance on this task (Block Design, 63th percentile).

Sam scored similarly on a spatial task that required the visualization of spatial relationships by identifying two or three pieces that form a complete target shape, become more difficult as drawings of the pieces are flipped, rotated, and more similar in appearance (WJ-III, Spatial Relations, 68th percentile).

*********[omitted other possible test results]

When Sam is not under time pressure, he can demonstrate that he possesses average skills in phonemic awareness, sight word reading, reading vocabulary, and reading comprehension. When Sam is under time pressure, however, his reading test scores clearly show that he is not able to demonstrate his reading comprehension skill. In an analysis of the discrepancy between Sam's verbal ability and his achievement in reading, the test results identify Sam as having a Specific Learning Disability in the area of reading, under timed conditions, with functional deficits in the areas of visual-motor integration and processing speed. The results of this evaluation also identify Sam as meeting diagnostic criteria for the inattentive type of ADHD.

This provides explanation for Sam's reported need to re-read material and to study for longer periods of time. With deficits in attention and processing speed, he needs much more time to review and practice in order to comprehend and to retain the information.

Social/Emotional Functioning: There are no significant concerns reported regarding Sam's functioning in these areas, but screening measures were administered to assess his current emotional functioning. Responses fell within normal limits.

Based upon information from these various sources, Sam has not displayed any serious emotional disturbance that would provide an explanation for learning inconsistencies. There is no alternate or co-morbid psychiatric diagnosis that explains Sam's learning issues.

SUMMARY and RECOMMENDATIONS

The results of this evaluation indicate that Sam possesses average to high average cognitive ability to learn. Sam exhibited relative strengths in his short-term auditory memory, in his fund of general knowledge, and in his spatial organization. Functional limitations that impact his learning process include attention, visual-motor integration, verbal fluency, and visual processing speed. When working without time pressure, Sam's academic achievement is commensurate with his verbal ability. However, when time limits are imposed, there is a significant discrepancy between Sam's average verbal comprehension ability and his lower achievement in the specific area of timed reading comprehension.

Based upon the results of this comprehensive psycho-educational evaluation, it is recommended that reasonable and appropriate educational accommodations and modifications be provided to Sam under the Americans with Disabilities Act (ADA) and Section 504 of the Rehabilitation Act of 1973.

Sam is diagnosed as having a Reading Disorder (timed conditions) and ADHD, Predominantly Inattentive Type, both of which substantially limit his learning activities.

The following educational accommodations are recommended:

1. Time and one-half for exams, including law school exams, the MPRE and Bar Exams. Sam's scores on several measures of reading comprehension illustrate a clear pattern of higher achievement when provided with unlimited time and lower achievement with specific time limits. Although unlimited time is best for him, it is not reasonable or possible to request this, but time and one-half would provide an appropriate and reasonable accommodation for him.

2. Separate room for test taking, in order to minimize distractions. With Sam's slower pace of processing, as well as distractibility, a setting separate from the larger group is recommended.

3. Preferential seating in the classroom, in order to minimize distractions.

4. Note-taking assistance, as needed. Processing speed and attentional deficits may interfere with writing down all of the necessary information in a lecture format of teaching.

5. Use of a computer for word processing, due to deficits in visual-motor integration and processing speed.

Additionally, It is also recommended that Sam become more knowledgeable about the diagnosis of ADHD, Predominantly Inattentive Type. Prior to this evaluation, Sam suspected that inattention and distractibility were interfering with his academic progress, and the results of this evaluation confirm that diagnosis. Sam has decided that he does not want to pursue a medication evaluation to determine if stimulant medication would be helpful to him, so it is of critical importance that he develops compensatory behavioral strategies.

Doctor Ph.D.

California Licensed Psychologist #XXXXXXX

Index